PHILOSOPHY &
EDUCATION

third edition

PHILOSOPHY &
EDUCATION

an introduction
in Christian perspective

by George R. Knight

ANDREWS UNIVERSITY PRESS
BERRIEN SPRINGS, MI

© 1998, 1989, 1980 ANDREWS UNIVERSITY PRESS
213 Information Services Building
Berrien Springs, MI 49104-1700
616-471-6915
aupress@andrews.edu

ISBN 1-883925-20-7
Library of Congress Catalog Card Number 98-72676

"An education that fails to consider the fundamental questions of human existence—the questions about the meaning of life and the nature of truth, goodness, beauty, and justice, with which philosophy is concerned—is a very inadequate type of education."

—Harold Titus

"At present, opinion is divided about the subjects of education. People do not take the same view about what should be learned by the young, either with a view to human excellence or a view to the best possible life; nor is it clear whether education should be directed mainly to the intellect or to moral character . . . [,] whether the proper studies to be pursued are those that are useful in life, or those which make for excellence, or those that advance the bounds of knowledge. . . . Men do not all honor the same distinctive human excellence and so naturally they differ about the proper training for it."

—Aristotle

"And this is eternal life, that they know thee the only true God, and Jesus Christ whom thou hast sent."

—Jesus

To my students in educational philosophy—
individuals whose probings
extended and refined my thinking

Contents

List of Figures

A Word to the Reader

The basic premise underlying this book is the seemingly obvious proposition that individuals cannot arrive at their destination unless they know where they are going. That premise leads to inquiries about goals, the issue of goals leads to reflection upon values, and questions concerning values lead to the consideration of such basic items as the nature of truth and reality. In other words, questions about purpose direct us to basic philosophic issues.

A second premise is that there is a definite connection between philosophic positions and educational practices. The implication of this statement is that educational practices are built upon philosophical beliefs. Philosophic perspectives, therefore, are major determinants of such practical educational considerations as teaching methodology, curricular focus, the role of the teacher, the function of the school in the social order, and the nature of the learner.

A third premise is that the greatest need of Christian schools is that they be Christian in the fullest sense of the word. In an era of soaring educational costs, the continued existence of Christian schools as an alternative to public systems of education may be predicated upon the ability of Christian educators to develop a genuinely Christian alternative. This need can only be realized as Christian educators clearly understand their basic beliefs and how those beliefs can and must affect their educational planning and practice. Christian educators will be aided in their task by the study of the ideas of historical and contemporary educational philosophers and theorists, but beyond this they must seek to develop a positive educational philosophy built upon a distinctly Christian world view.

The purpose of this text is to survey those aspects of philosophy that are relevant to the educational profession and to highlight the relationship between philosophical starting points and educational outcomes. This short book makes no claim to comprehensive treatment of either educational or philosophical categories. It is a survey, and, as such, it does not seek to answer all the issues raised. On the contrary, many questions have been deliberately left unanswered or unexplained in the hope that such an approach might stimulate discussion and continuing thought about those questions. Thinking is an ongoing process, and one of the most beneficial results of the study of educational philosophy is obtained if students reach the place where they are unable to think of educational practices in isolation from the basic questions of life and ultimate meaning that give those practices significance.

This book has been written with the college and university student in mind. Other readers, however, will find it to be a helpful guide for analyzing educational purposes and practices in the light of their basic beliefs. It can be used by itself as a textbook for a course providing only limited time for the treatment of educational philosophy, or it may be used in conjunction with readings from philosophers and educational theorists espousing the various positions that it describes. Teachers of courses in the philosophy of Christian education may decide not to require the entire text as reading for their students. In this case, Parts I and III provide the essentials for developing a Christian perspective. Beyond this, Chapter 6, which deals with contemporary theories of education, will prove especially helpful for students who need an overview of the forces in current educational thought.

Philosophy and Education is divided into three sections. Part I deals with basic concepts in philosophy and the relationship between philosophy and education. Part II is a survey of how traditional and modern philosophies have faced the basic philosophic questions and what that has meant for educational practice. Part III discusses the necessity of developing a personal philosophy of education, one possible approach to a Christian philosophy, and some of the ramifications of such a philosophy for educational practice in Christian schools.

I am indebted to many people for my ideas. I would particularly like to express my gratitude to Joshua Weinstein of the University of Houston for introducing me to the field of educational philosophy. Beyond this, I would like to express my appreciation to Robert Firth who edited this volume, and to George Akers of Andrews University, Peter DeBoer of Calvin College, and Maurice Hodgen of Loma Linda University for reading the manuscript and making many constructive criticisms that have enriched its content. Additional appreciation goes to Shirley Welch and Jill Doster, who aided me in proofreading; to Donna Wise, Nancy Sharp, and Gail Valentine, who did much of the typing; to Peter Erhard, who prepared the illustrations and cover design; to Denise Johnson, who prepared the manuscript for publication; and to the administration of Andrews University for providing me with financial support and time to develop the manuscript. Needless to say, I am also indebted to a host of writers, teachers, and speakers who have contributed to my education over the years. It should be recognized that many of the thoughts expressed in this volume have been gleaned from these sources. It should also be evident that originality is not a virtue of a survey text; that is particularly true of Parts I and II of this book.

—George R. Knight
May 1980

A NOTE ON THE THIRD EDITION

The reception of the first and second editions of *Philosophy and Education* far exceeded my expectations. The book's numerous printings and increasing use have validated the helpfulness of the general approach taken. As a result, the third edition makes no macro-changes in structure. It has, however, added a chapter on postmodernism and a section discussing critical pedagogy, multiculturalism, and feminism. It has also greatly expanded the material on the aims of Christian education as they relate to the role of the teacher and added a section on values education. Most of the other changes in the third edition have had to do with updating, clarifying, enriching, and cleaning up the rough spots.

I would like to thank Harro Van Brummelen, Paul Brantley, Jane Thayer, and George Akers for sharing insights and materials with me; Bonnie Beres for typing the manuscript; Carol Loree and Deborah Everhart who saw the book through the publication process; and Julius Nam and Sandra White for procuring library materials.

I trust that *Philosophy and Education* will be of benefit to its readers as they seek to approximate Christian ideals in both their personal and professional lives.

March 30, 1998

PART ONE: BASIC CONCEPTS

1

The Nature of Philosophy and Education

WHY STUDY PHILOSOPHY OF EDUCATION?

"Mindlessness"[1] is the most pertinent and accurate criticism of American education. There has been a great deal of activity in the field of educational innovation and experimentation, but most of it has not been adequately evaluated in terms of purpose, goals, and actual needs. Charles Silberman noted that education "has suffered too long from too many answers and too few questions."[2]

Neil Postman and Charles Weingartner have indicated that mindlessness in education is a natural outcome for a society which has traditionally been concerned with the "how" rather than the "why" of modern life. America has been making an unrelenting assault on technique for more than a century. As a nation it has been busy creating new techniques for traveling, communicating, healing, cleaning, dying, and killing. The American people, however, have seldom asked whether or not they wanted the improvements, needed them, should have them, or whether they would come at too high a cost. The very word "progress" has come to be seen in terms of new methods.

That mentality, claim Postman and Weingartner, has been adopted by the educationalists of America who are busy creating new techniques for teaching spelling, new methods for teaching arithmetic to two-year-olds, new ways of keeping school halls quiet, and new means of measuring intelligence. Educators have been so busy creating and implementing new methodology that they have often failed to ask such questions as whether two-year-old mathematicians are worth having.[3]

"Why all this education? To what purpose?"[4] These are two of the most important questions that must be faced. Yet they are generally not seriously confronted. Educators have been concerned more with motion than progress, with means than ends. They have failed to ask the larger question of purpose; and the professional training of educators, with its emphasis on methodology, has largely set them up for this problem. Lawrence Cremin met the issue squarely when he noted that

> too few educational leaders in the United States are genuinely preoccupied with educational issues because they have no clear ideas about education. And if we look at the way these leaders have been recruited and trained, there is little that would lead us to expect otherwise. They have too often been managers, facilitators, politicians in the narrowest sense. They have been concerned with building buildings, balancing budgets, and pacifying parents, but they have not been prepared to spark a great public dialogue about the ends and means of education. And in the absence of such a dialogue, large segments of the public have had, at best, a limited understanding of the whys and wherefores of popular schooling.[5]

There is a strong need for the preparation of a new breed of professional educators who are able to focus on "thought about purpose" and "to think about what they are doing and why they are doing it."[6] Certain educational thought leaders are calling for professional training that emphasizes studies in the humanities of education—those studies of the history, philosophy, and literature of education that will enable educators to develop a clear vision regarding the purpose of education and its relation to the meaning of life. These studies have been neglected in the training of educational professionals because their immediate utility has been difficult to demonstrate. But, notes Cremin, "it is their ultimate utility that really matters."[7] After all, it is not even possible to talk in terms of the utility of educational means unless individuals know what they desire as an outcome and why they desire one particular end product above other possible outcomes. When a desired goal is in mind, then a person is in a position to think in terms of the relative values of various methodologies that will aid in reaching a destination.

The task of educational philosophy is to bring future teachers, principals, superintendents, counselors, and curriculum specialists into face-to-face contact with the large questions underlying the meaning and purpose of life and education. To understand these questions the student must wrestle with such issues as the nature of reality, the meaning and sources of knowledge, and the structure of values. Educational philosophy must bring students into a position where they can intelligently evaluate alternative ends, relate their aims to desired ends, and select pedagogical methods that harmonize with their aims. Thus a major task of educational philosophy is to help educators think meaningfully about the total educational and life process so that they will be in a better position to develop a consistent and comprehensive program that will assist their students in arriving at the desired goal.

In summary, the study of educational philosophy is (1) to help educators become acquainted with the basic problems of education, (2) to enable them to evaluate better the wide variety of suggestions offered as solutions to these problems, (3) to assist them in clarifying thinking about the goals of both life and education, and (4) to guide them in the development of an internally consistent point of view and a program that relates realistically to the larger world context.

WHAT IS PHILOSOPHY?

Literally, the word "philosophy" means love of wisdom. It should be noted, however, that loving wisdom does not make one a philosopher. Philosophy in its technical sense might best be thought of in three aspects: an activity, a set of attitudes, and a body of content.[8]

Philosophy as an Activity

The activity aspect of philosophy is best seen by noting what philosophers do. Examining, synthesizing, analyzing, speculating, prescribing, and evaluating are activities that have traditionally been at the center of philosophic endeavors.

Examining is a first step in the philosophic process. Before thought takes place, philosophers must examine the evidence. That is true whether the evidence is external or an internal introspection of one's thoughts or emotions. The philosopher, of course, desires to examine the full range of evidence, a desire related to the attitude of comprehensiveness that will be discussed in the next section.

Analyzing in philosophy focuses on human language and our use of it in an attempt to clarify our understanding of problems and how they might be solved. In analysis the philosopher scrutinizes the use of logic in an argument and examines such words as "liberal," "good," "intelligence," and "motivation" in an attempt to evaluate their meanings in varying contexts. In analysis the philosopher operates on the assumption that basic misunderstandings in regard to meanings might lie at the root of human problems.

The synthesizing role of the philosopher rests on humanity's desire and need to possess a comprehensive and consistent view of life that provides a basis upon which it may unify its thoughts, base its aspirations, and interpret its experiences. To most people, rational existence demands a world view that adds significance to individual actions by placing them in their wider context. In their role as synthesizers, philosophers seek to unite and integrate specialized knowledges into a unified view of the world.

The speculative dimension of philosophy is based upon the limitations of human knowledge. There is not enough scientifically verified data to provide a base for action. Furthermore, the most important aspects of human and universal existence are not amenable to scientific treatment. If daily activity is not to be paralyzed, it is necessary to move beyond what can be demonstrated empirically. It is the speculative function of philosophy that allows a rational jump from the known to the unknown, and which permits movement with a relative degree of confidence into the undefined. The alternative to speculation is to be stymied by doubt.

Prescription in philosophy seeks to establish standards for evaluating values in conduct and art. Prescriptions are usually expressed in terms of how people "ought" to act or react in a given situation involving aesthetic judgments or moral alternatives. Intrinsic to prescribing is the task of defining what is meant by good, bad, right, wrong, beautiful, and ugly. The aim of prescriptive philosophy is to discover and illuminate principles for deciding what actions and qualities are most worthwhile. The alternative to prescription is to face every decision-making situation as if it were unique.

The evaluating function of philosophy involves making judgments about the adequacy of one's philosophic "project" in terms of a set of criteria. The nature of that criteria, of course, varies from philosopher to philosopher and is related to his or her philosophic orientation. We

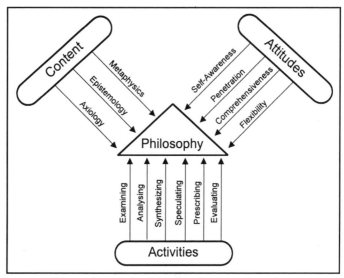

Figure 1. Aspects of Philosophy

will return to selected theories for evaluating philosophic ideas in our discussion of the validity of knowledge in Chapter 2.

In the mid-twentieth century many philosophers tended to avoid the synthesizing, prescriptive, and speculative activities of philosophy. That led to a narrowness that largely sterilized the discipline and robbed it of its meaning and relevance for the daily activities of social life (see Chapter 7). Meaningful and vital philosophy contains an interaction and balance of all its central activities.

Philosophy as an Attitude

Philosophers bring certain ways of thinking to their task. The characteristics of a person who is philosophically minded may be listed as self-awareness, comprehensiveness, penetration, and flexibility.

Self-awareness entails a commitment to being as honest as possible with one's self in regard to personal biases, assumptions, and prejudices. No one is neutral, and one of the most difficult and elusive activities of human existence is to come to grips with our personal predispositions. It might be said that it is impossible even to begin to arrive at a correct perspective of the world until people realize the color of the glasses they are wearing. Once individuals become aware of the effect of their personal predispositions, they need to take this information into account in both interpretation and communication.

Comprehensiveness involves an inclination toward collecting as much relevant data on a subject as possible from a wide spectrum of sources rather than being satisfied with a narrow sample. This attitude is related to the synthesizing function of philosophy in that it is interested in seeing the wholeness of phenomena rather than the parts.

Penetration is a desire that leads a person to go as deeply into a problem as skill, time, and energy allow. It is a squelching of the inclination toward the superficial in favor of a search for basic principles, issues, and solutions.

Flexibility might be thought of as the antithesis of rigidity or "psychological set." The attitude of flexibility is a form of sensitivity that enables one to be able to perceive old problems in new ways. It includes a willingness to restructure ideas in the face of sufficient evidence and the ability to envision viable alternatives to a viewpoint. Flexibility, however, should not be confused with indecisiveness or the inability to make a decision.[9] After careful study, one may decide that a position is the most reasonable and then act in accord with that decision. "The point at issue lies in one's willingness—even readiness—to change that position given sufficient reason."[10]

Philosophy as Content

It has been noted that philosophy is, in part, an activity and an attitude. If people are involved in such activities as examination, synthesis, speculation, prescription, analysis, and evaluation—and if they possess the attitudes of self-awareness, comprehensiveness, penetration, and flexibility—then they soon will be confronted with some bedrock questions related to the nature of reality, truth, and value.

The content of philosophy is better seen in the light of questions than in the light of answers. It can even be said that philosophy is the study of questions. Van Cleve Morris has noted that the crux of the matter is asking the "right" questions. By "right" he means questions which are meaningful and relevant—the kind of questions people really want answered and which will make a difference in how they live and work.[11]

There are three fundamental categories around which philosophical content has been organized: (1) *metaphysics* or the study of questions concerning the nature of reality; (2) *epistemology* or the study of the nature of truth and knowledge and how these are attained; and (3) *axiology* or the study of questions of value. A discussion of these three basic categories will form the subject matter of Chapter 2.

WHAT IS EDUCATION?

"I am not going to get married until after I finish my education," declared a young man to his friends. What did he mean by the term "education"? What was it that he hoped to complete before marriage? Was it education, learning, or schooling? Is there a conceptual difference between these words? If there is, one ought to come to grips with that difference and use the terms with precision. The following discussion will present some distinctions between these concepts and offer definitions[12] that will lead to a better understanding of these related but often confused processes.

In the above illustration the young man evidently meant that he would not get married until he was finished with school. Even though he used the term "education," he was referring to schooling. Schooling might be thought of as attendance at an institution in which teachers and students operate in a prescribed manner. Schooling can be equated with formal education—that education which takes place in a school.

Learning proves to be a more difficult concept to define, and different learning theorists have arrived at varying positions concerning the nature of learning. For present purposes, learning may be defined as "the process that produces the capability of exhibiting new or changed human behavior (or which increases the probability that new or changed behavior will be elicited by a relevant stimulus), provided that the new behavior or behavior change cannot be explained on the basis of some other process or experience"—such as aging or fatigue.[13]

From this definition it can be seen that learning is a process that, unlike schooling, is not limited to an institutional context. It is possible to learn individually or with the help of someone else. People can learn in a school but they can also learn if they have never seen a school. Learning is a lifelong process that may occur at any time and any place.

Education may be seen as a subset of learning. John A. Laska made a helpful distinction between learning and education when he defined education as "the deliberate attempt by the learner or by someone else to *control* (or *guide*, or *direct*, or *influence*, or *manage*) a learning situation in order to bring about the attainment of a desired *learning outcome (goal).*"[14]

Education, seen from this perspective, is not limited to schooling or to the traditional curriculum or methodologies of schools. Education, like learning, is a lifelong process that can take place in an infinite variety of circumstances and contexts. On the other hand, education is distinct from the broader concept of learning, since education embodies the idea of deliberate control by the learner or someone else toward a desired goal. Education might be thought of as directed learning as opposed to non-directed or inadvertent learning.

A fourth term that is sometimes confused with education is "training." The concept (not necessarily the way in which the word is always used) of training may be differentiated from the concept of education on the basis of the development of understanding. Understanding grows as one is led to think reflectively about cause and effect relationships rather than just responding to a set of stimuli. A development of understanding is inherent in education, while unreflective responsive activity is generally associated with training. Training can take place on the animal level, while education is essentially a human process. It should be noted that education may at times include some training aspects, since training is a subset of education just as education is a subset of learning.

Figure 2 illustrates the relationship of learning, education, training, and schooling. Education and training are specialized types of learning, while training, in turn, is a specialized type of education. Schooling is related to these three forms of learning in the sense that inadvertent learning,[15] education, and training may take place in the context of schooling. Figure 2 illustrates, however, that there are many other life experiences (such as eating lunch or going to the nurse) which take place in school but are not necessarily related to one of the various learning experiences. Figure 2 also illustrates that most learning, education, and training takes place outside the context of a formal school setting.

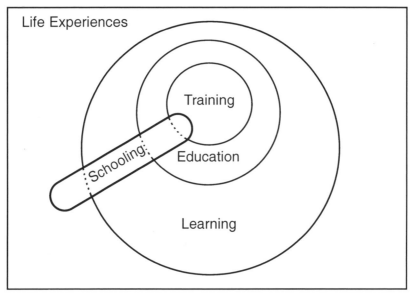

Figure 2. The Relationship of Selected Learning-Related Concepts

THE ROLE OF THE SCHOOL IN SOCIETY

The school is only one of society's agents for learning, education, and training. The family, media, peer group, and church are some of the other institutions that share this responsibility. In fact, the school may even be seen as a minor partner in the educational process, with the family and the media playing the major role in the lives of most children.[16] This vital point should be recognized even though the treatment of education in this book will tend to use categories that are most often linked with schooling. It should be understood, however, that the "teacher" in the fullest sense of the word may not be an employee of a school system—he/she may be a broadcaster, parent, pastor, or peer. Likewise, a television program or an individual home has a view of truth and reality and a set of values that leads it to select a certain "curriculum" and teaching methodology as it goes about its educational functions. In what follows, this idea may not always be explicitly stated, but it is implicit in the discussion and must be recognized if one is to gain the fullest understanding of education-related processes.

The school exists in a complex educational milieu. To complicate matters, the components of that milieu may not all be espousing the same message in regard to reality, truth, and value. This undoubtedly weakens the impact of the school (as well as the impact of society's other "educators") and gives children a garbled message about their world and what is important in life. It should ever be borne in mind that learning, education, training, and schooling take place in this complexity of forces.

Notes

1. Charles E. Silberman, *Crisis in the Classroom: The Remaking of American Education* (New York: Vintage Books, 1970), p. 11.

2. Ibid., p. 470.

3. Neil Postman and Charles Weingartner, *The School Book: For People Who Want to Know What All the Hollering Is About* (New York: Dell Publishing Co., 1973), pp. 295-97.

4. Lawrence A. Cremin, *The Genius of American Education* (New York: Vintage Books, 1965), p. 30.

5. Ibid., pp. 111-12.

6. Silberman, *Crisis in the Classroom*, p. 11.

7. Cremin, *The Genius of American Education*, p. 112.

8. Cf. Charles D. Marler, *Philosophy and Schooling* (Boston: Allyn and Bacon, Inc., 1975), pp. 5-11; and Philip G. Smith, *Philosophy of Education: Introductory Studies* (New York: Harper & Row, 1965), pp. 2-16.

9. Smith, *Philosophy of Education*, p. 14.

10. Marler, *Philosophy and Schooling*, pp. 10-11.

11. Van Cleve Morris, *Philosophy and the American School* (Boston: Houghton Mifflin Company, 1961), pp. 19-20.

12. Each of these definitions is presented as *a* possible definition and not *the* definition of the respective terms. As such they may be helpful in stimulating thought and discussion concerning the differences and similarities inherent in these concepts.

13. John A. Laska, *Schooling and Education: Basic Concepts and Problems* (New York: D. Van Nostrand Company, 1976), p. 6. Cf. Ernest R. Hilgard and Gordon H. Bower, *Theories of Learning*, 3rd ed. (New York: Appleton-Century-Crofts, 1966), p. 2.

14. Laska, *Schooling and Education*, p. 7.

15. In Figure 2 the largest circle refers to all learning processes, whereas only that learning outside the education subset represents inadvertent or non-directed learning.

16. The educational power of the family was highlighted in the influential studies of James Coleman and Christopher Jencks. Implicit in the findings of Coleman and Jencks is that improved families are more crucial to educational outcomes than better schools. Lawrence A. Cremin, in reflecting on these studies, concluded that their message is "not that the school is power*less* but that the family is power*ful*." Complicating the problem is the fact that the Carnegie Council on Children found that "by the age of 18, the average American child has spent more time watching television than in school or with his or her parents." (See James S. Coleman et al., *Equality of Educational Opportunity* [Washington, DC: U.S. Department of Health, Education, and Welfare, 1966]; Christopher Jencks et al., *Inequality: A Reassessment of the Effect of Family and Schooling in America* [New York: Harper and Row, 1972]; Lawrence A. Cremin, *Public Education* [New York: Basic Books, 1976], p. 68; Kenneth Keniston et al., *All Our Children: The American Family Under Pressure* [New York: Harcourt Brace Jovanovich, 1977], p. 7.)

2

Philosophic Issues in Education

Educational philosophy is not distinct from general philosophy; it is general philosophy applied to education as a specific area of human endeavor. Before understanding the structure of educational philosophy, it is imperative to learn something of the basic outline of philosophy. In order to do this, we must examine the categories of metaphysics, epistemology, and axiology.

METAPHYSICS

Metaphysics is the branch of philosophy that deals with the nature of reality. "What is ultimately real?" is the basic question asked in the study of metaphysics.

At first glance, it seems too simple a query to waste much time on. After all, average people seem to be quite sure about the "reality" of their world. Just ask them, and they will most likely tell you to open your eyes and look at the clock on the wall, to listen to the sound of a passing train, or to bend down and touch the floor beneath your feet. These things, they claim, are real.

Upon reflection, however, one is tempted to question these initial concepts of reality. For example, what exactly is the reality of the floor upon which you stand? It may seem to have a rather straightforward existence. It is obviously flat, solid, and smooth; it has a particular color; it is composed of an identifiable material, such as wood or concrete; and it supports your weight. At first glance, this is the reality of the floor upon which you are standing. Suppose, however, that a physicist enters the room and is questioned about the reality of the floor. She will reply that the floor is made of molecules; that molecules consist of atoms; atoms of electrons, protons, and neutrons; and these, finally, of electrical energy alone. To her, the real floor is a hotbed of molecular motion in which there is more space than matter. A third position on the reality of the floor is offered by a passing chemist who sees an alternate picture of "floor reality." To him, the floor is a body of hydrocarbons associated in a particular way and subject to certain kinds of environmental influences, such as heat, cold, wetness, dryness, and oxidation.

At this point it is evident that the question of reality is not as simplistic as it first appeared. If the reality of a common floor is confusing, what about the larger problems that present themselves as humanity searches for the ultimate reality of the universe?

Aspects of Metaphysics

A glimpse into the realm of metaphysics can be obtained by examining a list of major questions concerning the nature of reality. It will be seen that the queries of the metaphysician are among the most general questions that can be asked. It is important to realize, however, that the answers to these questions are needed before people can expect to find satisfactory answers to their more specific questions. The complete verification of any particular answer to these questions is beyond the realm of human demonstration. This does not, however, make the discussion of these issues irrelevant or a mere exercise in mental gymnastics, since people, whether they consciously understand it or not, base their daily activities and long-range goals upon a set of metaphysical beliefs. Even people dealing with the answers to more specific questions—physicists or biologists, for example—cannot escape metaphysical problems. Rather, it should be noted that metaphysical constructs lie at the foundation of the modern sciences.

"Metaphysics" is a transliteration from the Greek that literally means "beyond physics." It essentially represents the speculative and synthesizing activities of philosophy, and it provides the theoretical framework that allows scientists to create world views and develop hypotheses that can be tested according to their basic assumptions. Thus, theories of science are ultimately related to theories of reality, and the philosophy of science underlies scientific experimentation in much the same way that philosophy of education forms the foundation of educational practice.

It should be recognized that scientists are at times tempted to make interpretations that go beyond the "facts" of the answers to their relatively narrow questions. Such have invaded the realm of supplying metaphysical answers. That is the position of scientists who make positive statements about either creationism or evolution. They have gone beyond their experimental facts and assumed the role of metaphysicians. This may be all right in itself, as long as both they and their students consciously realize that they have exited the realm of science and entered that more basic world of metaphysics.

Metaphysical questions may be divided into four subsets. First, there is the cosmological aspect. Cosmology consists in the study of theories about the origin, nature, and development of the universe as an orderly system. "How did the universe originate and develop?" is a cosmological question. People have answered that question in a variety of ways, and their answers can be viewed as points on a continuum with design and accident as its polar extremes. Another cosmological inquiry is in regard to the purposefulness of the universe. Is there a purpose toward which the universe is tending? Affirmative replies to this query are referred to as being teleological. The Christian faith is teleological because it sees an end to earthly history with the second advent of Christ. Other philosophic schemes may be more prone to accept randomness or circularity in history. Two other widely discussed cosmological issues center around the nature of time and space.

A second metaphysical aspect is the theological. Theology is that part of religious theory that has to do with conceptions of and about God. Is there a God? If so, is there one or more than one? What are the attributes of God? If God is both all good and all powerful, how is it that evil exists? Are there such beings as angels, Satan, and the Holy Spirit? If so, what is their relationship to God? These and similar questions have been debated throughout human history.

People answer these questions in a variety of ways. *Atheists* claim that there is no God, while *pantheists* posit that God and the universe are identical—all is God, and God is all. *Deists* view God as the maker of nature and moral laws, but assert that God exists apart from, and is not interested in, humanity and the physical universe. On the other hand, *theists* believe in a personal creator God. *Polytheism* is opposed to *monotheism* in regard to the question of the number of gods. Polytheism holds that the deity should be thought of as plural, while monotheism insists that there is one God.[1]

A third aspect of metaphysics is the anthropological. Anthropology deals with the study of human beings. The anthropological aspect of philosophy is a unique category, since, unlike other areas of human investigation, humanity is both the subject and the object of inquiry. When people philosophize about humanity, they are speaking about themselves. The anthropological aspect of philosophy asks questions like the following: What is the relation between mind and body? Is there interaction between mind and body? Is mind more fundamental than body, with body depending on mind, or vice versa? What is humanity's moral status? Are people born good, evil, or morally neutral? To what extent are individuals free? Do they have free will, or are their thoughts and actions determined by their environment and inheritance? Does an individual have a soul? If so, what is it? People have obviously adopted different positions on these questions, and those positions are reflected in their political, social, religious, and educational practices and designs.

The fourth aspect of metaphysics is the ontological. Ontology is the study of the nature of existence, or what it means for anything to be. J. Donald Butler has coined the word "*isology*" as a synonym for "ontology," since the ontological task "is to determine what we mean when we say that something *is*."[2] There are several questions which are central to ontology: Is basic reality found in matter or physical energy (the world we can sense), or is it found in spirit or spiritual energy? Is it composed of one element (e.g., matter or spirit), or two (e.g., matter and spirit), or many? Is reality orderly and lawful in itself, or is it merely orderable by theorists? Is it fixed and stable, or is change its central feature? Is this reality friendly, unfriendly, or neutral in regard to humanity?

Metaphysics and Education

Even a cursory glance at either historical or contemporary societies will indicate the impact of the cosmological, theological, anthropological, and ontological aspects of metaphysics upon their social, religious, political, economic, and scientific beliefs and practices. People everywhere assume answers to these questions and then turn around and operate in their daily lives upon those assumptions. There is no escape from metaphysical decisions, unless one chooses merely to vegetate—and even that decision, in itself, would be a metaphysical decision about the nature and function of humanity.

Education, like other human activities, cannot escape the realm of metaphysics. Metaphysics, the issue of ultimate reality, is central to any concept of education because it is important that the educational program of the school be based upon fact and reality rather than fancy, illusion, or imagination. Varying metaphysical beliefs lead to differing educational approaches and even separate systems of education.

Why is it that Christian churches spend millions of dollars each year on private systems of education when free public systems are widely available? It is because of metaphysical beliefs regarding the nature of ultimate reality, the existence of God, the role of God in human affairs, and the nature and role of human beings as God's children. Men and women, at their deepest level, are motivated by metaphysical beliefs. They are willing to live and die for these convictions, and they desire to create educational environments in which these most basic beliefs will be taught to their children.

Later in this book it will be seen that metaphysical beliefs have a direct impact upon such educational issues as the most important content for the curriculum, what educational systems should attempt to do for both individuals and societies, and the role of teachers as they relate to learners.

The anthropological aspect of metaphysics is especially important for educators of all persuasions. After all, they are dealing with malleable human beings at one of the most impressionable stages of their lives. Views on the nature and potential of students lie at the very foundation of the educational process. Every educator must of necessity have some conception of the nature of human beings, their personal and social needs, and the ideal person. The very purpose of education in all philosophies is closely related to these views. Thus, anthropological considerations lie extremely close to aims in education. D. Elton Trueblood put it nicely when he asserted that "until we are clear on what man is we shall not be clear about much else." One spin-off of the centrality of anthropological considerations in education is the role of psychological study in the training of teachers. The same is true of sociology, but to a lesser extent in most teacher-training programs.[3]

It makes a great deal of difference in education if a student is viewed as Desmond Morris's "naked ape" or as a child of God. Likewise, it is important to know whether children are essentially good, as is asserted of Rousseau's Emile, or whether their goodness has been radically twisted by the effects of sin. Variation in anthropological positions will lead to significantly different approaches to the educational process. Other examples of the impact of metaphysics upon education will become evident further on in our study of educational philosophy.

EPISTEMOLOGY

The branch of philosophy which studies the nature, sources, and validity of knowledge is epistemology. It seeks to answer such questions as "What is true?" and "How do we know?" Due to the fact that the study of epistemology deals with such issues as the dependability of knowledge and the propriety of various methods of reaching warrantable truth, it stands—with metaphysics—at the very center of the educative process.

Dimensions of Knowledge
Can Reality be known? This is a logical question with which to begin the epistemological venture, since it demonstrates the close connection between epistemology and metaphysics. *Skepticism* in its narrow sense is the position claiming that it is impossible to gain knowledge and that any search for truth is in vain. This thought was well expressed by Gorgias (c. 483-376 B.C.), the Greek Sophist who asserted that nothing exists, and that if it did, we could not know it. A full-blown skepticism would make intelligent and consistent action impossible. Skepticism in its broader sense is often used to denote the attitude of questioning any assumption or conclusion until it can be subjected to rigorous examination. A term closely related to skepticism is "agnosticism." *Agnosticism* is a profession of ignorance, especially in reference to the existence or nonexistence of God, rather than a positive denial of any valid knowledge.

Most people claim that reality can be known. Once they have taken that position, however, they must decide through what sources reality may be known, and they must have some conception of how to judge the validity of their knowledge.

Is truth relative or absolute? Is all truth subject to change? Is it possible that what is true today may be false tomorrow? Truths that would answer yes to the previous questions are relative. Absolute Truth refers to that Truth which is eternally and universally true irrespective of time or place. If there is that kind of Truth in the universe, then it would certainly be helpful to discover it and place it at the very center of the school curriculum.

Is knowledge subjective or objective? This question is closely related to the relativity of truth. Van Cleve Morris has noted that there are three basic positions on the objectivity of knowledge. First, some hold that knowledge is something that comes to us from the "outside" and is inserted into our minds and nervous systems in much the same way that iron ore is dumped into a ship. Morris claims that mathematicians and physical scientists often see knowledge in this light.

Second, others believe that knowers contribute something in this engagement of themselves with the world in such a way as to be partially responsible for the structure of their knowledge. People in the social and behavioral sciences have often tended to see knowledge in this manner.

A third and final viewpoint is that we exist as "pure subjects" who become the manufacturers of truth rather than either its recipients or participants. This position, notes Morris, is most generally held in such areas as art, literature, and music.[4] Later it will be observed that the various philosophical schools tend to align themselves with one or another of these viewpoints on the objectivity of truth and knowledge.

Is there truth independent of human experience? This question is basic to epistemology. It can best be viewed in terms of *a priori* and *a posteriori* knowledge. *A priori* knowledge refers to truth that some thinkers claim is built into the very fabric of reality. It is independent of human knowers and is true whether any human knows and accepts it or not. This type of truth is said to exist prior to human experience of it and is independent of human awareness. An example of *a priori* knowledge is the ratio existing between the circumference and diameter of a circle (π). This relationship is a part of the very nature of circles.

On the other hand, the relation existing between two circles is not a given. One circle may be larger than the other, they may be in the same or different planes, or they may be concentric. Whatever knowledge one may have of the relationship of these two circles requires human experience for verification. Whatever knowledge is attained regarding their relationship is *a posteriori*—it is posterior to human experience of it and is dependent on human awareness.

Traditional philosophies have upheld the superiority of *a priori* knowledge, since, they claim, it is thought to represent the fixed and permanent world that is uncontaminated by human knowers. Modern philosophies have reversed this order and claim the superiority of *a posteriori* knowledge. In fact, some of them deny the existence of *a priori* knowledge.

Sources of Knowledge

The senses. Empiricism is the view that knowledge is obtained through the senses, that people form pictures of the world around them by seeing, hearing, smelling, feeling, and tasting. Empirical knowledge is built into the very nature of human experience. Individuals may walk out of doors on a spring day and see the beauty of the landscape, hear the song of a bird, feel the warm rays of the sun, and smell the fragrance of the blossoms. They "know" that it is spring because of the messages received through their senses. This knowledge is composed of ideas formed in accordance with observed data. Sensory knowing among humans is immediate and universal, and in many ways it forms the basis for much of our knowledge.

The presence of sensory data cannot be denied. Most people accept it at face value as representing "reality." The danger hidden in a naive acceptance of this approach is that our senses have been demonstrated to be both incomplete and undependable. (For example, most people have been confronted with the sensation of seeing a stick that looks bent when partially submerged in water but appears to be straight when examined in the air.) Fatigue, frustration, and common colds also distort and limit sensory perception. In addition, it should come as no surprise that there are sound and light waves beyond the range of unaided human perception.

Humans have invented scientific instruments to extend the range of their senses, but it is impossible to ascertain the exact dependability of these instruments since we do not know the total effect of the human mind in recording, interpreting, and distorting sensual perception. Confidence in these instruments is built upon speculative metaphysical theories whose validity has been reinforced by experimentation in which predictions have been verified in terms of a theoretical construct.

In short, sensory knowledge is built upon assumptions that must be accepted by faith in the dependability of our sensory mechanisms. The advantage of empirical knowledge is that many sensory experiences and experiments are open to both replication and public examination.

Revelation. Revealed knowledge has been of prime importance in the field of religion. It differs from all other sources of knowledge by presupposing a transcendent supernatural reality that breaks into the natural order. Revelation is God's communication concerning the divine will.

Believers in revelation hold that this form of knowledge has the distinct advantage of being an omniscient source of information that is not obtainable through other epistemological methods. The truth gained through this source is believed to be absolute and uncontaminated.

On the other hand, it is generally realized that distortion of revealed truth can take place in the process of human interpretation. Some people hold that a major disadvantage of revealed knowledge is that it must be accepted by faith and cannot be proved or disproved empirically.

Authority. Authoritative knowledge is accepted as true because it comes from experts or has been sanctified over time as tradition. In the classroom, the most common source of information is some authority, such as a textbook, teacher, or reference work.

Authority as a source of knowledge has its values as well as its dangers. Civilization would certainly be in a state of stagnation if each individual were unwilling to accept any statement unless he or she had personally verified it through direct, firsthand experience. The acceptance of authoritative knowledge generally saves time and enhances social and scientific progress. On the other hand, this form of knowledge is only as valid as the assumptions upon which it stands. If authoritative knowledge is built upon a foundation of incorrect assumptions, then that knowledge will of necessity be distorted.

Reason. The view that reasoning, thought, or logic is the central factor in knowledge is known as rationalism. The rationalist, in emphasizing humanity's power of thought and what the mind contributes to knowledge, is likely to claim that the senses alone cannot provide us with universally valid judgments that are consistent with one another. From this perspective, the sensations and experiences which we gain through our senses are the raw materials of knowledge.

These sensations must be organized by the mind into a meaningful system before they become knowledge.

Rationalism, in its less extreme form, claims that people have the power to know with certainty various truths about the universe which the senses alone cannot give. For example, if x is equal to y, and y is equal to z, then x is equal to z. It is possible to know that this is true quite independently of any actual instances or experiences, and that it applies to boxes, triangles, and other concrete objects in the universe. In its more extreme form, rationalism claims that humans are capable of arriving at irrefutable knowledge independently of sense experience.

Formal logic is a tool used by rationalists. Systems of logic have the advantage of having internal consistency, but they face the danger of not being related to the external world. Logical systems of thought are only as valid as the premises upon which they are built.

Intuition. The direct apprehension of knowledge that is not the result of conscious reasoning or of immediate sense perception is called "intuition." In the literature dealing with intuition we often find such expressions as "immediate feeling of certainty" and "imagination touched with conviction." Intuition occurs beneath the "threshold of consciousness." It is often experienced as a "sudden flash of insight." Many students have had such experiences while working out a mathematical problem for which they obtain the answer before they have been able to work through the steps of the problem.

Intuition is perhaps the most personal way of knowing. It is a direct apprehension of knowledge accompanied by an intense feeling of conviction that one has discovered what he or she is looking for. Intuition has been claimed, under varying circumstances, as a source for both religious and secular knowledge.

The weakness or danger of intuition is that it does not appear to be a safe method of obtaining knowledge when used alone. It goes astray very easily and may lead to absurd claims unless it is controlled by or checked against other methods of knowing. Intuitive knowledge, however, has the distinct advantage of being able to leap over the limitations of human experience.

The complementary nature of knowledge sources. There is no one source of knowledge that supplies people with all knowledge. The various sources should be seen in a complementary relationship rather than one of antagonism. It is true, however, that most thinkers choose one source as being more basic than the others. This most basic source is then used as a background against which other means of obtaining knowledge are evaluated. For example, in the modern world, empirical knowledge generally is seen as the most basic source. Most people hold any purported knowledge suspect if it does not agree with scientific theory. By way of contrast, biblical Christianity sees revelation as providing the basic framework within which other sources of knowledge must be tested.

Validity of Knowledge[5]

Recorded history shows that many beliefs once accepted as true were later discovered to be false. How can one say that some beliefs are true while others are false? What criteria can be used? Can we ever be certain that the truth has been discovered? Most people agree that tradition, instinct, and strong feelings are inadequate tests of truth. Universal agreement is also suspect, since all humans may have the same inherent shortcomings. Philosophers, in the main, have relied on three tests of truth—the correspondence, coherence, and pragmatic theories.

The correspondence theory. The correspondence theory is a test which uses agreement with "fact" as a standard of judgment. According to this theory, truth is faithfulness to objective reality. For example, the statement "There is a lion in the classroom" can be verified by empirical investigation. If a judgment corresponds with the facts, it is true; if not, it is false. This test of truth is often held by those working in the sciences.

Critics of the correspondence theory have put forth three main objections. First, they ask, "How can we compare our ideas with reality, since we know only our own experiences and cannot get outside of our experiences so that we can compare our ideas with reality in its 'pure' state?" Second, they note that the theory of correspondence also seems generally to assume that our sense data are clear and accurate. And, third, the critics point out that the theory is inadequate because we have ideas that have no concrete existence outside the area of human thought with which we can make comparisons. Many mental constructs in ethics, logic, and mathematics fall into this category.

The coherence theory. This theory places its trust in the consistency or harmony of all one's judgments. According to this test, a judgment is true if it is consistent with other judgments that have previously been accepted as true. The proponents of the coherence theory of truth point out, for example, that a statement is often judged to be true or false on the ground that it is or is not in harmony with what has already been decided to be true. This test of validity has generally been held by those who deal with abstract ideas and uplift intellectualism, as opposed to those who deal with the material aspects of reality.

Critics of the coherence approach have noted that false systems of thought can be just as internally consistent as true systems. They claim, therefore, that the theory falls short of what is needed because it does not distinguish between consistent truth and consistent error.

The pragmatic theory. There is a large group of modern philosophers who claim that there is no such thing as static or absolute truth. Pragmatists (to be discussed in Chapter 4) reject the correspondence theory due to their belief that people know only their experiences. They also dismiss the coherence theory because it is formal and rationalistic in a world in which we can know nothing about "substances," "essences," and "ultimate realities." Pragmatists see the test of truth in its utility, workability, or satisfactory consequences. In the thinking of John Dewey and William James, truth is what works.

Traditionalists have seen dangers in this test of truth, since it leads to relativism in the sense that there can be one truth for you and another for me. Critics also assert that "what works" in the limited range of human experience may be delusive when measured against what they see as an external reality built into the very essence of the universe.

Epistemology and Education

Epistemology, like metaphysics, stands at the base of human thought and activity. Educational systems deal in knowledge, and therefore epistemology is a primary determinant of educational beliefs and practices.

Epistemology makes a direct impact upon education in many ways. For example, assumptions about the importance of the various sources of knowledge will certainly be reflected in curricular emphases. A Christian school, with its belief in revelation as a source of certain knowledge, will undoubtedly have a curriculum and a role for the Bible in that curriculum that differ in substantial ways from an institution based upon a set of naturalistic premises.

Epistemological assumptions concerning the communication of

knowledge from one person or thing to another person will also impact teaching methodologies and the function of the teacher in the educative context. Educators must understand their epistemological presuppositions before they will be able to operate effectively.

The Metaphysical-Epistemological Dilemma

At this point it is evident that humanity is suspended, so to speak, in midair both metaphysically and epistemologically. Our problem is that it is not possible to make statements about reality without first having a theory for arriving at truth; and, on the other hand, a theory of truth cannot be developed without first having a concept of reality. We are caught in the web of circularity.

Through the study of basic questions, people are forced to realize their smallness and helplessness in the universe. They realize that nothing can be known for certain in the sense of final and ultimate proof that is open and acceptable to all people.[6] Every person—the skeptic and the agnostic, the scientist and the businessperson, the Hindu and the Christian—lives by a faith. The acceptance of a particular position in metaphysics and epistemology is a "faith choice" made by individuals, and it entails a commitment to a way of life.

The circular nature of the reality-truth dilemma is certainly not the most comforting aspect of philosophical thought; but since it does exist, we are obligated to make ourselves aware of it. Of course, this whole problem comes as no surprise to mature scientists who have come to grips with the limitations of their art and the philosophy upon which it is built. Neither does it pose a threat to believers in certain religious persuasions who have traditionally seen their basic beliefs in terms of personal choice, faith, and commitment. The whole problem, however, does come as a great shock and a disturbing issue to the average secular individual.

The conclusion of the metaphysical-epistemological dilemma is that all persons live by faith in the basic beliefs they have chosen. Different individuals have made different faith choices on the metaphysical-epistemological continuum and therefore have varying philosophic positions. The remainder of this book will examine the educational implications of distinctive philosophical choices. Before moving to that material, however, we will need to explore a third major area of philosophical content.

AXIOLOGY

Axiology is the branch of philosophy that seeks to answer the question, "What is of value?" People's interest in values stems from the fact that they are valuing beings. Humans desire some things more than others—they have preferences. Rational individual and social life is based upon a system of values. Value systems are not universally agreed upon, and different positions on the questions of metaphysics and epistemology determine different systems of value, because axiological systems are built upon conceptions of reality and truth.

The question of values deals with notions of what a person or a society conceives of as being good or preferable. A problem arises when two different conceptions of good or value are held by the same society or person. For example, a society may define a "good" as clean air and water. Yet that same society may turn around and pollute the earth in its acquisition of another good—money and material things. In such a case, there is a clear tension in values—a tension between what people say they value and what they act out in their daily lives. Thus, one might ask, "Which do they really value—what they say or what they do?"

Charles Morris has labeled the values that people verbalize, but may not actualize, as "conceived values." Those that they act upon he has referred to as "operative values."[7] Van Cleve Morris went one step beyond the problem of conceived and operative values by claiming that this whole problem is actually of mere "tactical" importance when compared to the "strategic" seriousness of discovering "what we ought to prefer."[8] In other words, he is claiming that the most crucial value issue for educators is determining what people ought to prefer rather than defining and clarifying those preferences that they act out or verbalize.

Axiology, like metaphysics and epistemology, stands at the very foundation of the educational process. A major aspect of education is the development of preferences. The classroom is an axiological theater in which teachers cannot hide their moral selves. In the area of axiology, by their actions teachers constantly instruct groups of highly impressionable young people who assimilate and imitate their teachers' value structures to a significant extent. Axiology has two main branches—ethics and aesthetics.

Ethics

Ethics is the study of moral values and conduct. It seeks to answer such questions as "What should I do?" "What is the good life for all people?" and "What is good conduct?" Ethical theory is concerned with providing right values as the foundation for right actions.

Harold Titus and Marilyn Smith claim that the question of morality is the central issue of our time.[9] World society has made unprecedented technological advances, but has not advanced significantly, if at all, in ethical and moral conceptions.

In 1952 George S. Counts noted that Western society had become so enraptured by technological advance that it tended to conceive of human progress largely in technological terms. Progress had come to mean more gadgets, more labor-saving devices, more speed in transportation, and more material comforts. "We are learning today, to our sorrow," said Counts, "that this advance, when not accompanied by equally profound reconstruction in the realms of understanding and value, of customs and institutions, of attitudes and loyalties, can bring trouble and disaster."[10] A decade later, writing on the same topic, he quoted Wernher Von Braun, an authority on rockets, as warning: "'If the world's ethical standards fail to rise with the advance of our technological revolution, we shall perish.'"[11]

The study of ethics is crucial in a world civilization that has the power to destroy the natural order through "peaceful" industrial processes or to obliterate more violently the present culture through nuclear warfare. Science and technology in themselves are morally neutral, but the uses to which they are put involve ethical considerations.

Both as a society and as individuals, we exist in a world in which meaningful ethical decisions cannot be avoided. Due to this fact, it is impossible to escape the teaching of ethical concepts in the school. Of course, one may choose to remain silent on these issues. That silence, however, is not neutrality—it is merely supporting the ethical *status quo*.

Ethical conceptions will enter the classroom in one form or another. The problem is that people differ in their ethical bases and feel quite strongly about having their children "indoctrinated" in a moral view that is alien to their fundamental beliefs. This issue is more of a problem in public school systems than in parochial schools, since the latter are generally established to teach a particular world view to a largely homogeneous group of pupils.

The following questions highlight the ethical problems that divide people:

- Are ethical standards and moral values absolute or relative?
- Do universal moral values exist?
- Does the end ever justify the means?
- Can morality be separated from religion?
- Who or what forms the basis of ethical authority?

Aesthetics

Aesthetics is the realm of value that searches for the principles governing the creation and appreciation of beauty and art. Aesthetics deals with the theoretical aspects of art in its widest sense and should not be confused with actual works of art or the technical criticism of them. Perhaps aesthetics ranks as the most controversial human study. If you want to get certain segments of any population excited, just begin to make authoritative judgments about the value of specific forms of literature, music, and visual art. Aesthetics is a realm of theory that relates closely to imagination and creativity, and it therefore tends to become highly personal and subjective.

Historians of past civilizations have usually considered artistic accomplishments to be an important mark of cultural development. By way of contrast, it should be recognized that some modern societies, such as the United States, have given primary importance to utilitarian and material concerns. Art "bakes no bread" for competitive individuals seeking to get ahead in the world, and it may not be seen as important by a culture embroiled in a race for survival in the technological and military spheres.

As a result, artistic works and aesthetic appreciation have found a rather low place in the hierarchy of American education. This priority was highlighted by the influential Conant Report, which did not recommend art as a requirement for high-school graduation. More recently, the National Commission on Excellence in Education also gave the arts only marginal recognition in its recommended curriculum.[12]

One must realize, however, that aesthetic valuation is a part of daily experience and cannot be avoided. The aesthetic experience often leads to a heightened sense of perception, an ability to apprehend new meanings, an elevation of feeling, and a broadened sensitivity. In one sense, the aesthetic experience is tied to the cognitive world of intellectual understanding; but, in another sense, it soars beyond the cognitive into the affective realm with its focus on feeling and emotion. The aesthetic experience enables people to move beyond the limits imposed by purely rational thought and the weakness of human language. A picture, song, or story may create an impression in a person that could never be conveyed through logical argument. Christ relied on aesthetic dynamics when He created word pictures in His parables.

Human beings are aesthetic beings, and it is just as impossible to avoid teaching aesthetics in the school, home, media, or church as it is to avoid inculcating ethical values. If educators do not consciously face up to their aesthetic responsibilities, they will make aesthetic impressions upon their students unconsciously and uncritically.

Areas of aesthetic importance in the school are usually thought of in terms of art, music, and literature classes. These aspects of the formal educational experience are certainly important in developing creativity and appreciation and in heightening a child's sensitivity to emotions and feelings, but perhaps the aesthetic experience is broader than these formal experiences.

Some philosophers and educators believe that the school and other educational agencies also have a responsibility to help students see the aesthetic dimension in the educational environment in such areas as architecture, the school grounds, personal neatness, and the neatly written paper. Aesthetics permeates the educational atmosphere, and the questions of "What is beautiful?" and "What should I like?" form one more part of the philosophic platform underlying education.

There are several issues that lay the basis for differences in aesthetic theory and choice. In evaluating these issues, individuals should keep in mind that aesthetic belief is directly related to other aspects of their philosophy. For example, if subjectivity and randomness are accepted in epistemology and metaphysics, they will be reflected in both aesthetics and ethics. Aesthetics is not a realm divorced from the rest of life. People's aesthetic values are a reflection of their total philosophy. The following issues form the basis for divergent aesthetic positions:

- Should art be imitative and representative, or should it be the product of the private creative imagination?

- Should the subject matter of artistic forms deal with the good in life only, or should it also include the ugly and grotesque?
- What is "good" art? By what standard, if any, can art be labeled "beautiful" or "ugly"?
- Should art have a social function and message, or should its meaning remain forever private to its creator?
- Can there be art for art's sake, or must it have a practical significance?
- Does beauty inhere in the art object itself, or is beauty supplied by the eye of the beholder?

Axiology and Education

The study of axiology has always been important, but it has a special relevance for educators in our day. The last century has seen an unprecedented upheaval in value structures, and today we live at a time when humanity's axiological position might best be described by the words "deterioration" and "flux."

John Gardner, a former United States Secretary of Health, Education, and Welfare, pointed out that a century ago it took a great deal of courage to become a rebel and attack certain dysfunctional aspects of a rigid social system. He noted, however, that these rebels were often highly moral people who were seeking a deeper level of value than could be seen from the surface. Gardner's conclusion was that the superficial has been destroyed and that the time has come to quit "pulverizing the fragments" and to begin asking what we intend to do "to protect ourselves from the elements." He made a crucial observation in noting that "once it was the skeptic, the critic of the *status quo*, who had to make a great effort. Today the skeptic is the *status quo*. The one who must make the effort is the man who seeks to create a new moral order."[13]

E. F. Schumacher demonstrated similar insight when he observed that the person "who conceived the idea that 'morality is bunk' did so with a mind well-stocked with moral ideas." He went on to point out that many of our generation no longer have a mind well-stocked with moral ideas; instead, such minds are well-stocked with the nineteenth-century concept that "morality is bunk." Schumacher concluded by calling for a reconstruction of our thought so that we can focus upon the deepest problems of our age. Without such a re-emphasis of axiological concerns, he postulated, education will prove to be an agent of destruction rather than a constructive resource.[14]

PHILOSOPHIC ISSUES AND EDUCATIONAL GOALS AND PRACTICES

Chapter 1 described education as a deliberate process that has a desired goal. If that is the case, then educators must have some basis for arriving at a conception of that goal. Concern with a goal presupposes a world view or a philosophical viewpoint that involves a set of beliefs in the nature of reality, the essence of truth, and a basis for forming values. As noted above, concepts of reality, truth, and value are the "stuff" of philosophy. Philosophy, therefore, is a basic constituent in the foundation of educational practice.

Figure 3 illustrates the fact that there is a definite relationship between philosophic beliefs and educational practices. For example, a distinct metaphysical and epistemological viewpoint will lead to a value orientation. That value orientation, in conjunction with its corresponding view of reality and truth, will determine the goals that will be deliberately aimed at in the educational process. The goals, in turn, will suggest preferred methods and curricular emphases.

Chapters 3 and 4 illustrate that varying positions on philosophic issues often lead to different educational practices when educators are consistent with their beliefs. This does not imply that different philosophic beliefs will always lead to different practices, since people may arrive at the same destination from different starting points. Neither does it mean that educators holding similar philosophic beliefs will choose the same practical applications. The point to note is that it is important for educators to choose, select, and develop practices that are in harmony with their beliefs.

It is also important to recognize that philosophy is not the sole determinant of specific educational practices. Figure 3 points out that elements in the everyday world play a significant role in shaping educational practice. Many factors—including political forces, economic conditions, the needs of the labor market, and the social conceptions of a particular population—impact upon educational practice.

Philosophy might be seen as providing the basic boundaries for preferred educational practices for any group in society. Within these

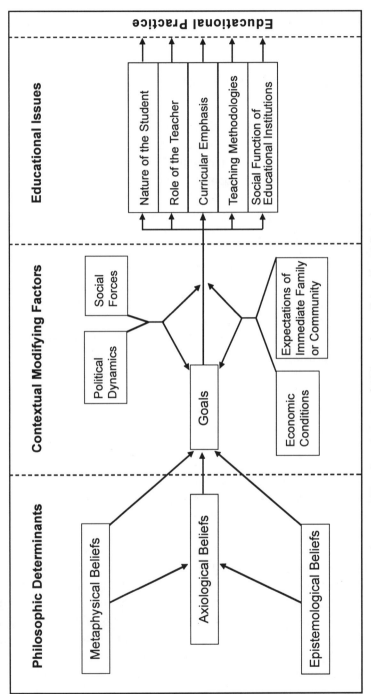

Figure 3. The Relationship of Philosophy to Educational Practice

boundaries, adjustments are made for particular situations in the everyday world. Parochial and private education sometimes arises when a subset of the population establishes a different set of philosophic foundations and educational boundaries from those of the larger culture. In such situations, an observer would expect to find some basic differences between the public system and the private alternative, since they are built upon different belief systems. The challenge for Christian educators is to select and develop educational practices that harmonize with their beliefs and are, at the same time, feasible in their social, political, and economic context.

SUMMARY OF PART I

Part I has indicated that the study of the philosophy of education is to help educators avoid the "mindless" fallacy of neglecting to root their educational practices in their basic beliefs. Education has been defined as a deliberate process that is goal-oriented. Philosophy has been set forth as a threefold entity (an activity, an attitude, and a body of content) that gives direction to education, since educational goals have a relationship to the metaphysical, epistemological, and axiological content of one's philosophy. It has also been noted that education and its related learning processes take place in a complex milieu in which the school is one of many dynamic forces. Philosophic beliefs determine the basic goals of education, but social dynamics modify both educational goals and practices.

Perhaps the central message of Part I is that educators must seek to establish educational environments and practices that are in harmony with their basic beliefs. That is true for all educators, but it may be even more crucial for Christian educators who have sought to develop an alternative educational system based on supernatural assumptions in the context of a society that is largely operating on naturalistic premises.[15] It is sometimes more natural, as well as easier, for the Christian to follow the plans and methodologies of the larger society than to deliberately examine those plans and methodologies in the light of the Christian world view. To follow the path of least resistance, however, may not always lead to Christian education.

The challenge is to examine Christian education in relation to Christian philosophy and then to select and/or develop methodologies and curricular patterns that best fit those philosophic starting points. Part II will examine some traditional and modern approaches to linking philosophy and education, while Part III will perform the same task from a Christian perspective.

Notes

1. For a helpful treatment of the various religious "isms," see Norman L. Geisler and William D. Watkins, *Worlds Apart: A Handbook of World Views*, 2d ed. (Grand Rapids, MI: Baker Book House, 1989). A broader treatment of "isms" is found in James W. Sire, *The Universe Next Door: A Basic Worldview Catalog*, 3d ed. (Downers Grove, IL: InterVarsity, 1997).

2. J. Donald Butler, *Four Philosophies and Their Practice in Education and Religion*, 3d ed. (New York: Harper & Row, 1968), p. 21.

3. Paul Nash, Andreas M. Kazamias, and Henry J. Perkinson, *The Educated Man: Studies in the History of Educational Thought* (New York: John Wiley & Sons, 1966); Paul Nash, *Models of Man: Explorations in the Western Educational Tradition* (New York: John Wiley & Sons, 1968); David Elton Trueblood, *Philosophy of Religion* (New York: Harper & Row, 1957), p. xiv.

4. Van Cleve Morris, *Philosophy and the American School*, p. 118.

5. Cf. Harold H. Titus and Marilyn S. Smith, *Living Issues in Philosophy*, 6th ed. (New York: D. Van Nostrand Co., 1974), pp. 266-73. See also John S. Brubacher, *Modern Philosophies of Education*, 4th ed. (New York: McGraw-Hill Book Co., 1969), pp. 227-30; David Elton Trueblood, *General Philosophy* (New York: Harper & Row, 1963), pp. 54-67.

6. D. Elton Trueblood has spoken to this point: "It is now widely recognized that absolute proof is something which the human being does not and cannot have. This follows necessarily from the twin fact that deductive reasoning cannot have certainty about its premises and that inductive reasoning cannot have certainty about its conclusions. The notion that, in natural science, we have both certainty and absolute proof is simply one of the superstitions of our age." *A Place to Stand* (New York: Harper & Row, 1969), p. 22; for a fuller discussion on the limits of proof, see Trueblood, *General Philosophy*, pp. 92-111.

7. Charles Morris, *Varieties of Human Value* (Chicago: The University of Chicago Press, 1956), pp. 10-11.

8. Van Cleve Morris, *Philosophy and the American School*, p. 221.

9. Titus and Smith, *Living Issues in Philosophy*, p. 115.

10. George S. Counts, *Education and American Civilization* (New York: Teachers College, Columbia University, Bureau of Publications, 1952), p. 130.

11. George S. Counts, *Education and the Foundations of Human Freedom* (Pittsburgh: University of Pittsburgh Press, 1962), pp. 27-28.

12. John Martin Rich, *Education and Human Values* (Reading, MA: Addison-Wesley Publishing Co., 1968), pp. 125, 146. See also James B. Conant, *The American High School Today* (New York: McGraw-Hill Book Co., 1959); National Commission on Excellence in Education, *A Nation at Risk: The Imperative for Educational Reform* (Washington, DC: U.S. Government Printing Office, 1983), p. 26.

13. John W. Gardner, *Self-Renewal: The Individual in the Innovative Society* (New York: Harper & Row, 1964), pp. 120-22.

14. E. F. Schumacher, *Small Is Beautiful: Economics as if People Mattered* (New York: Harper & Row, 1973), pp. 93-94.

15. An interesting discussion along this line is found in E. F. Schumacher, *A Guide for the Perplexed* (New York: Harper & Row, 1977), pp. 1-15. Schumacher notes that supernaturalism finds no place on philosophic maps developed upon naturalistic presuppositions by "scientific imperialists." In other words, much of the world treats a great deal of Christian reality as if it doesn't even exist. That leads to perplexity.

PART TWO: PHILOSOPHY AND EDUCATION

3

Traditional Philosophies and Education

Chapter 2 examined three central philosophic issues—metaphysics, epistemology, and axiology. Not everyone answers the questions spawned by these issues in the same way. Different approaches to these questions give rise to various "schools" of philosophy, such as idealism, realism, neo-scholasticism, pragmatism, and existentialism. These differences in philosophic belief lead to variance in educational theory and practice. There is a direct relationship between people's basic beliefs and how they view such educational components as the nature of the student, the role of the teacher, the best curricular emphasis, the most efficient instructional methods, and the social function of the school.

The remainder of this book will examine the connection between philosophy and education. The present chapter will discuss the relationship in terms of traditional philosophy, while Chapters 4 and 5 will perform the same task in the light of modern and postmodern philosophy. Chapter 6 will examine contemporary educational theories, and will, at first glance, look like a departure from the basic principle of organization. Upon a second viewing, however, these theories will be seen as educational extensions of the philosophic positions presented in Chapters 3 through 5. Part III will utilize the same model to study the relationship between Christian philosophy and education.

THE FUNCTION AND LIMITATION OF LABELS

The next two chapters will be using labels for groups of philosophers who approach the major issues of philosophy in basically the same manner. For example, some philosophers will be called pragmatists, while others will be referred to as idealists.

At the outset, it is important that the reader understands the limitations of any labeling system. First, any system for the classification of philosophic schools is, at best, only loosely accurate. One should not get the idea that philosophers may all be neatly categorized into five or six boxes and that each of these groups is completely distinct from the rest. The schools of philosophy might rather be seen as points on several continua on which there are differences but also agreements and overlapping. Therefore, no one classification is ever totally satisfactory.

Second, too much reliance upon labels may prove to be a substitute for thought about the significance of the differences between the systems and the variations between philosophers within a particular "school." Gaining an idea of the significance of the labels is the beginning rather than the end of understanding the nature of philosophy. Third, labels must be seen for what they are—a simplification of a complex field, so that neophytes will be able to find a starting place for their understanding.

Despite the limitations inherent in the use of labels, they still have a great deal of value. For one thing, the human mind demands classification systems. When faced with large banks of random data, the mind begins to search for understanding by dividing that data into manageable segments on the basis of distinctions and likenesses. It then applies names to the groups, so that the name or label is symbolic of a whole set of characteristics and affinities. Labels, therefore, help us focus on meaningful aspects and divisions of a topic. Thus, a first function of labels is to serve as handles by which we can get ahold of an area of thought; they help us gain control over a subject and clear up what would otherwise be a blur.

A second function of labels is to aid us in evaluating new material in the framework of what we already know. In this role, labels not only help us establish a knowledge system, but they also help us extend and enrich it. Used in a functional way, labels act as a general guide to help us make sense out of a complex universe. Labels become dysfunctional when they obscure the complexity that lies behind them and thus become a substitute for thinking rather than a tool of intelligence.

Labels have been used in this book to help the beginning student in educational philosophy see how basic differences regarding the nature of reality, truth, and value often lead to differing educational practices. This understanding is crucial, since it is imperative that our educational practices harmonize with our basic beliefs. It is unfortunate that this is sometimes not the case among educational practitioners. As a result, their practices all too often do not implement advancement toward their stated goals. It is such a state of affairs that has fostered a "bandwagon mentality" among many educators and has caused them to adopt educational innovations as panaceas before they have evaluated them in terms of basic beliefs and desired end products. This frantic activity is what has brought the charge of "mindlessness" against the educational establishment. Educators must realize that all educational practices are built upon assumptions rooted in philosophy, and that different philosophic starting points may lead to varying educational practices.

IDEALISM

Background

Idealism is a philosophic position that has had a great deal of influence upon education down through the ages. As an educational philosophy, idealism has had less direct influence in the twentieth century than previously. Indirectly, however, its ideas still permeate Western educational thought.

William E. Hocking, a modern idealist, has pointed out that the term "idea-ism" would be a better title than "idealism."[1] This is true because idealism is more concerned with "eternal" concepts (ideas), such as "truth," "beauty," and "honor," than with the high-minded striving for excellence which is referred to when we say, "She is very idealistic."

Idealism, at its core, is an emphasis on the reality of ideas, thoughts, minds, or selves, rather than a stress on material objects and forces. Idealism emphasizes mind as being basic or prior to matter, and even contends that mind is real while matter is a by-product of mind.[2] This is in direct contrast to materialism, which claims that matter is real and mind is an accompanying phenomenon.

Historically, idealism was clearly formulated in the fourth century before Christ by Plato (427-347 B.C.). Athens, during Plato's life-time, was in a state of transition. The Persian Wars had thrust Athens into a new era. Following the wars, trade and commerce grew rapidly, and foreigners settled within her walls in large numbers to take advantage of the opportunities for acquiring wealth.

That greater exposure of Athens to the outside world brought new ideas into all areas of Athenian culture. These new ideas, in turn, led people to question traditional knowledge and values. At this time, also, a new group of teachers, the Sophists, arose. The teachings of the Sophists introduced controversial ideas into the fields of politics and ethics. The Sophists focused upon individualism as they sought to pre-pare people for the new opportunities of a more commercial society. Their emphasis on individualism was a shift from the communal cul-ture of the past, and it led to relativism in such areas as belief and value.

Plato's philosophy[3] can, to a large extent, be seen as a reaction to the state of flux that had destroyed the old Athenian culture. Plato's quest was a search for certain truth. He defined truth as that which is perfect and eternal. It is evident that the world of daily existence is constantly changing. Truth, therefore, could not be found in the imper-fect and transitory world of matter.

Plato believed that there were universal truths upon which all peo-ple could agree. Such truths were found in mathematics. For example, $5 + 7 = 12$ has always been true (it is an *a priori* truth), is true now, and will always be true in the future. It was Plato's contention that uni-versal truths exist in every realm, including politics, religion, ethics, and education. To arrive at universal truths, Plato moved beyond the ever-changing world of sensory data to the world of ideas.

Idealism, with its stress on unchanging universal Truth, has had a powerful impact upon philosophical thought. The Christian church grew up in a world permeated by Neo-platonism and early amalga-mated idealism with its theology. This union was most clearly set forth by Augustine (354-430) in the fifth century. Idealism has been devel-oped in modern thought by such philosophers as Rene Descartes (1596-1650), George Berkeley (1685-1753), Immanuel Kant (1724-1804), and Georg Wilhelm Friedrick Hegel (1770-1831).

Perhaps the most influential American educational idealist was William T. Harris (1835-1909), who founded the *Journal of Specula-*

tive Philosophy, served as the dynamic superintendent of the Saint Louis schools during the 1870s, and later became the United States Commissioner of Education. Two twentieth-century idealists who have sought to apply idealism to modern education are J. Donald Butler and Herman H. Horne.[4] Throughout its history, idealism has been closely linked with religion since they both focus on the spiritual and otherworldly aspects of reality.

Philosophic Position of Idealism

A reality of the mind. Perhaps the easiest way to arrive at an understanding of idealist metaphysics is to go to the most influential of all idealists—Plato. Plato gives us a view of the idealist's concept of reality in his Allegory of the Cave.[5] Imagine, suggests Plato, a group of people in a dark cave, chained in such a way that they can see only the back wall of the cave. They cannot turn their heads or bodies to the right or left. Behind these chained beings is a fire, and between them and the fire is a raised pathway. Objects move along the pathway, and their shadows are cast upon the wall. The chained individuals cannot see the fire or the objects; they see only the shadows. If, questions Plato, they had been chained in this manner all their lives, would not they consider the shadows to be real in the fullest sense of the word?

Now, continues Plato, imagine that these individuals are unchained and are able to turn around and see the fire and the objects on the pathway. They would then have to readjust their conception of reality to fit the new perceptual data. Then, after having adjusted to a three-dimensional reality, they are led from the cave into the brilliance of the sunlit world. Would they not be dumbfounded by this fuller view of reality? Would they not also, in bewilderment, desire to return to the more manageable environment of the cave?

Plato's allegory suggests that the majority of humanity lives in the world of the senses—the cave. But to Plato this is not the world of ultimate reality; it is only a world of shadows and images of the "real" world. The more genuinely real world is a world of pure ideas that is beyond the world of the senses. One comes into contact with the ultimately real world through the intellect. The understanding of reality is a rare gift that is possessed by only a few people. These people (the thinkers and philosophers), therefore, should fill the most important posts in society if the social order is to be just. By way of contrast, most people live by their senses and are not in contact with reality. They maintain a definitely inferior existence.

In summary, it might be re-emphasized that reality for the idealist is dichotomous—there is the world of the apparent, which we perceive through our senses, and the world of reality, which we perceive through our minds. The world of the mind focuses on ideas, and these eternal ideas precede and are more important than the physical world of sensation. That ideas precede material objects can be illustrated, claim the idealists, by the construction of a chair. They point out that someone had to have the idea of a chair in mind before he or she could build one to sit on. The metaphysics of idealism might be defined as a world of mind.

Truth as ideas. The clue to understanding the idealists' epistemology lies in their metaphysics. Since they emphasize the reality of ideas and mind, we find their theory of knowing to be principally an enterprise of mentally grasping ideas and concepts. Knowing reality is not an experience of seeing, hearing, or touching; it is rather taking hold of the idea of something and retaining it in the mind.

Truth to the idealist lies in the realm of ideas. Some idealists have postulated an Absolute Mind or Absolute Self who is constantly thinking these ideas. George Berkeley, a Christian idealist, identified the concept of the Absolute Self with God. Down through history many religious thinkers have made that same identification.

Key words in idealistic epistemology are "consistence" and "coherence." Idealists are concerned with developing a system of truth that has internal and logical consistency. We know that something is true, they claim, when it fits into the harmonious nature of the universe. Those things which are inconsistent with the ideal structure of the universe must be rejected as false. Frederick Neff has noted that

> idealism is essentially a metaphysics, and even its epistemology is metaphysical in the sense that it attempts to rationalize and justify what is metaphysically true rather than to utilize experience and methods of knowledge as a basis for the formulation of truth.[6]

Truth for idealists is inherent in the very nature of the universe. Therefore it is prior to, and largely independent of, experience. Hence, the means by which ultimate knowledge is gained is not empirical.

Idealists of various strains rely heavily upon intuition, revelation, and rationalism in gaining and extending knowledge. These methods are those best able to handle truth as ideas, which is the basic epistemological stance of idealism.

Values from the ideal world. The axiology of idealism is firmly rooted in its metaphysical outlook. If ultimate reality lies beyond this world, and if there is an Absolute Self who is the prototype of mind, then the cosmos can be thought of in terms of macrocosm and microcosm. From this viewpoint, the macrocosm can be thought of as the world of the Absolute Mind, while this earth and its sensory experiences may be thought of in terms of microcosm—a shadow of that which is ultimately real. In such a conception, it should be evident that both ethical and aesthetical criteria of goodness and beauty would be external to humanity, would be inherent in the very nature of true reality, and would be based on fixed and eternal principles.

For the idealist, the ethical life can be thought of as a life lived in harmony with the universe. If the Absolute Self is seen in terms of macrocosm, then the individual human self can be identified as a microcosmic self. In this case, the role of the individual self would be to become as much like the Absolute Self as possible. If the Absolute is viewed as the final and most ethical of all things and persons, or as God who is by definition perfect and is thus flawless in morals, the idealist epitome of ethical conduct would lie in the imitation of the Absolute Self. Humanity is moral when it is in accord with the Universal Moral Law, which is an expression of the character of the Absolute Being. A problem arises in discovering the Moral Law. That problem is not difficult for religious idealists, who accept revelation as a source of authority. On the other hand, this discovery does pose a problem for the idealist with a secular orientation. Kant's categorical imperative[7] may be viewed as one means of arriving at the Moral Law by means other than revelation.

The aesthetics of the idealist can also be seen in terms of macrocosm and microcosm. The idealist sees as beautiful the approximation or reflection of the ideal. That art which attempts to express the Absolute is categorized as aesthetically pleasing. Artists seek to capture the ultimate and universal aspects in their work. The function of art forms is not to portray literally the world to our sensibilities, but to depict the world as the Absolute Self sees it. Art is an attempt to capture reality in its perfect form. From this viewpoint, photography, in general, would not be considered a true art form, since its business is to depict things the way they happen to be in our experience. Art from the idealist's point of view can be thought of as the idealization of sensory perceptions.

Idealism and Education

In terms of the idealist metaphor, the learner can be viewed as a microcosmic self who is in the process of becoming more like the Absolute Self. In one sense, the individual self is an extension of the Absolute Self and, as such, has the same attributes in an undeveloped form. Motivationally the idealist pupil "is characterized by . . . the will to perfection. Whatever he does, he does as well as he can. . . . He strives for perfection because the ideal person is perfect."[8]

In a universe whose reality is centered in idea and mind, the most important aspect of learners is their intellect; they are microcosmic minds. It is at the level of mind that the educational endeavor must be primarily aimed, since true knowledge can be gained only through the mind. From this perspective, Plato proclaimed that in the best of all worlds the rulers would be philosophers. Why? Because only they had dealt with the world of ultimate reality which lies beyond this sensory world. Due to their philosophic view, idealists concentrate on the mental development of the learner.

Teachers have a crucial position in an idealist school. It is the teachers who serve the students as living examples of what they can become. Teachers stand closer to the Absolute than do the students, because they have more knowledge about the ultimate world of the mind. They know more about "reality" and are thus able to act as intermediaries between the microcosmic self of the learner and the macrocosmic Absolute Self. The teachers' role is to pass on knowledge of reality and to be examples of the ethical ideal. They are patterns for the students to follow in both their intellectual and social lives.

The subject matter of idealism is viewed in terms of its epistemological position. If truth is ideas, then the curriculum must be formed around those subjects that bring students into contact with ideas. The idealist curriculum emphasizes, therefore, the study of the humanities. For many idealists, the proper study for people is humanity. History and the study of literature are found at the center of their curricular systems, because these subjects help students most in their search for the ideal humanity and ideal society. Pure mathematics is also an appropriate discipline, since it is based upon universal *a priori* principles and it provides methods for dealing with abstractions.

Words, either written or spoken, form the basis of idealism's method of instruction, because it is through words that ideas move from one mind to another. The aim of this method might be defined as the absorption of ideas. The library tends to be the center of educational activity in the idealist school. It is in the library that students come into contact with the world's truly significant ideas. The classroom, in one sense, may be seen as an operating arm or extension of the library—a place in which books and ideas form the center of attention. Teacher methodology in the classroom is often seen in terms of lecturing in a context in which knowledge is being verbally transferred from the teacher to the student. Teachers are also apt to initiate discussions through which they and their students handle the ideas of readings and lectures as they bring concepts into sharper focus.

The idealist teacher would not be especially excited about a field trip to the local dairy or the teaching of auto mechanics in high school, since such activities lie at the periphery of life's true meaning—they deal more with the shadowy sensory world than with ultimate reality. They are not, therefore, proper "educational" activities.[9]

Detractors of idealism have pointed to this type of education as an ivory-tower experience. That criticism does not bother the idealists, who claim that the real purpose of schools and universities is to provide a place where the mind can "think" and "know" without being bothered by the transitory experiences of everyday life.[10]

It should come as no surprise that idealism, with its emphasis on the ideas of the past (especially those ideas dealing with the Absolute), has a conservative social impact. For idealism, the changeless world of Ultimate Reality is of a higher order than the transitory world of the senses. Humanity, when it has finally come into contact with the unchanging ideas of reality, must order its life to fit into the context of that reality. The social function of the school, for the idealist, is to preserve the heritage and to pass on the knowledge of the past. The school is not an agent of change. It is rather a sustainer of the *status quo*.

REALISM

Background

Realism, to a certain extent, is a reaction against the abstractness and otherworldliness of idealism. The basic starting point for the realist is that the objects of our senses exist in their own right quite independently of their being known by a mind. The fundamental difference between realism and idealism might be illustrated by the example of a tree on a deserted island. The idealist would say that such a tree exists only if it is in some mind (including the mind of a transcendent being) or if there is knowledge of it. The realist, on the other hand, holds that whether or not anyone or anything is thinking about the tree, it nevertheless exists—matter is independent of mind.

Well-defined realism finds its genesis in Plato's pupil, Aristotle (384-322 B.C.). On the one hand, Aristotle was deeply influenced by Plato; but, on the other hand, his thinking showed a definite divergence from Platonic idealism. Aristotle held that the basic constituents of every object were form and matter. Form may be equated with Plato's conception of idea, while matter can be thought of in terms of the material making up any particular sensory object. According to Aristotle, form can exist without matter (e.g., the idea of God or the idea of dog), but there can be no matter without form. Aristotle did not downplay the importance of form or ideas. His radical departure from his teacher came with the belief that a better understanding of universal ideas could be obtained through the study of particular things or matter.

It was Aristotle's focus on the possibility of arriving at conceptions of universal form through the study of material objects that led him to lay the basic structure for what has evolved into the modern physical, life, and social sciences. Aristotle was a great organizer and categorizer. Even the beginning college student has probably seen Aristotle's name in the history of such diverse fields as physics, botany, zoology, sociology, psychology, logic, and the various aspects of formal philosophy. In Aristotle, people found the rationale upon which they have developed the modern sciences.

Realism found its way into the modern world largely through the influence of Francis Bacon's (1561-1626) inductive methodology (the scientific method) and John Locke's (1632-1704) proposal that the human mind is a blank sheet (*tabula rasa*) that receives impressions from the environment. Perhaps Harry S. Broudy has made as strong an argument as anyone for realism in modern education.[11]

Philosophic Position of Realism

A reality of things. For the realist, ultimate reality is not in the realm of the mind. The universe is composed of matter in motion, so it is the physical world in which people live that makes up reality. This is a straightforward approach to a world of things that operate according to laws which are built into the very fabric of the universe. The vast cosmos rolls on despite people and their knowledge. The universe is not unlike a giant machine in which humanity is both spectator and participant. The laws controlling the cosmos not only govern the physical universe, but they are also operating in the moral, psychological, social, political, and economic spheres. In other words, the realist sees reality in terms of things that operate according to natural law. In its variation of configurations, realism is found at the philosophic base of much modern science.

Truth through observation. The epistemology of realism is a common sense approach to the world that bases its method upon sensory perception. W. E. Hocking notes that "realism as a general temper of mind is a disposition to keep ourselves and our preferences out of our judgment of things, letting the objects speak for themselves."[12]

Truth, for the realist, is viewed as observable fact. Sense perception is the medium for gaining knowledge.[13] Realism utilizes the inductive method in investigating the natural world and in arriving at general principles from observations. The realist seeks to discover how the world works by examining it. The natural law thereby discovered is believed to be built into the nature of reality. It may be thought of as being absolute, prior to humanity's experience with it, and unchangeable. From that perspective, the existence of "Natural Law" for the realist may be viewed as having much the same magnitude as Absolute Mind for the idealist. Both positions are conceptions of the ultimate and "out-there" nature of truth and reality. Realism turns to the correspondence theory for validating its conception of truth—i.e., truth is that which conforms to the actual situation as perceived by the observer.

Values from nature. According to the realist, values are also obtained by the observation of nature. Through a study of the natural order, one comes to know the laws that provide the basis for ethical and aesthetic judgment. Values derived from this source are permanent, since they are rooted in a universe that is stable—even though, from the human point of view, it is being more fully understood all the time.

The ethical basis of realism might be viewed as the law of nature. Nature, claims the realist, has a moral law. All people have that law or at least have the possibility of discovering it. Just as gravity is a universal law in the physical world, so is supply and demand a law in the economic realm. It was with this concept of moral law in mind that Thomas Jefferson referred to the "inalienable rights" of individuals. Humanity must look to nature for a clearer definition of these rights.

Nature also contains the criteria for beauty. A beautiful art form, from the viewpoint of realism, reflects the logic and order of the universe. In one sense it is "re-presenting," or presenting anew, the rationality of nature as that rationality is revealed in pattern, balance, line, and form. In painting, the objective of artists should be to recreate what they perceive as realistically as possible. From this perspective, photography definitely qualifies as an art form.

Realism and Education[14]

To the realist, students are viewed as functioning organisms that can, through sensory experience, perceive the natural order of the world and thereby come into contact with "reality." Pupils can see, feel, and taste. The world is a "thing," and pupils can know the world through their senses.

Many realists view students as persons who are subject to natural law and are therefore not free in their choices. Students, claim these exponents of realism, respond to environmental stimuli. It is not uncommon to find realists advocating a behavioristic psychology. At its most extreme form, this approach sees students as part of the great universal machine. Such students can be programmed in a manner similar to the way computers are programmed. Of course, such programming may not at first be successful. In that case, students must be reinforced, disciplined, and shaped until they have learned to make the proper responses.

If the student is thought of as a spectator viewing the universal machine, then the teacher can be seen as a more sophisticated observer who knows a great deal about the laws of the cosmos. The role of the teacher, therefore, is to give accurate information about reality to the student in the quickest and most efficient manner. For this reason the teacher's own biases and personality should be as muted as possible. The function of teaching is to demonstrate the regularities and laws of nature and to pass on to the student those facts of the natural world that have been verified by research.

In harmony with its metaphysical and epistemological perspective, the curriculum in the realist school emphasizes the subject matter of the physical world taught in such a way that the orderliness underlying the universe is evident. The sciences stand at the center of the realist curriculum, since the laws of nature are best understood through the subject matter of nature. Mathematics also finds a central place in realist curricular thinking, since mathematics is an example of the highest form of order. Mathematics is a precise, abstract, symbolic system for describing the laws of the universe.

The realist's conception of the universe, with its emphasis on statistical and quantitative studies, has largely shaped much of our knowledge of the social sciences. The realist views the curriculum in terms of knowledge which can be measured. Many realists have taken for their credo the position espoused by Edward L. Thorndike in 1918: "Whatever exists at all exists in some amount. To know it thoroughly involves its quantity as well as its quality."[15]

Thus the focus of the realist curriculum is on demonstrable facts and the structural frameworks of the academic disciplines that give meaning to those facts.[16] The "symbolics of information" (language and mathematics) are also important in the curriculum, because they provide "the entrance to an academic discipline" as well as an encoded system for passing on accumulated knowledge.[17]

The instructional method of the realists is closely related to their epistemology. If truth is gained through sensory perception, then learning experiences should be organized, to a large extent, in a manner that utilizes the senses. It was from this perspective that John Amos Comenius, the seventeenth-century Moravian bishop and educator, became famous for his *Orbis Pictus*, in which he astonished the educational world by suggesting that visual aids—pictures—be used in instructing the young in Latin vocabulary. In the late eighteenth and early nineteenth centuries, Johann Heinrich Pestalozzi took the realist method a giant step forward when he called for the use of physical object lessons in the classroom, since students would learn best if they could feel, smell, and hear an object as well as see it.

The modern realist favors demonstrations in the classroom, field trips, and the use of audio-visual aids in situations where field trips would not be practical or would be too time-consuming. This does not mean that the realist denies the validity of symbolic knowledge (as found in books). It rather implies that the symbol has no existential status, but is viewed simply as a means of representing or communicating about the real world.

The method of realists involves teaching for the mastery of facts in order to develop an understanding of natural law. They are concerned that students comprehend the basic laws of nature. In this approach they rely heavily on inductive logic as they move from the particular facts of sensory experience to the more general laws inferable from that data.

The mechanistic world view of many realists also leads them to favor teaching machines and programmed learning. Through a machine a great deal of accurate information about the world may be passed to the student quickly and efficiently. The whole concept of teaching machines is compatible with the idea that people are machines and can be programmed. From this perspective, teaching is best when it is most objective and dehumanized, since humans are a source of error.

It should be apparent that the social position of the school in realism closely approximates that of the school in idealism. The purpose of the school is to transmit knowledge that has been settled upon by those who have a clear concept of empirical science and natural law and its function in the universe. The realist school focuses on the conservation of the heritage—it is concerned with passing on the proven facts and the structural frameworks that provide meaning for those facts.

NEO-SCHOLASTICISM

Background

Scholasticism was an intellectual movement that developed in western Europe between 1050 and 1350. This movement at first found its home in the monastic orders; but as universities arose in the thirteenth century, it came to dominate their curricula. Scholastic scholars were not as interested in seeking new truth as they were in proving existing truth through rational processes.

A major event that stimulated the rise of scholasticism was the emergence of Aristotle's writings in Christian Europe. Most of his writings had been lost to the Christian world during the Middle Ages. They had, however, been preserved in the Islamic world beyond the pale of medieval Christendom. Those of Aristotle's writings and ideas that had been available to Christian Europe had been largely neglected. Medieval theology and philosophy had been founded upon the Augustinian synthesis of Platonic and early Christian thought.

In the twelfth century, however, translations of Aristotle and Arabic and Jewish commentaries on his works began to appear in western Europe. These new ideas were not always in harmony with accepted Christian thought, and Aristotelian philosophy turned out to be just as divisive to medieval Christendom as Darwinism would later be to nineteenth-century Christianity. It soon became apparent that these two bodies of knowledge—medieval Christianity and Aristotelianism—had to be harmonized. The scholastics sought to organize the data of revelation systematically by the use of Aristotelian deductive logic and to harmonize the ideas of revelation with the philosophy of Aristotle. In essence, scholasticism can be seen as the attempt to rationalize theology in order to buttress faith by reason.

Thomas Aquinas (1225-1274) was the foremost scholar in this crisis. The results of his work have been preserved in his *Summa Theologica*. The basic approach developed by Aquinas was that a person should acquire as much knowledge as possible through the use of human reason and then rely on faith in that realm beyond the scope of human understanding. The philosophy of Aquinas (Thomism) eventually became the official philosophic position of the Roman Catholic Church.

The essence of scholasticism is rationalism. Neo-scholasticism is a new or updated form of scholasticism with its emphasis on, and appeal to, human reason. Neo-scholasticism is therefore a modern statement of a traditional philosophy.

In twentieth-century educational thought, neo-scholasticism was a philosophical position that had two branches. The most important segment, in terms of educational establishments, was the religious branch, which formed the substructure of Roman Catholic educational philosophy. In the literature this segment was often referred to as "scholastic realism," "religious realism," and "ecclesiastical neo-Thomism." Jacques Maritain was a leading advocate of religious neo-scholasticism.

The second division, the secular branch, was represented by such men as Mortimer J. Adler and Robert M. Hutchins.[18] Their beliefs were often labeled "rational humanism," "classical realism," and "secular neo-Thomism." The basic educational ideas of these groups find a united expression in the theory of perennialism, which will be discussed in Chapter 6.

Philosophic Position of Neo-scholasticism

A reality of reason (and God). As noted above, there are some differences of opinion among philosophers over the labeling of the neo-scholastics. This is due partly to the fact that neo-scholasticism overlaps other philosophic positions and partly to the fact that it has two distinct roots. The first of these roots is Aristotle, who laid the foundations of realism. The second root is Aquinas, who synthesized Aristotelian philosophy and Christianity.

Aristotle laid the groundwork of neo-scholasticism through his conception of people as rational animals and his development of deductive logic. For Aristotle, the most important question people can ask about things is their purpose. He held that since humans are the only creatures endowed with the ability to think, humanity's highest purpose is to use that ability. Aristotle also taught that the universe has design and order, and that every result has a cause. The design, order, and cause-and-effect relationships in the world, he claimed, point to a First Cause or an Unmoved Mover. Aquinas equated Aristotle's Unmoved Mover with the Christian God. God, Aquinas suggested, is pure reason; and the universe He created is therefore also reason. Humans, as rational animals, live in a rational world that they are capable of understanding.

The metaphysics of the neo-scholastics is a two-sided coin. On the one side is the natural world that is open to reason. On the other side is the supernatural realm, which is understood through intuition, revelation, and faith. Scientists deal with the natural aspect, but the spiritual side is beyond their reach. Neo-scholastics hold the nature of the universe to be permanent and unchanging.

Truth through rationalism (and inspiration). If, as the neo-scholastics claim, the rational human mind is naturally oriented toward the rationality of the universe, then it follows that the mind can take hold of certain truths by itself—it can intuit truth. Intuitive or self-evident truths, postulate the neo-scholastics, are found in analytic statements. An analytic statement is a statement that contains its predicate in its subject. Examples of analytic statements are "God is good" and "Two things equal to the same thing are equal to each other." These kinds of statements, in which the predicate is analyzed out of the subject, do not have to be tested in experience. One does not need to draw two lines equal to a third and then measure them to see if they are equal. The intellect reveals that this is true—it is self-evident and has been intuited as true.

A second form of truth for the neo-scholastic is found in synthetic statements. Synthetic truth depends upon our experience. An example of a synthetic statement is that "San Francisco is 3,224 miles from New York." Synthetic statements lie in the realm of science and empirical experience. They must be tested, since their predicates are not contained in their subjects. On the other hand, analytic statements are logically and intrinsically true.

Neo-scholastics hold, in contrast to empiricists, that analytic statements form first principles and are therefore of a higher order than synthetic statements. These self-evident statements open up a whole realm of truth to the neo-scholastic that cannot be reached by science. For the secular neo-scholastic, truth can be known through reason and intuition. The religious branch of this philosophic approach adds supernatural revelation as a source of knowledge that can put finite humans in contact with the mind of God.

Both branches of neo-scholasticism rely heavily upon reason and the deductive forms of Aristotelian logic. Induction is not rejected, however, since information gained through the senses forms a part of the raw material used in deductive thinking.

In summary, it should be noted that the neo-scholastics believe in a hierarchy of truth. At the lower level people rely on reason. This is the realm of nature and science and is quite limited. The higher level is the realm of first principles and faith. These two realms often overlap, and thus they form two routes to the same truth. For example, the existence of God is a matter of faith, even though Aquinas posited five logical proofs of God's existence in his *Summa Theologica*. The neo-scholastic values most highly those truths that are logical, permanent, and unchanging.

Values related to rationality. It has been noted that reason is the central pillar in both neo-scholastic metaphysics and epistemology. This is also true of its ethics. The moral life is the life that is in harmony with reason. Humans are basically rational beings, and the good act is controlled by rationality. People sometimes are controlled and led astray by their wills, desires, and emotions. Good people, however, are the ones whose desires and wills are subservient to their intellects; if they know what is right, they will do it, because it is reasonable to do what is good. The ethics of neo-scholasticism might be seen in terms of acting rationally.

Aesthetic theory is not as clear-cut in the neo-scholastic school of philosophy as in other philosophies. This may be due to the fact that the heavy stress of neo-scholasticism on the rational nature of humanity is antithetical to the faculties of will and emotion which we generally associate with art forms. Van Cleve Morris, after noting the inborn tendency of humans to creativity, has summed up the neo-scholastic approach to art as "'creative intuition,' a somewhat mystical, probing lurch of the intellect beyond itself," as if the art were seeking to escape from reason—as in the case of modern art and poetry.[19] This is a concept built upon the desire of people to give to their material the meaning that is, in Aristotelian terms, potentially already in it. Art, therefore, is self-evident to artists. They intuit meaning to art rather than approaching it logically, even though they may appreciate a work of art through the pleasure it gives the intellect.

Neo-scholasticism and Education

Both branches of neo-scholasticism are consistent in the relationship between their philosophic stance and their educational recommendations. The student, for both groups, is a rational being who has a natural potential to acquire Truth and knowledge. Religious neo-scholastics also see the learner as a spiritual being who may relate to God. The responsibility of the school is to help the student develop these capacities.

Faculty psychology is the perspective from which the rational powers of the learner are viewed by the neo-scholastics. In this view, the mind is thought to have different potentials, or faculties, which must be carefully developed. Therefore, the faculty of reason is trained through the formal discipline inherent in the study of those subjects having the most logical organization, the faculty of memory is developed by having students memorize, and the faculty of the will is strengthened by having students engage in tasks that require a high degree of perseverance for completion. Through such procedures, the faculties are developed and the will is brought under submission to reason.

Teachers in a neo-scholastic frame of reference are viewed as mental disciplinarians with the capability of developing reason, memory, and will power in their students. Initiative in education, claims the neo-scholastic (in agreement with idealists and realists), lies with the teacher. It is the teacher's responsibility, in conjunction with other educational authorities, to decide what knowledge the child should learn. It is helpful if this decision harmonizes with the child's interest and curiosity, but subject matter concerns, rather than student desires, are central to the educational endeavor. Intelligence demands the discipline of developing an understanding of those aspects of reality that are permanent and unalterable.

The ecclesiastical neo-scholastic sees the role of teachers to be that of spiritual leaders as well as mental disciplinarians. Teachers lead the child not only through the realm of reason, but also through the more important sphere of faith.

Secular neo-scholastics insist that, since humans are rational beings, the curriculum should give priority to the cultivation of their rational aspects. The mind, therefore, must be trained to think, and education should focus on sharpening the intellect, so that people will be able to understand the Absolute Truth of the cosmos. The mind must be strengthened and toughened if it is to reach that Truth.

From this perspective, it is felt by neo-scholastics that those subject matters having internal logic are best able to achieve the aim of education and should therefore be at the center of the curriculum. Mathematics is seen by many secular neo-scholastics as the nearest approach humanity has made to Pure Reason. Mathematics is uncontaminated by the irregularities of the ordinary affairs of life and therefore most nearly approximates the rational nature of the universe.

Of somewhat less precision, but of great importance in strengthening the mind, are foreign languages—especially those that are most rigorously systematic. Thus Latin and Greek have often stood at the top of the recommended linguistic studies, while the less regular modern languages are lower in the hierarchy. Other topics of study considered especially important are logic and the works of the great minds of the past. The religious branch of neo-scholasticism is in basic agreement with its secular relative, but would hasten to include the systematic study of dogma and doctrine as subjects of primary importance.

The subject matter of the neo-scholastic tradition has two functions: (1) to explain the world to the student and (2) to train the intellect to understand that world. Their curricular stress is upon those subjects that emphasize the intellectual and spiritual aspects of culture.

Neo-scholastic methodology generally focuses on training the intellectual powers. This approach is rooted in the concept of mental discipline. The intellect is strengthened through exercises in reason and memory in relation to the discipline inherent in the subject matter. This training of the intellect has been likened by some to mental calisthenics. The idea runs parallel to building up the physical body. Just as the corporeal muscles are developed through rigorous exercise, so the mind is strengthened by strenuous mental exertion. The training of the will to accept the idea of performing naturally demanding tasks is a by-product of the methodology.

Like other traditional philosophies, neo-scholasticism has a conservative social function. In the eyes of many, it is a regressive social philosophy that faces modern social problems on the basis of thirteenth-century thought patterns.

CRITIQUE AND PERSPECTIVE

Despite their differing viewpoints, the traditional philosophies have certain characteristics in common. Each has metaphysics as its primary concern, each holds that the universe contains truth of an *a priori* and objective sort that is awaiting discovery by people, and each believes that both truth and value are eternal and unchanging rather than relative and transient.

In education the traditional philosophies also have likenesses as well as differences. For example, each sees the teacher as an authoritative person who knows what the student needs to learn; each has set forth a curriculum based on its version of the "solid" subjects that are "heavy" in intellectual content; and each views education and schooling in a conservative vein, since their function is to transfer the heritage of the past to the present generation.

All of these philosophies have made an impact upon recent education. Certainly the traditional bookishness and intellectualism of Western education have been heavily influenced by idealistic and neo-scholastic presuppositions. One of the interesting chapters in the history of education has been the struggle of realism against an entrenched idealism and neo-scholasticism as realistic educators and philosophers sought to make room in educational institutions for sensory experience and the sciences. This struggle began in the eighteenth-century Enlightenment, and the final victory was not achieved until the twentieth century. The influence of Darwinism aided realism in a powerful manner in the final phases of this struggle. It will be seen in Chapter 6 that the impact of the traditional philosophies on twentieth-century education is largely felt through the influence of essentialism, perennialism, and behaviorism.

From a Christian perspective, it appears that each of the traditional philosophies has something of value to offer. Christianity in its different varieties has often aligned itself with either idealism, neo-scholasticism, or realism. Many Christian philosophers and theologians, for example, have equated God with the Absolute Being of idealism, the Unmoved Mover of realism, or the Being of Pure Reason of neo-scholasticism. Christians, traditionally, have also tended to appreciate the *a priori* aspects of these philosophies, along with their affirmation of the existence of certainty and permanence in the realm of knowledge and value.

On the other hand, many Christians have been disturbed by the dichotomy of the spiritual and the material in idealism, and by the emphasis of idealism and neo-scholasticism on the mental and intellectual side of education to the detriment of the affective, physical, and vocational aspects of human existence. This has been particularly offensive to those Christians who have viewed biblical humanity as a unity of mental, physical, and spiritual attributes and have stressed the need for a balance of each of those aspects in education. These Christians find that the idealistic and neo-scholastic emphasis on the mental and rational side of human nature has not provided a base for the practical and physical in education. Beyond these points, others have held that idealism does not provide an adequate explanation for the existence of evil in the world, and that both neo-scholasticism and idealism have tended to provide an elitist education for the few and vocational training for the many in a Christian community espousing the priesthood of each believer.

Other Christians have questioned the naturalistic presuppositions of realism that seem to them to be more in harmony with deism, agnosticism, or even atheism than with personal Christianity. They find even more disturbing the tendency of realism to be deterministic and to minimize the importance of humanity in its attempt to be objective and scientific. From their viewpoint, the lack of free will and human dignity implied in realism is dehumanizing and does not harmonize with the Christian revelation.

In conclusion, it can be said that Christians will probably find something in each of these philosophies that they see as helpful, true, or good. They also probably will find some things that do not fit the biblical picture.

The task is not to accept one of these (or some other) philosophies, but to gain insight into the basic issues of life and some possible answers to those issues. With this heightened awareness of alternative possibilities, the task of individual Christian educators is to seek to build a personal philosophy that will not only guide their educational practice, but will provide a basis for decision-making in every aspect of their lives. Chapter 4 turns from traditional philosophies to modern philosophies. The modern philosophies approach the basic issues of life from a different perspective than the traditional ones, and their answers will provide a broader base from which individual Christians can begin to develop personal philosophies.

Notes

1. William Ernest Hocking, *Types of Philosophy*, 3d ed (New York: Charles Scribner's Sons, 1959), p. 152.

2. In this discussion of idealism the reader should note that even though there are many types of idealism, they all have a common emphasis on ideas and mind. The following pages will

build upon the implications of this central position and will not seek to deal with variations within the idealistic approach to basic philosophic and educational issues. This level of treatment will serve the purposes of this introductory text. What has been said in regard to this simplified approach to idealism will also hold true for the other philosophies studied.

3. A delightful and easy-to-read portrayal of the thought of the various philosophers is found in Jostein Gaarder, *Sophie's World: A Novel About the History of Philosophy* (London: Phoenix House, 1995).

4. J. Donald Butler, *Idealism in Education* (New York: Harper & Row, 1966); Herman Harrell Horne, *The Democratic Philosophy of Education* (New York: The Macmillan Co., 1932).

5. Plato *Republic* 7. 514-17.

6. Frederick C. Neff, *Philosophy and American Education* (New York: The Center for Applied Research in Education, 1966), p. 36.

7. Act only on that maxim which will enable you at the same time to will that it be a universal law.

8. Herman Harrell Horne, "An Idealistic Philosophy of Education," in *Philosophies of Education*, National Society for the Study of Education, Forty-first Yearbook, Part I (Chicago: University of Chicago Press, 1942), pp. 156-57.

9. Following from Plato's aristocratic notions of society and education, idealists have tended to view formal education as being for the select few rather than for the masses. Plato divided people into three basic levels, according to whether they lived by their appetites, passions, or intellects. The type of education that most idealists have been concerned with is for those who are chiefly governed by their intellects. Those outside the intellectual elite should receive vocational and technical studies. For people in the latter group, instruction in the world of things (through either apprenticeships or vocational schooling) would be appropriate, since this harmonizes with their needs and the cast of their minds—minds unable to transcend the world of shadows.

10. Van Cleve Morris, *Philosophy and the American School*, p. 183.

11. Harry S. Broudy, *Building a Philosophy of Education*, 2d ed. (Englewood Cliffs, NJ: Prentice Hall, 1961).

12. Hocking, *Types of Philosophy*, p. 225.

13. It should be noted that the New Realists and the Critical Realists differ over whether the mind perceives the object itself or a representation of that object. That difference, however, is not of major importance for the level of argument being followed in this presentation.

14. A systematic approach to this topic is found in Wm. Oliver Martin, *Realism in Education* (New York: Harper & Row, 1969).

15. Edward L. Thorndike, "The Nature, Purposes, and General Methods of Measurements of Educational Products," in *The Measurement of Educational Products, National Society for the Study of Education*, Seventeenth Yearbook, Part II (Bloomington, IL: Public School Publishing Co., 1918), pp. 16-17.

16. Gerald L. Gutek, *Philosophical and Ideological Perspectives on Education* (Englewood Cliffs, NJ: Prentice Hall, 1988), pp. 46-49.

17. Harry S. Broudy, *The Uses of Schooling* (New York: Routledge, 1988), p. 81; Harry S. Broudy, "What Schools Should and Should Not Teach," *Peabody Journal of Education*, October, 1976, p. 36.

18. Jacques Maritain, *Education at the Crossroads* (New Haven, CT: Yale University Press, 1943); Mortimer J. Adler, "In Defense of the Philosophy of Education," in *Philosophies of Education*, National Society for the Study of Education, Forty-first Yearbook, Part I (Chicago: University of Chicago Press, 1942), pp. 197-249; Robert M. Hutchins, *The Higher Learning in America* (New Haven, CT: Yale University Press, 1936).

19. Van Cleve Morris, *Philosophy and the American School*, pp. 266-67.

4

Modern Philosophies and Education

Chapter 3 surveyed the relationship between education and the traditional philosophies of idealism, realism, and neo-scholasticism. It was noted that different philosophic positions lead to variations in educational emphases and practices. This chapter will continue examining that relationship in terms of the modern philosophic stances of pragmatism and existentialism.

Traditional philosophies had a basic similarity in the fact that they were primarily concerned with metaphysics—the issue of reality. The modern philosophies brought a definite shift in the hierarchical importance of the three basic philosophic categories. That shift was stimulated by the findings of modern science.

For centuries, humanity's knowledge and philosophic perspective had remained fairly stable. Newly discovered knowledge was generally not of such a quantity or quality that societies had difficulty fitting it into their world view and daily practice. That stability, however, began to change in the seventeenth and eighteenth centuries. First came the new scientific discoveries and theories. They were soon followed by technological breakthroughs that made the industrial revolution possible and brought disruption and major discontinuities to the traditional social and philosophic patterns of the Western world.

Throughout the nineteenth and twentieth centuries these advances in scientific knowledge, with their corresponding effects upon society, continued to accelerate; and, as a result, many people came to reject an absolute reality that is static or even one that can be known. From the human point of view, it seemed to many people that truth, as well as human knowledge of truth, is relative and that there are no universal certainties.

That conclusion led the modern philosophies to avoid the issue of ultimate reality and to focus on relativist approaches to truth and value from the perspective of social groups (pragmatism) and from the viewpoint of individuals (existentialism). In the shift from metaphysics, pragmatism set forth epistemology as the central philosophic issue, while existentialism moved the focus of priority to axiology. It will be seen that this shift in philosophic interest led to major alterations in educational ideas concerning the nature of the student, the role of the teacher, the content emphasis of the curriculum, the preferred methods of instruction, and the social function of education and the school.

PRAGMATISM

Background

Pragmatism is America's contribution to the history of philosophical thought. It has come to prominence during the past one hundred years and is associated with such names as Charles S. Peirce (1839-1914), William James (1842-1910), and John Dewey (1859-1952).

Traditional philosophies were static and tended to account for things as they were. The last half of the nineteenth century, however, saw unprecedented change as the industrial revolution reached high gear. Industrialism, urbanization, and mass migrations of populations were central factors on the American scene. Change appeared to be a central feature of human existence. The intellectual arena saw the development and wide acceptance of the theories of biological and social Darwinism as people sought to rationalize and deal with the concept of change. Pragmatism (also called "experimentalism" and "instrumentalism") was the philosophic reaction to the changing world.

William James defined pragmatism as *"the attitude of looking away from first things, principles, 'categories,' supposed necessities; and of looking towards last things, fruits, consequences, facts."*[1] Pragmatism was critical of the older systems of philosophy, which, claimed the pragmatists, made the mistake of looking for ultimates, absolutes, and eternal essences. The pragmatists emphasized empirical science, the changing world and its problems, and nature as the all-inclusive reality beyond which their faith in science would not allow them to go.

Pragmatism has intellectual antecedents in those Greek thinkers, such as Heraclitus (fifth century B.C.), who postulated the inevitability of change, and the British empiricists (seventeenth and eighteenth centuries), who maintained that people can know only what their senses experience. Pragmatic thought in education has been most influentially expressed in the writings of Dewey,[2] whose ideas stimulated widespread experimentation in twentieth-century theory and practice.

The impact of pragmatism upon education has been most widely felt through the influence of the progressives. Pragmatism has also affected education, both directly and indirectly, through reconstructionism, futurism, critical pedagogy, and educational humanism. All of these theories will be discussed in Chapter 6.

Philosophic Position of Pragmatism

An experiential reality. Some pragmatists deny that their philosophic position even has a metaphysics. That is undoubtedly due to the fact that traditional metaphysics has been concerned with an "ultimate" and "absolute" realm of reality beyond the grasp of human empirical experience. The pragmatist, on the other hand, claims that if there is such an order of reality, people have no way of knowing about it. From the pragmatic viewpoint, mind and matter are not two separate and independent substances. People know about matter only as they experience it and reflect upon that experience with their minds. Reality, therefore, is never divorced from the human knower.

From the pragmatists' perspective, humanity lives in what Plato described as the cave of sensory perception. This, they claim, may not be the sum total of reality; but, like it or not, the cave is all we have. We live in a world of experience and have no way of knowing whether what some people claim lies beyond human experience has any truth or reality.

With the passage of time, humanity's experience changes, and therefore the pragmatists' concept of reality changes. Their metaphysical scheme allows for no absolutes, no *a priori* principles, or unchangeable natural laws. Reality is not an abstract "thing." Rather, it is a transactional experience that is constantly undergoing change. As William James put it, people live in "a universe with the lid off." Dewey, like James, turned away from the older notions of a closed world with fixed limits and restricted possibilities.

The pragmatist points out that cosmological reality has been undergoing change across time. For example, cosmic reality for many centuries centered around the geocentric theory, which placed a stationary earth at the center of the universe; then the broadened experience of Copernicus allowed the development of a heliocentric "reality"; and subsequent extensions of experience in the twentieth century led to a new view of "reality" focused upon universal relativity.

Therefore, claim the pragmatists, reality is not fixed, but is in a constant state of flux as humanity's experience broadens. What is "real" today may not be real tomorrow, since reality cannot be divorced from experience any more than matter may be separated from mind. We live in a dynamic universe that is undergoing a constant state of change; and such things as scientific laws, which are based upon humanity's limited experience, must be stated in terms of probability, rather than in terms of absolutes.

Truth as what works. Pragmatism is basically an epistemological undertaking. Knowledge, according to the pragmatist, is rooted in experience. People have active and exploratory minds, rather than ones that are passive and receptive. As a result, individuals do not simply receive knowledge; they make it as they interact with the environment. The seeking of knowledge, therefore, is a transaction. Human beings act upon the environment and then undergo certain consequences. They learn from this transactional experience with the world around them.

The clearest and most extensive discussion of the pragmatic epistemological method for transforming experience into knowledge was given by Dewey in *How We Think* (1910). According to Dewey, the process of reflective thinking may be seen as having five steps. First, individuals, as they actively move through life, meet up with a problem or a disturbing situation that temporarily inhibits their progress. This situation provides a moment of hesitation, during which the process of thought is initiated as the mind begins to focus on the problem at hand.

The second step is an intellectualization of what was at first an emotional response to blocked activity. During this phase, steps are taken by the individual to diagnose the situation and to come to grips with the precise nature of the problem.

The third stage involves an inventory of possible solutions. People let their minds freely suggest every conceivable potential solution to the problem. These possible solutions take the form of "guiding ideas" or hypotheses.

Phase four is an exercise in reasoning as the possible solutions of the third stage are conjectured upon for their probable consequences if put into action. The mind operates in a line of thought running from cause to effect in an attempt to narrow the choices to the hypothesis that will be successful in overcoming the current difficulty.

The fifth stage is concerned with testing the most reasonable hypothesis by action to see if the conjectured consequences do in fact occur. If the hypothesis or proposed answer works when applied to the world of experience, then it is true—truth is what works. If the hypothesis does not work or does not enable a person to overcome the problem, then it remains unverified and fails to come under the pragmatic definition of truth. If an acted-upon hypothesis proves to be false, then the person must go back to at least phase four and seek truth in an alternate hypothesis.

At this point it is important to recognize that knowledge, from the pragmatic perspective, needs to be carefully distinguished from belief. The authenticity of what persons may claim to believe is a matter of private concern, but what they claim to know must be capable of demonstration to any impartial, qualified observer. In other words, beliefs are private, while knowledge is at all times regarded as public. The pragmatist notes that although some beliefs may be founded on knowledge, certainly many of them are not. From the pragmatist's viewpoint, a statement that purports to be true is one that can be phrased in "if . . . then" language and can be tested by public empirical experience.

The pragmatic epistemological position gives no place to such things as *a priori* concepts and Absolute Truths. Humanity lives in a constantly expanding and changing experiential world, and what "works" today may prove to be an insufficient explanation tomorrow. Therefore, truth is relative, and what is true today may not be true in the future or in a different situational context.

Values from society. The axiology of pragmatism is directly related to its epistemology. Just as humanity is ultimately responsible for truth and knowledge, so it is also responsible for values. Values are relative, and there are no absolute principles on which we can lean. As cultures change, so do values. This does not mean that morality must of necessity fluctuate from day to day, but it does mean that no axio-logical precept may be regarded as universally binding.

In the realm of ethics, the criterion of good conduct can be defined from the position of the pragmatist as the social test. That which is eth-ically good is that which "works." It should be noted, however, that just as the epistemological test is of a public nature, so we find that the ethical test is based on the good of society and not merely upon a pri-vate or personal good. For example, if my goal is to gain wealth, then I might assume that it would be good (it would achieve my goal) if I became a thief. In this way I would personally achieve a position of wealth. Since the results are satisfactory, in the sense that my course of action worked to make me rich, I might be tempted to think that my thievery was moral. But, claims the pragmatist, while this may work for an individual, it could not possibly work for the entire social sys-tem, since no one would be able to accumulate wealth if everyone else was stealing it. Therefore, when put to the public test, stealing fails to work and cannot be defined as good or moral, since it makes civilized living an impossibility.

By this view of ethics the early pragmatists were able to validate the last six commandments (those dealing with relationships between people) of the Judeo-Christian Decalogue while ignoring the first four (those dealing with the relationship between people and God), which were impossible to test by empirical means. This was a crucial devel-opment in their approach to ethics for several reasons: (1) the ethical value system of Western civilization was based upon these moral pre-cepts; (2) moral education had been tied to the Hebrew-Christian tra-dition; (3) the accepted way of teaching these morals in their religious context was being undermined by Darwinism and biblical criticism; and (4) if civilization was to have continuity, then a new foundation for morality needed to be found—one that could be taught in the pub-lic schools. The pragmatists put forth an axiological test that they believed would solve this crucial social problem.

It should not be inferred from the above discussion that the prag-matists were in favor of such things as universal commandments or moral codes. On the contrary, they advocated that the individual should learn how to make difficult moral decisions, not by falling back on rigidly prescribed rules, but by determining which course of intel-ligent action was likely to produce the best results in human terms. It just so happens that traditional Western values could be validated by the pragmatic method, while they were at the same time being purged of their unscientific "religious" elements, which were not amenable to the public test of experience. Thus a new rationale could be developed for teaching traditional ethics in what was becoming a secular society.

Aesthetic criteria for the pragmatist are also found in human experience, as opposed to the traditional philosophies which found their aesthetic determinants beyond the confines of experience. Dewey, in *Art as Experience,* provides the clue to the pragmatist's approach to aesthetics. The way in which aesthetic evaluation is arrived at may be called "social taste." Concepts of beauty depend upon how people feel when they have an "aesthetic" experience. If, in the presence of a given work, they see new meanings in life and have new dimensions of feeling which enable them to make better emotional contact with their fellow beings, then they are experiencing a work of true art. From this perspective, the pragmatist would abolish the distinction between fine and practical art. Both of these traditional categories enter into the human experience and can lead to aesthetic appreciation.

Pragmatism and Education

The important thing about students, from the pragmatists' epistemological viewpoint, is that they have experiences. They are experiencing individuals who are capable of using their intelligence to resolve problematic situations. Students learn as they act upon their environment and are, in turn, acted upon by that environment as they undergo the consequences of their actions.

For the pragmatist, the school experience is a part of life, rather than a preparation for life. As such, the way people learn in school is not qualitatively different from the way they learn in other parts of life. As they move through the day, students face problems which cause them to go through the "complete act of reflective thought." The resultant use of their intelligence causes growth, and that growth enables them to interact with, and adapt to, their changing world. Their developing ideas become instruments for successful living.

Teachers in a pragmatic educational context are not teachers in the traditional sense of the word. That is, they are not individuals who "know" what the students will need for the future and therefore have the function of imparting such essential bodies of knowledge to their students. For one thing, claims the pragmatist, no one "knows" what students will need since we live in a world that is constantly changing. This fact, coupled with the idea that there are no such things as *a priori* or absolute truths which all students must know, modifies the role of the teacher.

Teachers in a pragmatic school can be seen as fellow learners in the educational experience, as their entire classes daily face a changing world. Teachers, however, are more experienced fellow travelers and can therefore be viewed as guides or project directors. They advise and guide student activities that have arisen out of the felt needs of their students; and they perform this role in the context of, and with the benefit of, their wider experiences. But, it is essential to note, they do not base class activities on their own felt needs.

Traditional educational philosophies put subject matter at the center of the educational focus. The child was supposed to conform to the demands of the structure of the several curricular areas. Pragmatism rejected that approach and placed students and their needs and interests on center stage. Subject matter, it claimed, should be chosen with an eye to the needs of the student.

The curriculum, according to Dewey and other pragmatists, should not be divided into restrictive and unnatural subject-matter areas. It should rather be built around natural units that grow out of the pressing questions and experiences of the learners. The specific units of study might vary from one fourth-grade class to the next, but the idea was that the traditional subjects of the school (art, history, math, reading, etc.) could be woven into a problem-solving technique that utilized the innate curiosity of the students to learn the traditional materials as they worked on problems and issues that were of current interest to them in their daily experience.

Methodology, for the pragmatist, centers around giving students a great deal of freedom of choice in seeking out the experiential (learning) situations that will be the most meaningful to them. The classroom (which is seen not just as a "school" setting, but as any place where experiences may be had) is viewed in terms of a scientific laboratory where ideas are put to the test to see if they are capable of verification.

Field trips, note the pragmatists, have distinct advantages over such activities as reading and audio-visual experiences, since the student has a better chance to participate in firsthand interaction with the environment. It is true that field trips and other actual experiences with the environment are time-consuming. On the other hand, they are held to be more motivating, since they have intrinsic interest; and they are more meaningful, because they involve people in direct rather than indirect experience. For example, one learns more about a dairy and cows by going to the barn and milking, smelling, and hearing a cow than by a week of reading and viewing the process on a movie screen.

Thus, the methodology of the pragmatists is in direct line with their experiential epistemology. One favorite technique of the pragmatists is the project method, which will be described in Chapter 6 under the discussion of progressivism.

This experiential methodology, it should be noted, does not imply that all pragmatists are opposed to books, libraries, museums, and other organized knowledge resources. Dewey, for example, held that all study "at the outset" should "fall within the scope of ordinary life-experience." As students mature and build a significant knowledge base upon experience, however, they should be able to come to the place where they can learn through indirect and logical approaches to organized subject matter.

In other words, the child, according to Dewey, should gradually move from learning based upon direct experiences to vicarious learning methods. These vicarious methods should then be all the more meaningful, since they are built upon a knowledge base founded upon significant experiences in everyday life.[4]

The social policy of the school, as viewed by pragmatism, is that of liberalism in the sense that pragmatists are not afraid of social change. In fact, they claim that social change is inevitable and that the function of the school should be to teach the younger generation to manage change in a healthy manner. The aim of the school is not to have students memorize a set body of content, but rather to have them learn how to learn, so that they can adapt to the constantly changing world of the present and future. From this perspective, it can be claimed that the curriculum of the pragmatic school will be more concerned with process than content.

The political viewpoint of pragmatism is that of democracy. The pragmatists see the school, ideally, as a democratic living and learning environment in which everyone participates in the decision-making process in anticipation of soon having a wider participation in the decision-making process of the larger society. Societal and school decisions in this framework are evaluated in the light of their social consequences, rather than in terms of some hallowed tradition. Social, economic, and political change is viewed as good if it betters the condition of society.

Neopragmatism

Classical pragmatism was an influential force in philosophical circles (especially American) for the first half of the twentieth century, but in the 1950s it was marginalized by philosophical analysis (see Chapter 7). The analytic hold on the field lasted for about twenty-five or thirty years, but the last two decades of the century witnessed a breaking down of the analytic dominance and a resurgence of pragmatic concerns.

One of the central figures in that resurgence was Richard Rorty, who in 1979 shocked his colleagues in an address to the American Philosophical Society announcing "the end of philosophy." For Rorty, philosophy in both its traditional and analytic guises was dead. To him philosophers had no special knowledge, special access to knowledge, or special methods for ascertaining knowledge. Knowledge, as he saw it, did not have a basis in ideas that faithfully corresponded to reality. Such correspondence was an illusion. In the spirit of William James, the neopragmatic philosophic conversation would have to be based on satisfying social beliefs rather than "truths once regarded as timeless, necessary, and unconditional."[5] Rorty called for philosophy as continuing "conversation" of significant issues rather than a quest for metaphysical or epistemological certainty. Other important neopragmatists include Hilary Putnam in America and Jürgen Habermas in Germany.

While the neopragmatic philosophers have their differences, they also have their commonalities, which are quite in harmony with classical pragmatism. Those commonalities include (1) a criticalness toward all appeals to absolutes, (2) an insistence upon "a robust plurality of experiences, beliefs, and inquiries," (3) a continuing emphasis on ethical, political, and social responsibility, (4) a strong sense of the precariousness of human existence, (5) a commitment to democratic action, (6) a felt need to communicate in a language that all social classes can understand and participate in, and (7) a positive outlook on the possibilities of human action based on a "reconstruction" philosophy.[6]

The neopragmatists' ideas are being felt most directly in the educational world through some of the implications of postmodernism (see Chapter 5), and especially through the various democratizing reform programs set forth under the critical pedagogies umbrella (see Chapter 6).

EXISTENTIALISM

Background

Existentialism is one of the newer arrivals on the philosophic scene. It is nearly all a twentieth-century product. In many ways it is more closely related to literature and the arts than it is to formal philosophy. That is undoubtedly due to the fact that it is deeply concerned with the emotions of individuals, rather than being primarily concerned with the intellect.

Existentialism, due to its very nature, is difficult, if not impossible, to define. Walter Kaufmann, one of the more perceptive American existentialists, introduces his *Existentialism from Dostoevsky to Sartre* by noting that

> existentialism is not a philosophy but a label for several widely different revolts against traditional philosophy. Most of the living "existentialists" have repudiated this label, and a bewildered outsider might well conclude that the only thing they have in common is a marked aversion for each other.[7]

Existentialism must not be seen as a "school" of thought in the same sense as the other four philosophic positions that we have studied. Kaufmann has identified the heart of existentialism as: (1) the refusal to belong to any school of thought; (2) the repudiation of the adequacy of philosophic systems and bodies of belief; and (3) a marked dissatisfaction with traditional philosophy as superficial, academic, and remote from life.[8]

Individualism is the central pillar of existentialism. The existentialist does not seek for such things as purpose in the universe. Only the individual has purpose.

Existentialism finds its roots in the works of Søren Kierkegaard

(1813-1855) and Friedrich Nietzsche (1844-1900). Both men reacted against the impersonalism and formalism of ecclesiastical Christianity and the speculative philosophy of Hegel. Kierkegaard strove to revitalize Christianity from within by uplifting the place of the individual and the role of personal choice and commitment. Nietzsche, on the other hand, denounced Christianity, declared the death of God, and uplifted his version of the superman.

Existentialism became especially influential after World War II. A renewed search for meaning seemed especially crucial in a world that had suffered a prolonged depression and had been torn apart by two global wars of unprecedented magnitude. A further stimulant for the existentialists' renewed search for meaning and significance was the dehumanizing impact of modern industrialism. Existentialism is largely a revolt against a society that robbed humanity of its individuality. Influential spokespersons for twentieth-century existentialism include Karl Jaspers, Gabriel Marcel, Martin Heidegger, Jean-Paul Sartre, and Albert Camus.

Existentialism has focused mainly on philosophical issues and has not been too explicit on educational practices. Its relative silence on education has also undoubtedly been influenced by its concern for the individual rather than the social group. Exceptions to this neglect of educational topics are found in the works of such writers as Martin Buber, Maxine Greene, George Kneller, and Van Cleve Morris.[9]

Existentialists have contended that philosophy is not a speculative activity that can be calmly detached from the matrix of the fundamental realities of death, life, and freedom. Philosophy that relies primarily on the intellect is rejected by existentialist thinkers. Philosophy must be "informed by passion," because it is in states of heightened feeling that ultimate realities are discovered. Thus Miguel de Unamuno can condemn those who do philosophy only with their brains as "definition-mongers" and "professionals of thought."[10]

Existentialism, then, is not a "systematic" philosophy. As a result, existentialism does not communicate to educators a set of rules to be mastered or a program to be institutionalized. On the other hand, it does provide a spirit and attitude that can be applied to the educational enterprise. It is from this perspective that we will look at the underlying philosophy of the existentialist.

The reader should realize, when studying the material on existentialism, that existentialists do not generally frame their thought in metaphysical, epistemological, and axiological terms. There is, however, a position from which they speak. It is in this cautious spirit that the following analysis is made, with the realization that existentialist thinkers would object to any analysis. This task is performed for philosophic neophytes who need the starting point that can be provided by analysis and labeling if they are to gain a foundation from which to develop insight and make evaluations and comparisons.

Philosophic Position of Existentialism

Reality as existence. Individual existence is the focal point of existentialism's view of reality. One way to look at the metaphysical foundation of existentialism is to contrast it with the neo-scholastic dictum that essence precedes existence in relation to time. For example, some neo-scholastics have looked upon God as the Creator of all things—including people. When God made humans, they claim, He had the idea of humanity (its essence) in mind before actually creating any persons.

Existentialism begins by reversing this priority, so that existence precedes essence. A person first is, and then he or she must attempt to define his or her whatness or essence. A person is faced with such questions as "Who am I?" and "What is the meaning of existence?" in a world that gives no answers. The act of daily living is a process of defining personal essence. As an individual goes through life, he or she makes choices and develops preferences and dislikes. It is through this activity that persons define who they are as individuals. Through this process a person comes to the realization that he or she is what he or she chooses to be. Individuals face an existence that they had no voice in accepting, and are confronted by the absolute and inescapable necessity of making responsible choices.

The focus of reality resides within the self of the individual human person. Existing is the focal point of the existentialist's philosophy. Each person is faced with the stark realities of life, death, and meaning; and each has the unutterable freedom of being responsible for his or her own essence. A person has no external authority upon which to fall back, since philosophic systems are viewed as unauthentic cop-outs. The traditional philosophers surrender the individual's authenticity to a logical system, the Christian leans on God, the realist looks to nature for meaning, and the pragmatist relies on the community. All of these avenues are ways of removing people from the frightful reality of being individually responsible for their choices. They remove the individual from coming to grips with the crucial and primary reality of personal existence and its meaning in a world without meaning apart from that existence.

Jean-Paul Sartre, an atheistic existentialist, put the human predicament this way:

> If man, as the existentialist conceives him, is indefinable, it is because at first he is nothing. Only afterward will he be something, and he himself will have made what he will be. Thus, there is no human nature, since there is no God to conceive it. Not only is man what he conceives himself to be, but he is also only what he wills himself to be after this thrust toward existence. Man is nothing else but what he makes of himself. Such is the first principle of existentialism.[11]

Some readers will react to the existentialist perspective with the thought that it doesn't make sense. Many existentialists would not be threatened by that problem; to them life doesn't have to make intellectual sense—in fact, it might even be called "absurd."

Truth as choice. The individual is the center of epistemological authority in existentialism—not humanity as a species, but persons as individuals. Meaning and truth are not built into the universe. Rather, it is the individual who gives meaning to such things as nature. Note, for example, states the existentialist, how the "laws" of nature have changed through the ages as individuals have endowed nature with different meanings. People have a desire to believe in external meanings; and, as a result, individuals choose to believe what they want to believe.

If existence precedes essence, then first came the individual person, and then came the ideas that the individual has created. All knowing resides in the individual self, and it is the self that makes the ultimate decision as to what is true. Truth, therefore, can be seen in terms of existential choice, which is based upon the authority of the individual.

This epistemological stance is a radical departure from traditional epistemologies. It is interesting to note that some Christian and Jewish philosophers and theologians have espoused existentialism.[12] It should be realized, however, that they are not Christian and Jewish believers in the historical sense of the term, since they themselves have become the locus of authority, rather than the God who is "out there" and who has traditionally given meaning and teleological direction to the universe. These modern religious philosophers have accepted a view that allows them to act "as if" the external authority and reality of God have meaning. This has had its effect on the traditional Hebraic- Christian view of revelation, which has seen revelation as God's authoritative word to humanity. From the religious existentialist's viewpoint, the Bible may be viewed as the report of a series of "encounters" with God. Modern individuals, they claim, can also have encounters; and these may be just as valid as the encounters of Moses, Abraham, or Paul. Thus the meaning of scriptural authority has been updated, modernized, and (in its traditional usage) abolished in the hands of religious existentialists.

value

Values from the individual. The focus of existentialist philosophy is in the realm of axiology, just as the center of traditional philosophy was in metaphysics, and the emphasis of pragmatism was on epistemology. If existential metaphysics can be summed up in the word "existence," and if its concept of epistemology is seen in terms of the word "choice," then it follows that the major portion of life's activities and philosophy's concerns must be bound up in the axiological interests of the individual, who is an existential chooser.

Existentialists are faced with the frightful task of producing values out of nothing. Individuals have been thrown into life without their consent, and each is free to become whatever he or she desires. Individual persons are not determined. Rather, they are "condemned to be free." Because of this freedom, each person is responsible for his or her choices and actions. In this vein, Carl Rogers has noted that individuals cannot rely on either the Bible or the prophets, on Freud or research, or on the revelations of God or the decisions of other people.[13] Individuals have personal experiences and make private decisions which are authoritative. Individuals have no excuse for their actions. Each person has, in the idea of Sartre, "no exit" from his or her freedom and responsibility.

In the realm of ethics there are no absolutes, and there is nobody to spell out the nature of good conduct. If there were such an external authority, life would be much simpler—all an individual would have to do is comply with the requirements. The anguish of being free to make individual ethical decisions comes about because individuals must make their own choices and bear responsibility for those choices. An individual cannot fall back on any source of authority outside of his or her self.

The anguish of responsible freedom is felt all the more when it is realized that individuals can make choices that are harmful when put into practice. However, if individuals can make harmful choices, they can also make ethical choices that can counteract those ideas and actions which have proven to be injurious. Each person has the great potential of bettering, worsening, or even destroying human existence.

Living the responsible life also includes acting upon one's decisions, if a person is to be true or authentic to himself or herself. Unfavorable consequences to a person who acts out his or her ethical convictions are not the main concern in the eyes of the existentialist. It is important to act regardless of the consequences. The only typically moral question, claims Sartre, is "What, here and now, would be the least *phoney* thing for me to choose?"[14] Not to act is to be irresponsible; it is to seek a world without tension and anguish. Existentialists note that there is no tension after death, but that some people try to make their own lives like death by avoiding conflict at all cost. The opposite of death is life, and life for the existentialist necessitates a degree of tension as individuals act out their personal ethical convictions.

The aesthetic viewpoint of the existentialist can be described as a revolt against the public standard. Each individual is the supreme court in regard to what is beautiful. As in other areas of existence, no one can make decisions for other individuals. What is beautiful to me is beautiful, and who can contradict me?

Existentialism and Education

The relative silence of existentialism on education, previously noted, should not be seen as satisfaction with the schools. On the contrary, existentialists are quite disturbed at what they find in the educational establishment. They are quick to note that much of what is called education is nothing but propaganda served to a captive audience. They also point out that much of what currently passes for education is actually harmful, since it prepares students for consumerism or makes them into cogs in the machinery of industrial technology and modern bureaucracy. Instead of helping to bring out individuality and creativity, the existentialists cry, much education stifles and destroys these essential human attributes.

In a philosophy that revolts at the regimentation of individuals, it is only to be expected that the individual will be the center of the educational endeavor. Van Cleve Morris claims that existentialist educational concern will focus on helping the individual self come into a fuller realization of the following propositions:

1. I am a *choosing* agent, unable to avoid choosing my way through life.
2. I am a *free* agent, absolutely free to set the goals of my own life.
3. I am a *responsible* agent, personally accountable for my free choices as they are revealed in how I live my life.[15]

The role of the existentialist teacher will not be that of the traditional teacher. The existentialist teacher will not be one who is mainly concerned with cognitive transference and who has the "right" answers. He or she will rather be a person who is willing to help students explore possible answers.

The teacher will be concerned with the unique individuality of each student. Existentialist teachers will realize that no two students are alike, and that, consequently, no two need exactly the same education. The existentialist will seek to relate to every student in what Buber refers to as an "I-Thou," rather than an "I-It," relationship. That is, such teachers will treat the student as an individual with whom they can personally identify, rather than an "It" that needs to be externally directed and filled with knowledge.

The existentialist teacher might be described as what Rogers calls a "facilitator." In this role the teacher will respect the emotional and irrational aspects of individuals and will endeavor to lead students into a better understanding of themselves. Such teachers and the youngsters who are with them will face the ultimate questions of life, death, and meaning as they explore human experiences from a variety of viewpoints. In all of these experiences, both teachers and students will learn and share roles as they increase in awareness of how to find and be themselves in a mechanized world seeking to rob them of selfhood and individuality.

The curriculum in an existentialist school will of necessity be open to change, since existentialism's concept of truth is ever expanding and changing. From that perspective, student choice should be a deciding factor in the selection of subject matter. That conclusion does not mean, however, that traditional subject matter finds no place in the existentialist's curricular approach. It rather indicates curricular flexibility as opposed to the traditional hierarchy of subjects in terms of importance.

Existentialists are in general agreement that the fundamentals of traditional education—such as the three R's, science, and social studies—should be studied. These so-called basics are the foundation of creative effort and of an individual's ability to understand himself or herself. These basic subjects, however, should be presented in relation to the student's affective development rather than being isolated from individual meaning and purpose as they often are in traditional education.

The humanities also loom large in the existentialist curriculum, because they give a great deal of insight into the major dilemmas of human existence. The humanities develop themes around people making choices in relation to sex, love, hate, death, disease, and other meaningful aspects of life. They present a total view of humanity from both a positive and a negative perspective and are therefore superior to the sciences in helping individuals understand themselves.

Beyond the fundamentals and the humanities, the existentialist curriculum is wide open. Any subject that has meaning for an individual can be justified in the course of studies.

Methodology for the existentialists has an infinite number of possibilities. They decry uniformity of materials, curriculum, and teaching, and declare that there should be many options open to students who desire to learn. These options do not have to be restricted to the traditional school, but might be found in alternative types of schools, or in the realm of business, government, or personal affairs. Ivan Illich put forth some suggestions for educational variations in his *Deschooling Society* (1970) that can be appreciated by many existentialists.

The criteria of existentialist methodology center around the concepts of noncoerciveness and those methods that help each student to find and be himself or herself. Perhaps the prototypes of existentialist methodology can be viewed through such approaches as Carl Rogers' *Freedom to Learn* (1969) and A. S. Neill's *Summerhill: A Radical Approach to Child Rearing* (1960).

Existentialists are not generally concerned with the social policy of education or the school. Their philosophy lends itself to an emphasis on the individual, rather than to the social aspects of human existence.

CRITIQUE AND PERSPECTIVE

The modern philosophies of pragmatism and existentialism, despite their differences, have several points in common. In contrast to the traditional philosophies, both reject *a priori* epistemological considerations and downplay metaphysical ultimates and essences beyond the reach of humanity. In addition, both are relativist in terms of values and truth, and both are humanistic or human-centered. A major difference between pragmatism and existentialism is that the former bases its relativism and humanism on the authority of society, while the latter stresses the role of the individual.

In education, the modern philosophies, in addition to the differences discussed in this chapter, also have likenesses. For example, both see the teacher as being more of a guide or facilitator than an authority figure; both believe the curriculum should center in one way or another around the needs of the child, rather than around a solid core of unchanging "Truth"; and both reject the role of the school as primarily an institution for the transmission of past knowledge to future generations.

Both existentialism and pragmatism have affected recent education. By far, the largest impact has been made by pragmatism. In fact, the pragmatic influence made an impression on every aspect of modern education—from architecture, movable classroom furniture, and activity centers to a curriculum at all levels of education that has been broadened to include the practical and useful in addition to the academic. Many observers have noted that pragmatism has "transformed" schooling in the United States and other countries. The impact of existentialism has been more recent and, thus far, less dramatic. Certainly, however, the movements in alternative education, educational humanism, and deschooling that arose in the 1970s found a major portion of their roots in existentialism. Both existentialism and pragmatism were having a renewed impact upon education in the 1990s through postmodernism. We will examine that impact in Chapter 5.

From a Christian point of view, it appears that both pragmatism and existentialism have some aspects of belief and educational practice that are related to Christian philosophy and its educational implications. Pragmatism, for instance, has brought philosophy "down to earth," so that it deals with living issues in everyday life. In doing this, pragmatism has attempted to break up the dichotomy between academic formality and daily living—a dichotomy that has spelled death to living spirituality in those who have separated the formal aspects of religious belief from their daily activities.

Beyond this, pragmatism has uplifted the unity of the practical and the theoretical in education and has given people a view of education that helps them see it as a lifelong process that can take place anywhere, rather than a process that is confined to specialized institutions (schools). Many Christians have seen these elements, along with other aspects of pragmatism, to be more in harmony with Judaic-Christian thought than are the Greek frames of reference adopted by the traditional philosophies.

Many Christians have also found certain elements in existentialism to be congruent with the biblical revelation. For example, existentialism is a revolt against the materialistic and conformist emphasis of modern society. Existentialism emphasizes each individual's alienation from his or her self, fellows, and world, along with each person's need to face the basic issues of existence—life, death, and meaning. The result of this emphasis has led to self-examination, an awareness of the uniqueness of each individual person, and the responsibility of each individual for making personal choices. Certainly these aspects of existentialism lie at the heart of what Jesus, Paul, and the biblical prophets stressed. In this sense, the existentialists have not developed new information as much as they have stimulated a clearer focus and a renewed interest in old questions and truths—questions and truths that tend to be smothered by bureaucratic societies, hierarchical churches, and formal academic philosophies.

It should be noted, however, that what Paul Tillich correctly called the "existential elements in early Christian theology"[16] and a full-blown existential philosophy are two separate entities. Historic Christianity has uplifted the existential aspects of humanity's predicament, but it has viewed those elements in a philosophic framework in which reality is God-centered rather than human-centered, revelation is authoritative rather than merely experiential and relative, and values have been given by God rather than chosen by people. Individuals in historic Christianity have had the frightful responsibility of choosing whether or not to relate to the "God who is there" and who has spoken to humanity, but Christianity has not seen individuals as having the authority to create God in their own image or to choose to read meaning into His revelation.

Historical Christianity has focused upon the existence of a transcendent God and the authoritative and accurate nature of His revelation as found in the Bible. Many modern people, however, have come to believe that the Bible is rooted in myth rather than fact, and they have tended to see it as a production of people rather than a revelation from God. Belief in the accuracy of the Bible has become an impossibility for them, and they have thereby lost the foundation of their faith. Their sense of helplessness, however, has driven many of them to desire to believe in God anyway. This ungrounded belief of the "Christian existentialist" has been likened to a "leap into nothingness." The leap has been taken, not because of religious certainties, but because there are no satisfactory alternatives to the driving inadequacies and needs of individuals in a hopeless world.[17] One cannot help but appreciate the insight of Albert Camus, who identified this frantic leap as "philosophical suicide" by individuals who cannot face the reality of absurdity and hopelessness. Truly existential persons, he claimed, must have the courage to "live *without appeal*" to that which is beyond themselves.[18]

The crucial point of error in many Christians' evaluation of existentialism is the failure to discern the important difference between the "existential elements" of historic Christianity and existentialism as a philosophy. The former are central to historic Christianity, while the latter may be seen in terms of its antithesis. A major difficulty for some Christians in relation to understanding existentialism is that religious existentialists often use the same words (e.g., God, creation, or redemption) as traditional Christianity, but with different meanings. It is therefore important to examine a writer's philosophic roots, rather than to gain a mere surface knowledge of a work through the author's use of particular words.

Christians have generally found pragmatism to have much less of an appeal than existentialism. That is undoubtedly due to the fact that pragmatism is unapologetically naturalistic and humanistic. Pragmatism, at the outset, rejects certain knowledge of reality beyond the sensory experience of human beings. It has therefore been seen, by most Christians, as having an insufficient perspective on reality, truth, and value.

The religious implications of pragmatism have been illustrated by William James in his doctrine of the "will to believe." For James, certain doctrines are comforting and strengthening, such as the doctrine of the belief in the existence of God. Because this and other doctrines are comforting and strengthening, they are useful (i.e., they work). It is their usefulness that establishes their validity.[19]

James's argument has been seen by many Christians as something quite distinct from biblical Christianity. Christians are quite ready to agree that belief in God is comforting; but, they claim, it is comforting because God exists in His own right, rather than because the idea of God makes people feel better. Elton Trueblood, in his critique of the modern philosophies, was certainly correct when he wrote: "'I prefer to believe' is an un-Christian statement."[20]

In conclusion, it can be said that the modern philosophies can lead Christians to a heightened awareness of certain aspects of the biblical message that historical Christianity, through its alignment with Greek philosophy, has overlooked. The task, once again, is not to accept a total philosophic package that may have philosophic roots that are incompatible with the biblical message. The individual Christian should rather seek to utilize the insights offered by the modern philosophies to develop a personal philosophy of education that roots itself in the Christian world view but has been enriched by noting the insights of other viewpoints.

Finally, a caution that must be emphasized in the study of philosophic systems is that it is not always possible or even desirable to fit either ourselves or formal philosophers into neat little boxes called "idealism," "realism," or "existentialism." These systems, as has been noted, are merely labels to help guide our thinking as we relate to possible answers to the basic issues that have faced humanity through the ages. Chapter 6 will develop some of the educational extensions of the traditional and modern philosophies as they were expressed in the twentieth century. But before turning to that topic, we need to examine postmodernism.

Notes

1. William James, *Pragmatism* (New York: Longmans, Green and Co., 1907), pp. 54-55.

2. See especially, John Dewey, *Democracy and Education* (New York: The Macmillan Company, 1916); and John Dewey, *Experience and Education* (New York: The Macmillan Company, 1938).

3. John Dewey, *How We Think: A Restatement of the Relation of Reflective Thinking to the Educative Process,* new ed. (New York: D. C. Heath and Co., 1933), pp. 106-118.

4. Dewey, *Experience and Education,* pp. 86-112.

5. John Patrick Diggins, *The Promise of Pragmatism: Modernism and the Crisis of Knowledge and Authority* (Chicago: University of Chicago Press, 1994), pp. 11, 15, 416; Richard Rorty, *Philosophy and the Mirror of Nature* (Princeton, NJ: Princeton University Press, 1979).

6. Richard J. Bernstein, "The Resurgence of Pragmatism," *Social Research* 59 (Winter 1992):813-40. See also, C. A. Bowers, *Elements of a Post-Liberal Theory of Education* (New York: Teachers College Press, Columbia University, 1987), pp. 137-57.

7. Walter Kaufmann, *Existentialism from Dostoevsky to Sartre,* rev. ed. (New York: New American Library, 1975), p. 11.

8. Ibid., p. 12.

9. Martin Buber, *Between Man and Man* (London: Kegan Paul, 1947); Maxine Greene, *Teacher as Stranger: Educational Philosophy for the Modern Age* (Belmont, CA: Wadsworth Publishing Co., 1973); George Kneller, *Existentialism and Education* (New York: John Wiley & Sons, 1958); Van Cleve Morris, *Existentialism in Education: What It Means* (New York: Harper & Row, 1966).

10. Miguel de Unamuno, *Tragic Sense of Life,* trans., J. E. C. Flitch (New York: Dover Publications, 1954), p. 14.

11. Jean-Paul Sartre, *Existentialism and Human Emotions* (New York: Philosophical Library, 1957), p. 15. Commenting on the human predicament, William Barrett writes that "the Self . . . is in Sartre's treatment . . . a bubble [that] has nothing at its center. . . . The only meaning" an individual "can give himself is through the free project that he launches out of his own nothingness." *Irrational Man: A Study in Existential Philosophy* (Garden City, NY: Anchor Books, 1962), p. 247.

12. Existentialism is divided into two camps: (1) the religious existentialists, who profess belief in the existence of God; and (2) the atheistic existentialists, who claim that the idea of God is a human creation.

13. Carl R. Rogers, *On Becoming a Person: A Therapist's View of Psychotherapy* (Boston: Houghton Mifflin Co., 1961), p. 24.

14. Quoted in Mary Warnock, *Ethics Since 1900,* 3d ed. (New York: Oxford University Press, 1978), p. 131.

15. Van Cleve Morris, *Existentialism in Education,* p. 135.

16. Paul Tillich, "Existentialist Aspects of Modern Art," in *Christianity and the Existentialists,* ed. Carl Michalson (New York: Charles Scribner's Sons, 1956), p. 130.

17. It is from this viewpoint that some persons claim to believe in Jesus, while at the same time rejecting the virgin birth, His resurrection, and other central pillars of the biblical revelation. It is not a belief in the historical Christ.

18. Albert Camus, *The Myth of Sisyphus and Other Essays,* trans., Justin O'Brien (New York: Vintage Books, 1955), pp. 21-48.

19. William James, *Essays in Pragmatism,* ed. Alburey Castell (New York: Haffner Publishing Co., 1948), pp. 88-110, 154-58.

20. Trueblood, *A Place to Stand,* p. 27.

5

The Postmodern Impulse

The final quarter of the twentieth century witnessed the rise of a philosophical perspective known as postmodernism. The term itself is problematic because it means various things to different people.

PRELIMINARY OBSERVATIONS

One way to come to grips with the term "postmodernism" is to see it as a reaction to modernism.[1] The heart of modernism was the desire to understand the world through reason. The underlying assumption of the early modernists was that the world is a reasonable place and that the reality that exists can not only be understood by the human mind, but that there is a system of fixed laws which undergird both reality and human thought at its best.

In the eighteenth century, such men as Isaac Newton began to more intensively apply their rational way of thinking to the world around them. That procedure led to the rise of science, the findings of which the modernists believed were true reflections of reality. The nineteenth century would see such individuals as August Comte and Herbert Spencer extend the scientific approach into the realm of human society. The result was the development of the social sciences.

The modern frame of mind came to believe that the discoveries of the natural and social sciences provided human beings with certain truth, truth that was beyond doubt, human understandings that mirrored reality as it existed. Such knowledge was believed to be objective and neutral, as was the scientific method itself. The various facts of the modern outlook were utilized to form theories (metanarratives) to explain the world and the meaning of life.

Modernism also viewed knowledge as being good by its very nature. Thus discovering the truths of nature would enable people to control their world, eventually overcome human limitations, and even eradicate those destructive evils (such as diseases) that had plagued humankind throughout its recorded history. The idea of continuous progress, of course, was an important aspect of the modernist scheme of things.

Modernism, however, didn't fulfill its promise. Science and technology, for example, brought about environmental degradation, totalitarianism, and global wars with atomic potential based on technological knowledge. Thus, as one scholar put it, "reason and science did not lead to . . . utopia."[2]

The reactions were many. One was the despair of existentialism. Another is what we have come to know as postmodernism. Postmodernism, as we will shortly see, is in large part a rejection of the modern view of things.

At the very outset it should be recognized that postmodernism is not a unified world view. Various proponents set forth their own theories, which at times contradict other postmodern ideas. In spite of their differences, however, the postmoderns are united in their rejection of modernism. We will note other shared ideas at the close of the section below entitled "Varieties of Postmodernism."

Before moving beyond preliminary remarks on the nature of postmodernism, it should be noted that scholars are not agreed as to its exact significance. Some hold that postmodernism represents a new historical period that people are entering, while others view it as an extension of some of the basic concepts undergirding modernism itself. Still others see postmodernism as a kind of in-between period in which old ways are being questioned but the new era has yet to arrive. That uncertainty is reflected in the title of this chapter, which views postmodernism in its present state of evolution as an impulse or mood rather than as a well-developed and well-integrated philosophy. Only time will tell if the impulse will have permanence. In the meantime, postmodernism has raised significant issues that are at the center of educational discussion as the world moves into the twenty-first century.

PHILOSOPHIC ROOTS

Postmodernism is not primarily a product of philosophers, but rather of those whose fields of interest range from art to literature and architecture. That, however, does not mean that philosophers haven't made important contributions to the field. Historically, David Hume (1711-1776) cast doubt onto the question of cause and effect and onto the human ability to truly know the external world. Immanuel Kant (1724-1804) sought to answer Hume's philosophy but ended up by claiming that the human mind really couldn't know things in themselves, but only interpreted external reality in terms of mental categories already present in the mind.

While Hume and Kant laid the groundwork for the postmodern frame of mind, it was Friedrich Nietzsche (1844-1900) who fleshed out the ideas. According to Nietzsche, there is no foundation on which to rest beliefs. Truth is dead and people have no option but to create their own world. Thus knowledge became a human construction based in the subjective use of language. Nietzsche arrived at the frontiers of postmodernism even though he lived nearly a century before his ideas would become "mainstream."

Beyond the ideas of such philosophers as Kant and Nietzsche, the ideas of three philosophic movements have been especially influential in postmodernism. The first is pragmatism. Pragmatism's commitment to the idea that knowledge is provisional, its rejection of metaphysical schemes, its socially active position in the face of human problems, and its concern for social (rather than merely individual) issues have all found a place in postmodernism. Such neopragmatists as Richard Rorty are closely identified with postmodernism.

A second philosophic base of postmodernism is existentialism. Such concepts as Jean-Paul Sartre's I-am-what-I-choose-to-be approach not only add to the relativistic basis of postmodernism, but also involve people in the *construction* of knowledge. And knowledge construction, as we will soon see, stands at the very basis of postmodern epistemology and curriculum.

A third basic philosophic outlook undergirding postmodernism is Marxist thought. Marxism's preoccupation with class struggle and economic concerns informs both postmodern theory and practice, even though postmoderns reject the Marxist scheme of history (its metanarrative). Postmodernism's concern with class struggle and economic issues will be most evident in our discussions of the thought of Michel Foucault in the next section and in the section on critical pedagogy in Chapter 6.

Before moving away from the philosophic roots of postmodernism, it should be recognized that the movement represents a rejection of behaviorism (see Chapter 6) with its scientific objectivity and technological approach to human engineering. Postmodernism also largely rejects the positivistic and objective views of philosophical analysis (see Chapter 7). On the other hand, postmodern theorists respond positively to certain analytic philosophers in their sensitivity to language and in their understanding of the interconnectedness of the meanings of language.

VARIETIES OF POSTMODERNISM

One way to get a better grip on postmodernism is to examine the ideas of some of its leading theorists. This section will examine the major contributions to postmodern theory by Richard Rorty, Jacques Derrida, Jean-François Lyotard, and Michel Foucault.

We had a glimpse of Rorty in our discussion of neopragmatism in Chapter 4. Rorty strikes at the foundation of modern epistemology by criticizing what he sees as its central metaphor—the image of the mind as a mirror of reality. Rorty, as we saw previously, rejects that view with its correspondence view of truth. To Rorty, language and thought may be tools for coping with experience, but they certainly do not supply us with pictures of reality. Thus with Rorty we are faced with epistemological subjectivity. One can have opinions but not truth. As a result, people can and must keep the philosophic conversation going even though they are unable to objectively ground their opinions.[3]

The subjectivity found in Rorty is also in the work of Derrida. Derrida has attacked what he calls the "logocentrism" of Western society. As he sees it, the central task of philosophy has been to understand *logos* or the central controlling rational principle of the universe. Unfortunately, philosophers have failed in that attempt because they have not been in touch with reality itself but rather with the language that they think represents that reality. Thus all they really have is their writings or texts and not an understanding of objective reality.

The problem is that both author and readers bring to the text personal emphases and meanings that have been shaped by their unique experiences. Thus what they get when they read a text is not an objective account or even what the author may have meant, but their own interpretation based upon generally unconscious presuppositions.

What needs to be done, Derrida suggests, is to "deconstruct" the texts by unpacking the presuppositions expressed by such things as word choices, the hidden meanings in puns, and so on. When people unpack texts they will discover that the Western philosophical perspective has tyrannized, suppressed, excluded, or marginalized other perspectives.

Derrida holds that rather than merely being held captive by the dominant perspective, people need to celebrate diversity. This has encouraged some minority groups and feminists to ally themselves with deconstructionists in the equal rights struggle.[4]

A third strain of postmodernism is found in the work of Michel Foucault. Foucault explored the power implications in language. He suggests that Western society has for centuries erroneously believed that there is an objective body of knowledge that is just waiting to be discovered, that that knowledge is value-free, and that knowledge benefits all people rather than merely a special class.

Foucault rejects each of those propositions and puts forth the thesis that knowledge is socially constructed by those who seek to legitimize their power and that that knowledge power is used to control and subject other people and peoples. In such works as *The Archeology of Knowledge*[5] Foucault argues that concepts such as madness are parts of speech rather than necessarily being facts of life. These speech forms are developed by people and used to control other people. At bottom, however, they are human constructions rather than reflections of reality.

What is needed is opposing discourse so that marginal groups might be liberated from subjection to dominant classes. As might be expected, marginal groups (such as racial minorities, feminists, and homosexuals) are more than happy to utilize Foucault's thesis on socially-constructed knowledge as power in their attempts to change the existing order of things.

A final postmodern theorist that we will examine is Jean François Lyotard. "I define *postmodern*," he penned, "as incredulity [skepticism] toward metanarratives."[6] By metanarrative he means those grand philosophical/historical understandings of the shape of reality that legitimize the way things are by providing reasons for the correctness of the status quo. These metanarratives are not reality, claims Lyotard, but systems of myths used to sustain social relationships in a given society. Religious philosophies fall under the heading of metanarratives and are thus ruled out along with so-called secular metanarratives. Metanarratives, of course, are based upon the use of language and are used to control people.

The philosophers that we have discussed in the last two sections disagree on many of their ideas, but, as Gary Land puts it,

> they laid the philosophical foundations for postmodernism through three primary contributions. First, human beings have no access to reality and, therefore, no means of perceiving truth. Second, reality is inaccessible because we are caught up in a prison-house of language that shapes our thought before we think and because we cannot express what we think. Third, through language we create reality, and thus the nature of reality is determined by whoever has the power to shape language.[7]

In spite of the fact that the theories we have been discussing seem rather esoteric and remote from practical concerns, they soon found their way into educational discussions. That took place because postmodern concepts dealt with such basic issues as reality, knowledge, and social control—topics at the heart of what schooling and education are all about. We will now turn to some of the educational implications of postmodernism.

POSTMODERNISM AND EDUCATION

If postmodernism as a philosophic outlook is somewhat unsettled and in a state of flux, postmodernism's meaning for education is even less developed. Most writings in the field have focused on the social aspects of education, which will be treated in Chapter 6 in the discussion of critical pedagogy, multi-culturalism, and feminism. The present chapter will focus on the more general implications of postmodernism for education.

The bedrock of any postmodern educational philosophy includes the following concepts: it is impossible to determine objective truth, language does not put us in contact with reality, language and meaning are socially constructed, metanarratives are social constructions developed by dominant groups to legitimize their position and privileges, knowledge is power, and schools have traditionally functioned as agents of that power for social control via the manipulation of knowledge. Also important to a postmodern approach to education are such ideas as the importance of understanding the plurality of various perspectives, the need for people to listen to everybody's story (especially the unheard stories of the oppressed), the importance of opposing groups listening to one another, and the need for democratic communication, which is crucial in creating change.

As noted above, it is the social function of schools that has generally caught the attention of postmodern educational theorists. For postmoderns, the ultimate educational sin is the mere passing on of the stored up knowledge of the past. Rather than being agents for preserving and transmitting the past, as proposed by the traditional philosophies, schools, in line with the sentiments of the pragamatists, must function as change agents.

The aim of the curriculum from a postmodern perspective is the reconstruction of knowledge as a basis for reconstructing the larger culture and its power relationships.[8] Postmodern curriculum theory to date represents a turning away from the hard and fast subject-matter categories of modernism. William E. Doll, for example, begins his book on postmodern curriculum by rejecting Herbert Spencer's nineteenth-century dictum that science should form the basis of the curriculum.[9]

According to Doll, the *"adoration of science*, its deification," is a thing of the past. What is true of science is equally true regarding classical literary education. Curriculum and the whole of education, Doll suggests, is going through a "megaparadigm" shift. He admits that "the implications of a post-modern perspective for education are enormous but by no means clear."[10]

On the other hand, there does seem to be a general consensus among postmodern educational theorists that education in the future cannot rely on the curriculums and methods of the past. Whereas the curriculum of the modern era came to the schools prepackaged by experts, Joe L. Kincheloe suggests that in postmodern education students and teachers must "learn to produce their own knowledge."[11]

That thought brings us to constructivism, one of the more developed aspects of the interface between postmodernism and education.
John Zahorik points out that constructivist teaching theory is based on
three propositions. First, *"knowledge is constructed by humans."* It is
not a set of facts, concepts, or laws independent of the knower that is
waiting to be discovered. Rather, humans create knowledge and everything they know is made by them. Whereas that knowledge may represent an external reality, any possible correspondence is unknowable.
"All that humans can know is that their constructions are compatible
with other constructions they may have made."[12]

Second, *"knowledge is conjectural and fallible."* Knowledge can
never be stable since it is a human construction and people live in a
constant state of change. Thus human understandings are by their very
nature tentative, incomplete, and imperfect, even though all of them
may not be equally imperfect.[13]

Third, *"knowledge grows through exposure."* These exposures
can be to individuals, events, or objects. Because the experiences
inherent in those exposures can be encoded in language, they can be
shared socially. Social sharing leads to the pooling of various understandings. That pooling makes it possible for people to develop agreed-
upon social constructions.[14]

Although Zahorik doesn't discuss them, his third point raises two
issues closely related to the curricular concerns of many postmodern
theorists. The first is the importance of language in both its construc-
tionist and deconstructionist aspects. Postmodern education, given the
postmodern philosophic position on language, should help students
become both conscious and self-conscious of the way that language
and presuppositions interact in both the formation of their own concepts and in the unpacking of the hidden meanings in the "text(s)" of
other people.

A second issue raised by Zahorik that is fraught with postmodern
curricular potential is the idea of exposure. The postmodernist emphasis on diversity postulates broad cultural exposure that moves beyond
the ideas and values of the dominant culture to those of minority and
suppressed cultures. To put it in a Lyotardian frame of reference, students must be exposed to the marginalized individual narratives of the
powerless rather than merely to the controlling metanarratives.

That exposure and the education that it is embedded in, as postmodern theorists tend to see it, is not an individual affair but is communal. Thus C. A. Bowers can advocate the "restoration of community"[15] as the essential aim of education. That community, however, will democratically include the marginalized as well as those currently making up the dominant groups. In fact, creating such a community is at the heart of much postmodern educational philosophizing.

Postmodern curricular theorists tend to view the curriculum in terms of process rather than content. Thus Doll writes that

> curriculum will be viewed not as a set, a priori "course to be run," but as a passage of personal transformation. This change of focus and subject will place more emphasis on the runner running and on the patterns emerging as many runners run, and less emphasis on the course run, although neither the runners nor the course can be dichotomously split. Organization and transformation will emerge from the activity itself, not be set prior to the activity.[16]

Patrick Slattery pictures the postmodern curriculum in kaleidoscopic terms. "The kaleidoscope," he notes, "creates constantly changing images and yet is always symmetrical within its own context," whereas the telescope charts what is perceived as a fixed and unchanging universe. In his view, curricular designs, like a kaleidoscope, will constantly change and become something new. On the other hand, they remain interrelated. "Postmodernism celebrates the diverse and complex understandings within each unique context."[17]

Doll realizes that postmodern comments about curriculum and methods will seem strange or even absurd from the perspective of modernism. But, he points out in line with his postmodern way of thinking, the modernist paradigm "is historical—the product of a particular, Enlightenment-oriented, Western mind-set—developed over the past three to four hundred years." He assures his readers that the new ways of thinking about curriculum seem quite normal and natural to those espousing the newly emerging postmodern mind set.[18]

Postmodern educational theorists generally view teachers as social activists who are out to change the status quo by helping students take personal and social responsibility for the future. Henry A. Giroux asserts that in the democratic struggle against racism, class structures, and sexism, teachers must move beyond critique of the existing social order toward transformation and hope. That, he notes, suggests that educators must combine with others engaged in public struggles in order to invent languages and provide spaces both in and out of schools that offer new opportunities for social movements to come together. By doing this we can rethink and reexperience democracy as a struggle over values, practices, social relations, and subject positions that enlarge the terrain of human capacities and possibilities as a basis for a compassionate social order.[19]

The teacher in a postmodern framework must be more than the technicist of the behaviorist model, who functions as a repository of right answers and hand-me-down knowledge supplied by research experts. To the contrary, postmodern teachers are generators of knowledge within the daily uncertainty of the classroom experience. The teacher must be a person who is able to respond within the context of ever-changing settings. Thus, teacher training needs to produce "teacher thinkers" rather than technicists.[20]

CRITIQUE AND PERSPECTIVE

From a Christian perspective, postmodernism, like the other philosophies we have studied, provides some helpful insights as well as some that are less than helpful. On the helpful side is postmodernism's critique of the faith Western cultures have placed on human reason and the scientific method. Ever since the Enlightenment, Western thinkers have placed too much optimism in the unaided abilities of the human mind.

A second helpful insight is the attention given to social ethics and individual and group responsibility for the social whole. The individualistic tendencies inherent in modernism too often led to the rich getting richer while neglecting those segments of world society that were needy and at the mercy of dominant cultures or social groups. The postmodernists' social concern certainly lines up with the biblical message.

A third beneficial insight is the recognition that language is closely related to power. As James Sire puts it, "We do tell 'stories,' believe 'doctrines,' hold 'philosophies' because they give us or our community power over others. The public application of our definitions of *madness* does put people in mental health wards."[21]

In the educational realm, postmodernism is to be congratulated for uplifting moral education, for helping educators see more clearly the political (power) aspects of education, and for encouraging teachers to help students take up their social responsibilities.

Of course, not all of postmodernism's philosophical and educational contributions seem to be valid. Many scholars, for example, have pointed out that the very rejection of metanarratives is itself a metanarrative, a view of the philosophical shape of things. Second, in spite of its denial of absolutes, postmodernism's concern with oppression and dominance reveals its own set of moral absolutes. Such terms as "democracy," "tolerance," and "justice" constantly undergird their value judgments. Their literature doesn't set these concepts forth as preferences, but as judgmental criteria.

A third criticism is that many believe that postmodernism has carried the social construction of knowledge to an absurd extreme. John R. Searle of the University of California at Berkeley, for example, argues that there are portions of the real world that "are only facts by human agreement." Yet, as he puts it, there "are 'objective' facts in the sense that they are not a matter of your or my preferences, evaluations, or moral attitudes." In the first category he puts such things as the value of money, while in the second are such facts as that his sister got married on December 14. He is quite convinced that "realism and a correspondence conception are essential presuppositions of any sane philosophy, not to mention of any science."[22]

The basic issue of conflict between Christianity and postmodernism is that the first is founded upon revealed absolutes, while the second denies both the concept of absolutes and the possibility of revelation. From the postmodern perspective, even "God" is a social construct.

Again, in the face of postmodernism's denial of metanarratives, the central core of the biblical picture is a grand metanarrative that begins with creation and runs through the incarnation and second advent. The Bible provides both an overarching view of history and a comprehensive world view. Such conceptions find no place in the postmodern scheme of things. Christian educators, in fact, see the telling of the biblical metanarrative as one of the primary reasons for the existence of their schools.[23]

Notes

1. For a helpful treatment of the interface between modernism and postmodernism, see Stanley J. Grenz, *A Primer on Postmodernism* (Grand Rapids, MI: Wm. B. Eerdmans Pub. Co., 1996).

2. Gary Land, "The Challenge of Postmodernism," *Dialogue* 8 (1996):1:5.

3. See Rorty, *Philosophy and the Mirror of Nature.*

4. Jacques Derrida's seminal work is *Of Grammatology* (Baltimore: The Johns Hopkins University Press, 1976).

5. Michel Foucault, *The Archeology of Knowledge and the Discourse of Language* (New York: Pantheon Books, 1972).

6. Jean-François Lyotard, *The Postmodern Condition: A Report on Knowledge* (Minneapolis: University of Minnesota Press, 1984), p. xxiv.

7. Land, "The Challenge of Postmodernism," p. 6.

8. Joe L. Kincheloe, *Toward a Critical Politics of Teacher Thinking: Mapping the Postmodern* (Westport, CT: Bergin & Garvey, 1993), p. 35.

9. William E. Doll, Jr., *A Post-Modern Perspective on Curriculum* (New York: Teachers College Press, Columbia University, 1993), p. 2.

10. Ibid., pp. 2, 3.

11. Kincheloe, *Toward a Critical Politics of Teacher Thinking*, p. 34.

12. John A. Zahorik, *Constructivist Teaching* (Bloomington, IN: Phi Delta Kappa Educational Foundation, 1995), p. 11.

13. Ibid., p. 12.

14. Ibid.

15. Bowers, *Elements of a Post-Liberal Theory of Education*, p. 137.

16. Doll, *A Post-Modern Perspective on Curriculum*, p. 4.

17. Patrick Slattery, *Curriculum Development in the Postmodern Era* (New York: Garland Publishing, 1995), p. 243.

18. Doll, *A Post-Modern Perspective on Curriculum*, p. 4.

19. Henry A. Giroux, *Pedagogy and the Politics of Hope: Theory, Culture, and Schooling* (Boulder, CO: Westview Press, 1997), p. 227.

20. Kincheloe, *Toward a Critical Politics of Teacher Thinking*, pp. 217, 34.

21. Sire, *The Universe Next Door,* p. 187.

22. John R. Searle, *The Construction of Social Reality* (New York: The Free Press, 1995), pp. 1, xiii.

23. For a helpful treatment of this thesis, see Brian J. Walsh, "Education in Precarious Times: Postmodernity and a Christian World View," in Ian Lambert and Suzanne Mitchell, eds., *Crumbling Walls of Certainty: Towards a Christian Critique of Postmodernity and Education* (Sydney: Centre for the Study of Australian Christianity, 1997), pp. 8-24.

6

Contemporary Theories of Education

The preceding three chapters discussed six major philosophical viewpoints and their implications for education. The treatment thus far has been an extrapolation of what philosophers have said about education. The present chapter will examine what educators have had to say about their field in the light of philosophy. In other words, this chapter will focus on theories which take educational problems as their starting point and seek answers by appealing to philosophy.

The educational theorists referred to in this chapter have generally not framed their theories in terms of philosophic concerns (i.e., metaphysics, epistemology, and axiology). This does not mean, however, that their educational proposals have no philosophic undergirding. On the contrary, their proposals are thoroughly permeated with assumptions, even though those assumptions may not always be explicit. This chapter, in the spirit of the theorists, will focus on educational principles rather than philosophic categories. Figure 4 illus-

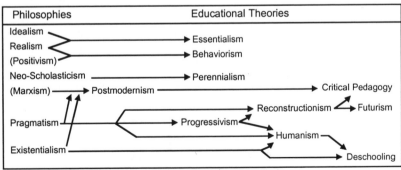

Figure 4. The Relationship of Educational Theories to their Philosophic Sources

trates the relationship between the contemporary educational theories and their philosophic roots.

The formation of these theories has been largely a phenomenon of the twentieth century. Many of their attributes previously existed in an informal manner, but their detailed elaboration has awaited the educational conflict that has been consciously fought since the early 1900s.

PROGRESSIVISM

Background

Progressivism in education was part of a larger socio-political movement of general reform that characterized American life in the late-nineteenth and early-twentieth centuries as America sought to adjust to massive urbanization and industrialization. Progressivism in politics was evident in the careers of such leaders as Robert La Follette and Woodrow Wilson, who attempted to curb the power of trusts and monopolies and to make the system of political democracy truly operative. In the social arena, progressives of the stamp of Jane Addams worked in the settlement-house movement to improve social welfare in Chicago and other urban areas. The reforms and attempted reforms of the progressives were many, and educational progressivism must be seen in its wider context.

Progressivism as an educational theory[1] arose as a definite reaction against traditional education, which had emphasized formal methods of instruction, mental learning, and the literary classics of Western civilization. The major intellectual influences underlying progressive education were John Dewey, Sigmund Freud, and Jean-Jacques Rousseau. Dewey made his contribution as a philosopher of the pragmatic school who wrote a great deal on the philosophic undergirding of education and attempted to validate his ideas in his laboratory school at the University of Chicago. Pragmatism, therefore, may be seen as a central influence in progressive educational theory.

A second influence undergirding educational progressivism was the psychoanalytic theory of Freud. Freudian theory bolstered many progressives to argue for more freedom of self-expression among children and a more open learning environment in which children could release the energy of their instinctive impulses in creative ways. A third influence was Rousseau's *Emile* (1762). This book particularly impressed those progressives who were opposed to the interference of adults in establishing the learning goals or curriculum of children. It should be noted that the excesses of the child-centered progressives were more in harmony with the thought of Rousseau and Freud than with that of Dewey, even though Dewey has generally received the blame by the many critics of progressive education.

These underlying intellectual influences were developed into progressive educational theory by a remarkable group of educators who were also active in applying their theory to school practice. Carleton Washburne, William H. Kilpatrick, Harold Rugg, George S. Counts, Boyd H. Bode, and John L. Childs were instrumental in developing the different strains of progressive thought. Through their influence and energy, progressive education became the dominant theory in American education from the 1920s to the l950s.

By the middle of the fifties, when progressive education lost its organizational existence, it had changed the face of American education. Perhaps part of the reason for its organizational demise was the fact that many of its ideas and programs had been adopted, to some extent, by the public school establishment, and the progressives, therefore, had less to "holler" about. From that point of view, it appears that their success led to their dissolution. On the other hand, it should be recognized that progressive theory in its completeness never did become the consistent practice in the vast majority of school systems. What was adopted were bits and pieces of progressivism that were amalgamated with other educational ideas in eclectic fashion.

The progressives should not be seen as a group who were unified on all theoretical matters. They were, however, united in their opposition to certain school practices. Allan Ornstein has noted that they generally condemned the following: (1) the authoritarian teacher, (2) heavy reliance on textbooks or bookish methods of instruction, (3) passive learning by memorization of information and factual data, (4) the four-walls approach to education that sought to isolate education from social reality, and (5) the use of fear or physical punishment as a form of discipline.[2]

The major organizational force of progressivism in education was the Progressive Education Association (1919-1955). Progressive education must be seen as both an organized movement and as a theory if one is to understand its history and impact. In both of these aspects it advocated a central core of principles. Many progressive ideas found renewed vitality in the educational humanism of the late 1960s and early 1970s.

In addition, the last decades of the twentieth century witnessed some progressive emphases being resurrected by the neopragmatists. That is especially true in the democratic desire to "help everybody's children take part in making culture."[3]

Progressive Principles

The process of education finds its genesis and purpose in the child. This position is in direct opposition to the traditional approach to education. The traditional school started with a body of organized subject matter and then sought to impose that corpus of learning on students, whether they desired it or not. The progressives reversed this model by putting the child at the focal point of the school. They then sought to develop a curriculum and teaching method that grew out of students' needs, interests, and initiatives.

According to progressive theory, children have a natural desire to learn and discover things about the world around them. Not only do they have this inborn desire, but they also have certain needs that must be fulfilled in their lives. These desires and needs give children a definite interest in learning those things that will help them solve their problems and thereby fulfill their desires.

Children's interests are, therefore, the natural starting point for the learning experience. That does not mean that children's interests should be the only factor in determining what they should learn. After all, children are still immature and may not be able to define significant purposes. On the other hand, the doctrine of child interest does stipulate that children naturally tend to oppose whatever they feel is imposed on them by others. Child interest, therefore, should be harnessed by the teacher, who will develop a learning environment in which this motivational force will naturally lead to the desired learning outcomes. The teacher uses the children's natural interests to help them learn those skills that will assist them in meeting their current needs and desires. This will, in turn, help students develop problem-solving skills and build the cognitive store of information needed for socialized living.

From the progressive viewpoint, starting with the child is the way that education most easily and naturally takes place. It utilizes the motivational force of genuine child interest and therefore helps students and teachers work together, rather than pitting them against one another in an adversarial relationship. This opens the way for more humaneness in the classroom and allows the teacher to relate to children in all their complexity—as individuals who have needs, desires, feelings, and attitudes.

Pupils are active rather than passive. Children are not passive beings who are just waiting for a teacher to stuff their minds full of information. Students are dynamic beings who naturally want to learn and will learn if they are not frustrated in their learning by adults and authorities who seek to impose their wills and goals upon them. Dewey noted that "the child is already intensely active, and the question of education is the question of taking hold of his activities, of giving them direction."[4]

The teacher's role is that of advisor, guide, and fellow traveler, rather than that of authoritarian and classroom director. This position is tied closely to both the pragmatists' belief in continual change and the progressives' position on the centrality of the child in education. The teacher cannot be an authority in the traditional sense of being a dispenser of essential information. That is true because a major reality of human existence is change. As a result, no one knows the shape of the future and the essential information that will be needed in the future. Thus, there can be no authoritative teaching of a restricted body of essential knowledge.

On the other hand, teachers possess greater knowledge and have had more experience than their students. That puts them in the position of being guides in territory through which they have already passed, advisors in situations in which students reach an impasse, and fellow travelers in those circumstances which are new to them in an ever-changing and ever-evolving world. They are individuals who will learn with their students as they seek to harness student energies and direct student interests in the learning enterprise. The role of teachers can be seen as that of helping students learn how to learn by themselves, so that they will develop into self-sufficient adults in a changing environment.

The school is a microcosm of the larger society. The school should not be seen as a distinct social setting in which education takes place in a unique way. Education and learning are constantly taking place in a person's life. For example, a boy watches his father change a tire. He learns from this experience because of his felt need, his natural curiosity, and his interest. This is a learning experience, and learning experiences take place in the same manner inside of schools as they do in the world at large. Learning and educative experiences in the everyday world are not artificially divided into cubicles of time, space, and content. Therefore, the education offered in the schools should not be artificially divided and punctuated by separating English from social studies, or by calling an unnatural halt to an educative experience by ringing the bell at a prearranged time. In the larger world, the subject matter of social studies, English, and math is integrated in its usage, and individuals stay at a task until they complete it or come to a natural break.

Education in schools should be seen in terms of how people are educated and learn in the larger world around them, because meaningful education is life itself and does not take on a distinct nature inside the walls of a school. That position is a departure from that of the traditionalists, who see education as a period of preparation for life—a time when the minds of children are being filled with the information they will need for real living.

Classroom activity should focus on problem solving rather than on artificial methods of teaching subject matter. This position rests upon the pragmatists' emphasis on experience and their problem-solving epistemology. Knowledge, declare the progressives, does not come through the reception of information as an abstract substance that is somehow transferred from the teacher to the pupil. Knowledge, they claim, is an instrument for managing experience.

That conclusion is not a rejection of traditional subject matter, but it is a rejection of the traditional method of attempting to transfer that subject matter to the younger generation. The progressives based their curricular and teaching approaches on problems of significance to their students. In doing this they developed the project method of instruction.

The project method can be illustrated by a fourth-grade class that wants to study Native Americans and decides to build a village. In the process of building their village, the students run across many problems. For example, they have to decide what kind of Native Americans they want to be. That problem leads them into the realm of reading, and then into geography and anthropology, as they discover that different tribes related to their environment in varying ways. If they decide to build a tepee, they will have an industrial experience in tanning leather, a geometrical experience in developing the pattern, a mathematical experience as they make the measurements, a biological experience in deciding what type of wood will be best for the poles, and a writing experience when they compose a report concerning their accomplishments.

From this short (and incomplete) example, it is evident that building the village would present the children with a series of problems which they would be interested in solving, since the decision to study Native Americans had been theirs in the first place. The process of solving these problems would allow a skillful teacher-guide to lead students through a large part of the traditional curriculum in an almost painless manner. Through the problem-solving process, the students would not only have learned facts, but, more importantly, they would have learned how to think and how to use their thoughts in the world of experience. A project might be as short as three days or as long as a year, depending on the nature of the project, the perseverance of the students, and the skill of the teacher.

The social atmosphere of the school should be cooperative and democratic. This position is a natural outgrowth of the progressive belief that the school is a microcosm of the larger society and that education is life itself rather than a preparation for living. The schools, claim the progressives, are unnaturally competitive. In the world of work, if a person has a problem, he or she is generally allowed to seek help from a fellow worker. In the school, however, children are punished for moving about, talking, or even trying to help one another solve a problem. Traditional education places an undue emphasis on competition that is neither socially healthy nor educationally efficient. Competition has its place if it serves the general good, but society and learning are more often advanced through cooperation.

Democratic forms of school and classroom direction and control were also advocated by the progressives. They were ardent supporters of political democracy, and they noted that students could not be prepared for democratic adulthood if they were raised in autocratic educational institutions. The school should promote student government, the free discussion of ideas, and the involvement of students and faculty in both learning and educational planning.

EDUCATIONAL HUMANISM IN RELATION TO PROGRESSIVISM

Background

Organized progressivism came to an end in the mid-fifties, but the ideas of the progressives continued to make themselves felt through a diversified movement generally referred to as educational humanism. The humanists adopted most of the progressive principles, including child-centeredness, the non-authoritative role of the teacher, the focus on the active and involved pupil, and the cooperative and democratic aspects of education.

Progressivism, however, is not the only source of educational humanism. Existentialism has also acted as a stimulus for the movement. As a result, educational humanism has placed even more stress on the uniqueness of the individual child than did the progressives, who tended to think of children more in terms of social units. The existentialist strain in educational humanism has led to an emphasis on a search for personal meaning in human existence.

This focus on the individual child in humanistic education has been strengthened even more by a third major contributor to educational humanism—the humanistic or existential psychologists. Psychologists of this strain include such people as Carl Rogers, Abraham Maslow, and Arthur Combs. These psychologists, along with many of their colleagues, made a direct and significant impact upon humanistic education. Their focus has been on helping the student become "humanized" or "self-actualized"—helping the individual student discover, become, and develop his or her real self and full potential.

A fourth stimulus for educational humanism has been the romantic critics. These writers arose in the social turbulence of the 1960s in a storm of protests over the repressive, mindless, and inhumane conditions of modern schools. They argued that schools had become intellectually deadening and psychologically destructive because they were preoccupied with order and punishment rather than human health and growth. Typical of their genre of educational writing are John Holt's *How Children Fail* (1964), Herbert Kohl's *36 Children* (1967), Jonathan Kozol's *Death at an Early Age* (1967), and George Dennison's *The Lives of Children* (1969). The literature produced by the romantic critics was eloquent, poignant, and popular. As such, it made a large impact on the reading public and developed a grassroots sympathy for experimentation in humanistic education.

Humanistic Principles

The present discussion of educational humanism will not seek to give a detailed summary of humanistic principles, since that would of necessity include much of the material surveyed in the treatment of progressivism. It will rather highlight humanistic emphases and examine some of the institutional formats through which the humanists have sought to give expression to their convictions.

Central to the humanistic movement in education has been a desire to create learning environments in which children are free from intense competition, harsh discipline, and the fear of failure. The humanists sought to move away from the adversary relationship so often found between students and teachers and, on the other hand, to create educational relationships permeated with trust and a sense of security. It was their belief that such an atmosphere would free students from destructive and energy-consuming fears and would allow more energy to be expended toward individual growth and the development of creativity. Holt captured the humanistic view of human nature as it relates to learning when he wrote

> that children are by nature smart, energetic, curious, eager to learn, and good at learning; that they do not need to be bribed and bullied to learn; that they learn best when they are happy, active, involved, and interested in what they are doing; that they learn least, or not at all, when they are bored, threatened, humiliated, frightened.[5]

In short, the humanists sought to move beyond the "jail mentality" of most schools in an attempt to provide learning environments that would lead to individual growth. Hence, the fundamental purpose of education for the humanists centered on self-actualization rather than a mastery of knowledge as an end in itself. As a result, openness, the use of imagination, and experimentation in fantasy were encouraged, while standardized testing and mass teaching were frowned upon. The humanists proposed that teachers could most easily reach their ends through working with individuals and small groups. True to its existential root, educational humanism was seeking to avoid the herd orientation of modern society.

Institutional Formats

The humanistic educators' emphasis on individuality spawned a great deal of diversity in approaches to schooling. Three of the most influential approaches have been the open classroom, the free school, and schools without failure. These became widespread alternatives to traditional educational approaches in the late 1960s and early 1970s.

The open classroom provides a schooling experience that seeks to break up the rigidity of the traditional classroom. The open classroom is a decentralized classroom in which the desks are separated into clusters and space is divided into learning areas. These areas are separated by screens, bookcases, and other objects. Such a classroom might have activity areas for reading, math, and art. Each area is equipped with a variety of learning materials which the students can use, manipulate, or read as needed. The open classroom does not have a rigid schedule in terms of either time or materials to be covered. Ample provision is made for student cooperation and physical mobility. The teacher and teacher aides generally spend their time with individuals and small groups rather than with the entire class. The open classroom seeks to provide a learning community in which both teachers and students work together. Kohl notes that in the open classroom

> the role of the teacher is not to control his pupils but rather to enable them to make choices and pursue what interests them. In an open classroom a pupil functions according to his sense of himself rather than what he is expected to be. It is not that the teacher should expect the same of all his pupils. On the contrary, the teacher must learn to perceive differences, but these should emerge from what actually happens in the classroom during the school year, and not from preconceptions.[6]

The free school movement can be seen largely as a revolt from a public education that cannot provide the proper conditions for humanistic education because of its custodial (baby-sitting) and indoctrination functions.[7] The free schools were developed by dissatisfied parents and teachers who wanted to get their children away from an authoritative system with its emphasis on a structured curriculum and demands of conformity.

Free schools have been established in all types of locations, from slum storefronts to converted army barracks and barns. No two of these schools are alike, and each has its own reason for existence.

They charge little or no tuition, are frequently held together by "spit and string, and run mainly on the energy and excitement of people who have set out to do their own thing." Most of them are quite small, and their mortality rate has been extremely high—many have lasted for only one or two years.

Free schools have appealed to varied social groups, from suburban whites to inner-city blacks. "Some seem to be pastoral escapes from the grit of modern conflict, while others are deliberate experiments in integrated multicultural, multilingual education." All of them seek to develop "free children," who will be independent and courageous people able to deal with the changing complexities of the modern world.[8]

William Glasser, the psychiatrist who developed "reality therapy," proposed a humanistic approach to education in his *Schools Without Failure*. Glasser holds that there are two kinds of human failure— "failure to love and failure to achieve self-worth." Schools have traditionally failed, according to Glasser, because they have not established warm interpersonal relationships through which the students' need for love and a sense of self-worth has been satisfied. The role of the school should be to provide a warm and nonthreatening environment in which those needs can be met. This atmosphere will provide an effective context for learning. At the same time, Glasser calls for individual responsibility from each student, since being responsible is intimately related to self worth.[9] *Schools Without Failure* provides suggestions as to how such goals might be reached.

The open classroom, the free school, and schools without failure are just three of the many variations proposed by the educational humanists to humanize schooling. It should be noted that most of the humanistic proposals have been aimed at elementary education.

PERENNIALISM

Background

Perennialist educational theory arose as a formal position in the 1930s as a reaction against the progressives, who, the perennialists felt, were destroying the intellectual fabric of American life by their emphasis in the schools on child-centeredness, presentism, and life adjustment. Modern perennialism generally represents a wholesale rejection of the progressive perspective.[10]

For the perennialist, permanence, despite significant social and political upheavals, is more real than the pragmatists' concept of change. The perennialists, therefore, advocate a return to the absolutes and focus on the time-honored ideas of human culture—those ideas that have proven their validity and usefulness by having withstood the test of time. Perennialism stresses the importance of mind, reason, and the great works of the intellectual past. Early perennialism was traditional, classical education in a revived form that was more specific in its theoretical formulations because it now had a visible and powerful enemy in educational progressivism.

The key to understanding the perennialist protest is the concept of liberal education. Liberal education in the classical tradition revolved around those studies that made people free and truly human, as opposed to the training that people received to do specific tasks in the world of work. In the Greek world, people were divided into two groups—those who worked and those who thought. It was believed that those who worked performed an essentially animal function, since they relied upon their muscles. On the other hand, those who thought used the distinctively human capacity of rationality. Individuals in the latter group were free individuals who were fit to govern. Since they were free, they needed an education that would develop their human—rational—capacity. Education, therefore, focused on the rational and mental aspect of humanity and tended to dwell on the influential ideas of Western culture. Training for work was not seen as an educational task; and, as a result, it was nearly always obtained through apprenticeship rather than schooling. Formal education through schooling was left to bestow its attention on developing the free or liberal person. Thus the liberal arts formed the curriculum in traditional education.

The liberal arts educational tradition was passed from Greece to Rome and from Rome to Christian Europe. Up until the late-nineteenth and early-twentieth centuries it represented the main line of education in Europe and the United States. The rise of industrialism, however, brought problems and changes to education. The machine freed more people from the task of the "slave" and provided a base of wealth that enabled them to partake of the educational privileges that had once been restricted to the ruling classes. Traditional education, however, did not enlist the interest of, and did not seem to be of meaning for, and did not seem to be of meaning for, many of the people who came from working-class backgrounds.

The progressives had arisen in an attempt to make education more meaningful to the new masses in the schools. But by the 1930s the traditionalists were ready to take a stand against what they considered to be the threat of anti-intellectualism in the American schools. Their basic position was that machines could do for every modern person what slavery did for the fortunate few of Athens. In a democracy, therefore, all people could be free and rulers. Thus all people needed a liberal education so that they could think and communicate, rather than merely a training for animal existence through schooling for work.[11]

The two most influential spokesmen for the perennialists have been Robert Maynard Hutchins and Mortimer J. Adler, who led their campaign from the University of Chicago where Hutchins became president in 1929 at the age of thirty. Both men were active lecturers and writers and sought to mold public opinion in favor of perennialism for over fifty years.

Hutchins and Adler made a major contribution for the perennialists when they undertook the editing of the massive collection entitled *Great Books of the Western World*. That collection consists of about one hundred of the works of the West that contain the "best" in ideas and thought.

The perennialist educational position found its purest implementation at St. John's College in Annapolis, Maryland, where President Stringfellow Barr made the study of the great books the basis for the bachelor's degree. The late 1980s saw a forceful plea for perennialism in higher education in the form of Allan Bloom's best-selling book, *The Closing of the American Mind* (1987).

Philosophically, perennialism finds its roots in neo-scholasticism. It therefore relies heavily on the thought of Aristotle. Perennialism in America has been largely associated with secular education, even though neo-scholasticism rests upon the writings of Thomas Aquinas as well as upon those of Aristotle. Roman Catholic educational theory has many affinities to the secular mainstream of perennialism, but it lays more emphasis on the spiritual, the theological, and Thomistic thought. The educational writings of Jacques Maritain are representative of perennialism's ecclesiastical branch.

Up through the early 1980s, perennialism had made most of its recommendations with the secondary school, and especially the college, in mind. The role of elementary education was seen as that of providing students with tools that they could later use to study and understand the liberal tradition. The year 1982, however, saw the publication of *The Paideia Proposal*, in which a group led by Adler set forth an agenda and a program directly aimed at "basic schooling" for the first twelve years of American education. While the Paideia Group gave at least outward lip service to some of the insights of John Dewey, the findings of educational psychology, and the exigencies of modern society, its recommendations were in harmony with traditional perennialist concerns and goals.[12]

Perennialist Principles

People are rational animals. As previously noted, those with perennialist presuppositions see people as largely sharing with the animal world many desires, enjoyments, and tasks. For instance, dogs enjoy riding in cars, can carry burdens and do other forms of work, and relish food that has been prepared for humans. In this sense, humans and the animals share much in common. What makes people distinctly human is the fact that, of all the animals, only humans possess a rational intellect. That is humanity's most unique and valuable characteristic. Aristotle claimed that "man is a rational animal," and perennialists share that viewpoint. Their view of education, therefore, focuses on the education of the rational aspect of people. Hutchins noted that "one thing is essential to becoming human, and that is learning to use the mind."[13] As individuals develop their minds, they can then use their reason to control their appetites and passions.

Human nature is universally consistent; therefore, education should be the same for everyone. One important fact about the rational nature of humanity is that it has been shared by all persons throughout all periods of human history. If humans are rational animals, and if people are universally the same in this respect, then it follows that all people should have the same education. On this point, Hutchins wrote:

> Every man has a function as a man. The function of a citizen or a subject may vary from society to society, and the system of training, or adaptation, or instruction, or meeting immediate needs may vary with it. But the function of a man as man is the same in every age and in every

society, since it results from his nature as a man. The aim of an educational system is the same in every age and in every society where such a system can exist: it is to improve man as man.[14]

Knowledge is universally consistent; therefore, there are certain basic subject matters that should be taught to all people. If knowledge were not the same everywhere, learned people would not be able to agree on anything. Individuals may have different opinions, but when they do agree, opinion becomes knowledge. The educational system should deal with knowledge, not opinion, because knowledge leads people to eternal truth and acquaints the student with the world's permanencies. Hutchins set forth the curricular uniformity of education in the following deduction: "Education implies teaching. Teaching implies knowledge. Knowledge is truth. The truth is everywhere the same. Hence education should be everywhere the same."[15]

Education, claim the perennialists in opposition to the progressives, should not adjust individuals to the world, but rather should adjust them to the truth. The curriculum should not focus on students' immediate interests, what seems important at the moment, or what may appeal to a particular society in a unique time and place. Neither is vocational or professional training a function of education. The school should focus on educating the intellect to grasp and understand the essential and eternal truths that relate to the role of individuals in human society. This shared knowledge base will help people understand one another and will better equip them to communicate and build a more satisfactory social order.

The subject matter, not the child, should stand at the center of the educational endeavor. Most perennialists are in agreement that if the educational system is to acquaint the student with eternal truth, it will have to have a curriculum emphasizing languages, history, mathematics, natural science, philosophy, and the fine arts.

The focal point of learning in perennialism lies in activities designed to discipline the mind. Difficult mental exercises, including reading, writing, drill, rote memory, and computation, are significant in training and disciplining the intellect. Learning to reason is also important. Thus exercises in grammar, logic, and rhetoric are imperative activities. These tasks may be somewhat distasteful to the average student, but even that is beneficial, since the will is developed as students persevere in hard intellectual tasks. The externally enforced mental discipline of the classroom helps children internalize the will power that later will be needed as they face difficult tasks in adult life, when there is no "enforcer" to urge them to complete unpleasant duties.

The great works of the past are a repository of knowledge and wisdom which has stood the test of time and is relevant in our day. The great books program associated with Hutchins, Adler, and St. John's College has been the avenue through which perennialism has received its widest publicity, even though not all leaders in the movement support the program. Those who endorse the great books approach maintain that studying the works of the leading minds down through history is the best means of coming into contact with humanity's greatest ideas and of thereby developing the intellect.

The greatness of a book lies in its status as a classic. A classic is a work relevant to every age, and is therefore superior to culture's lesser works. Those works which belong to this category are those that have stood the test of time. Since these books have been found valuable in varying centuries, civilizations, and cultures, they must contain a great deal of truth. If that assumption is valid, claim the perennialists, then the study of such works is imperative. Adler noted that the reading of the great books

> is not for antiquarian purposes; the interest is not archaeological or philological. . . . Rather the books are to be read because they are as contemporary today as when they were written, and that because the problems they deal with and the ideas they present are not subject to the law of perpetual and interminable progress.[16]

This emphasis on reading the original great works is in opposition to the essentialist tradition in education, which has uplifted the textbook as the major way to transmit organized subject matter. Hutchins stated that "textbooks have probably done as much to degrade the American intelligence as any single force. If the student should know about Cicero, Milton, Galileo, or Adam Smith, why should he not read what they wrote?"[17]

Those perennialists who do not favor the great books program maintain that contemporary sources of great ideas may be used to acquire knowledge. They are, however, just as concerned that students deal directly with the great intellects, rather than with the predigested mental food contained in textbooks.

The educational experience is a preparation for life, rather than a real-life situation. By its very nature, the school is an artificial arrangement in which immature intellects become acquainted with humanity's greatest achievements. The school is not, and should not be, as the progressives would have it, a microcosm of the larger society. Human life, in its fullest sense, can be lived only after the rational part of a person is developed. The school is a specialized institution that seeks to accomplish this all-important mission. It is not concerned with such things as the occupational or recreational aspects of human existence. These have their place in the lives of people, but they lie outside the proper activities of educational institutions.

ESSENTIALISM

Background

A second reaction to progressivism in education also arose in the 1930s under the banner of essentialism. Essentialists agreed with the perennialists that progressive educational practice was too "soft," since, in its attempt to make learning a painless enterprise, it had moved away from the difficult problem of grappling with the educational basics, such as the mastery of the tools of learning (the three R's) and the established facts. On the other hand, the approach of the perennialists appeared to be too aristocratic for many Americans and, to some observers, even smacked of anti-democratic ideals.

Essentialists, unlike the progressives and perennialists, do not have a singular philosophic base. The underlying philosophies of essentialism are idealism and realism. In addition, the essentialist tradition also contains a large number of "concerned citizens," who feel that the schools have "gone to pot" and that they need to get back to stricter discipline and a study of the "basics."

Essentialism forms the main stream of popular educational thought in most countries, including the United States. It is a conservative position and, as a result, is more concerned with the school's function of transmitting tested facts and truth than it is with innovation and educational frills.

Since the 1930s the essentialists have put forth a great deal of effort to warn the American public of "life-adjustment education," the child-centered school, and the deterioration of learning in the United

States. In 1938 a major voice was organized in the form of the Essentialist Committee for the Advancement of American Education under the leadership of William C. Bagley, Issac L. Kandel, and Frederick Breed.

A second major essentialist organization was formed in the 1950s as the Council for Basic Education. The leading spokesmen for this group were Mortimer Smith and Arthur Bestor. The general position of the Council can be viewed through the titles of Bestor's important works on education—*Educational Wastelands: The Retreat from Learning in Our Public Schools* (1953) and *The Restoration of Learning: A Program for Redeeming the Unfulfilled Promise of American Education* (1955).

Bestor's remark that "the men who drafted our constitution were not trained for the task by 'field trips' to the mayor's office and the county jail" is representative of essentialism's critique of progressivism's "contribution" to American education.[18] The Council for Basic Education was not only concerned with the deterioration of American public education, but it was also skeptical of the value of formal educational studies by professional specialists in education.

Another influential essentialist spokesman was Admiral Hyman G. Rickover, father of the atomic submarine, who deplored the lack of developed minds in America. He recommended the adoption of a European-type educational system, such as that of the Dutch or the Russians, so that American youth would have a good grasp of the basics upon high school graduation and would be adequately prepared to enter an intensive and rigorous professional or technological course of study.

The launching of *Sputnik* in 1957 added weight to the essentialist campaign, since many Americans interpreted the Soviet success as an indication of American educational inferiority. As a result, the late fifties and early sixties saw massive programs of curricular revision.

At the other end of the continuum of educational reform, however, the sixties also saw a powerful movement to humanize the schools along progressive lines. The predictable reaction to the new wave of educational humanism was a renewed call back to the basics, a call that became progressively strident throughout the 1970s.

By the early 1980s the United States government had entered the fray. In 1983 the National Commission on Excellence in Education issued an evaluation of American education entitled *A Nation at Risk*. The report warned that "the educational foundations of our society are presently being eroded by a rising tide of mediocrity that threatens our very future as a nation and a people."[19] The report called for renewed emphasis on the "Five New Basics," which would include, as a minimum standard for high school graduation, four years of English, three years of mathematics, three years of science, three years of social studies, and one-half year of computer science. It also recommended two years of foreign language for college-bound students.[20]

A Nation at Risk stimulated several other national reports that emphasized the need to return to the teaching of basic subjects and skills in the schools. Among these were the College Board's *Academic Preparation for College* (1983) and a report by the Task Force on Education for Economic Growth entitled *Action for Excellence* (1983).[21]

Besides the push in the 1970s and early 1980s to get back to the academic basics, the right wing of American Protestantism opened up a renewed drive to get the basic of all basics—religion—back into the school curriculum. Upset with the Supreme Court rulings against Bible reading and prayer in the public schools, and shocked by the moral breakdown of American culture in the 1960s, fundamentalist leaders such as Jerry Falwell and Tim LaHaye crusaded not only to get the three Rs back into the classroom, but especially to get the fourth R—religion—into the center of education. As they saw it, educational humanism was a threat that paled into relative insignificance in the face of the peril of its underlying philosophy of "secular humanism."

The upshot was not only a move to put religion back into the public classroom, but the creation of thousands of Christian day schools by conservative Protestant groups that had traditionally supported the public system. By the early 1980s the new wave of Christian day schools was perhaps the most rapidly growing sector of American education.[22]

Essentialism is alive and well in the late 1990s. In 1996 E. D. Hirsch, Jr. published *The Schools We Need and Why We Don't Have Them*. According to Hirsch, the United States has the "best public universities" but "the worst public schools of the developed world." In line with Bestor and Rickover, Hirsch lays the blame for the K-12 disaster at the feet of the progressive and humanistic educators. "Most current 'reforms,'" he notes, "are repetitions or rephrasings of long-failed Romantic, antiknowledge proposals that emanated from Teachers College [the home of educational progressivism], Columbia University, in the teens, twenties, and thirties of this century."[23]

Hirsch laid the foundation for his solution in 1987 in his *Cultural Literacy: What Every American Needs to Know.* "To be culturally literate," he argued in that volume, "is to possess the basic information needed to thrive in the modern world." Since that time he has shifted his terminology from "Cultural Literacy" to "Core Knowledge," since the word "cultural" was confusing to some. To operationalize his program, Hirsch founded the Core Knowledge Foundation and edited a series of books for the guidance of elementary schools. By 1996 some six volumes in the Core Knowledge Series had been published under such titles as *What Your First Grader Needs to Know.* Several hundred schools had adopted his basic principles by the late nineties.[24]

Essentialism, like other theories, does not find all of its proponents in total agreement as to the best course for the schools, but they are in agreement on several major principles.

Essentialist Principles

The school's first task is to teach basic knowledge. For the essentialists, education finds its center in the teaching and learning of the basic skills and subject matters that will, upon their mastery, prepare the student to function as a member of a civilized society. The elementary school, according to the essentialists, should focus its attention on a curriculum engineered to cultivate the basic tool skills that contribute to literacy and the mastery of arithmetical computations. Thus the three R's—the elementary essentials—are stressed. The secondary curriculum would aim at developing competency in history, mathematics, science, English, literature, and foreign languages. The essentialist program implies that educational nonessentials, such as tap dancing and basket weaving, are not the business of the school. The school should aim at teaching the hard core of fundamental learning to all youth.

Essentialists are outraged by the fact that many high-school graduates are functionally illiterate and that a large number of college freshmen need "bonehead" English. Schools, they claim, have catered too long to the desires of students. That has made a farce of education. What children need is to get to know the world as it really is by coming to grips with basic and essential subject matter.

Learning is hard work and requires discipline. Learning those things that are essential cannot always be related to the interest of the child. Although progressivism's problem-solving approach to learning is often helpful, it should be recognized that not all subject matter can be broken up into problems and projects. Much of it will have to be learned by such straightforward methods as memorization and drill. The immediate needs of the child are not as important as more distant goals. Effort is more important than interest, even though interest should be used as a motivational force whenever it is evident. For many students, interest develops as they put forth the amount of effort necessary to understand a field of subject matter.

Students, like adults, are easily diverted from tasks that take effort. They need, therefore, to discipline themselves to focus their attention on the task at hand. Many students, however, do not have this ability and need the assistance of a teacher who can tactfully provide an external context that will help them get down to the hard work of performing a difficult assignment.

The teacher is the locus of classroom authority. The essentialists hold that the teacher is not a fellow learner or a guide. Rather, the teacher is one who knows what the students need to know and is well acquainted with the logical order of the subject matter and the way it should be presented. In addition, the teacher, as a representative of the adult community, is in a position that demands respect. If this respect is not forthcoming, the teacher has the right and responsibility to administer disciplinary measures that will lead to an atmosphere conducive to orderly learning.

Essentialism and Perennialism Compared

In our discussion of essentialism and perennialism it has been seen that these two conservative theories have a great deal in common. Christopher Lucas has expressed their commonality in the following manner:

> First, traditionalists or conservatives of varied persuasions have tended to agree that considerations of technocratic utility and efficiency should be subordinated to the paramount intellectual, spiritual, and ethical purposes of general education. Secondly, essentialists and perennialists concur that the crux of the educational enterprise is the transmission and assimilation of a prescribed body of subject matter, one incorporat-

ing the basic elements of the social cultural heritage. Thirdly, both groups acknowledge the cardinal importance of effort, discipline, and self-control in the learning process, as opposed to self-indulgent gratification of immediate needs and transitory interests. Fourthly, conservatives come together in endorsing the idea of curricular continuity: the foundations for a collegiate-level liberal education are laid in a systematic, planned, and sequential exposure to the rudiments of learning skills, beginning with the three R's in the elementary school and extending through to an orderly introduction to the basic subject matter disciplines at the secondary school level.[25]

Even though there is a lot of similarity between essentialism and perennialism, there are also several pivotal differences which make them quite distinct as educational theories. These differences have been succinctly summarized by George F. Kneller. One major point of variation, according to Kneller, is that essentialism is less totally intellectual than perennialism. Essentialism is less concerned with the supposedly eternal truths, and is more concerned than perennialism with the adjustment of students to their physical and social environment.

A second point of departure is that essentialism is more willing to absorb the positive contributions of progressivism to educational method. A third area of variance is found in a different attitude to the great works of the past. Perennialists place much more emphasis on these works as timeless expressions of humanity's universal insights. Essentialists, on the other hand, see the great works of the past as one of many possible sources for the study of present problems.[26]

A fourth point, one not brought out by Kneller but one that should help the reader to understand better the differences between these two theories, is that the major thrust of perennialism has traditionally been directed at higher education, while the essentialists seem to be primarily concerned with the elementary and secondary levels.

RECONSTRUCTIONISM

Background

The 1930s was a decade of crisis. Worldwide depression had crippled the capitalistic nations economically, totalitarianism was raising its head in Europe and Asia, and social unrest was a growing feature in America. To some observers in the United States it appeared that democracy itself might be in its last hour. These observers noted that the depression of the thirties was not a problem of a lack of food or material goods. There was an abundance of those things. The depression has been accurately described as a famine in the midst of plenty. America's problem centered upon the distribution of goods and foodstuffs rather than upon their production. In the early thirties, the business sector was partially paralyzed, and the politicians appeared to be helpless in the face of massive economic disaster.

It was in this context that George S. Counts developed a rousing approach to education through several provocative speeches that in 1932 found their way into print as *Dare the School Build a New Social Order?* Counts called to educators to throw off their slave mentality, to deliberately reach for power, and then to make the most of their conquest by helping to shape a new social order based on a collective economic system and democratic political principles. He called for the educational profession to organize from the kindergarten through the university and to use its organized power in the interests of the great masses of the people.[27]

This position represented a reversal of the traditional role of the school from being a passive transmitter of the culture to being an active and leading agency of societal reform. The 1930s saw a group known as the "Frontier Thinkers" form around Counts and Harold Rugg at Teachers College, Columbia University. Their ideas were largely an extension of the social aspects of Dewey's progressive thought. The philosophical base of reconstructionism is found in pragmatism.

The postwar period saw a renewed thrust at reconstructionism through the work of Theodore Brameld. Some of Brameld's more influential writings have been *Patterns of Educational Philosophy* (1950), *Toward a Reconstructed Philosophy of Education* (1956), and *Education as Power* (1965).

Principles of Reconstructionism

World society is in a state of crisis, and civilization as we know it will come to an end unless current practices are reversed. The problems of population, pollution, limited natural resources, global inequality in the distribution of resources, nuclear proliferation, racism, nationalism, and the naive and irresponsible uses of technology threaten our present world order and will destroy it if not corrected as soon as possible. These problems, note the reconstructionists, are coupled with the challenge of modern totalitarianism, a loss of humanistic values in a mass society, and the increase of functional ignorance among the world's population. In short, the world is facing economic, military, and social problems on an unprecedented scale. The problems faced are of such a magnitude that they can no longer be ignored.

The only effective solution to world problems is the creation of a planetary social order. Just as the problems are worldwide, so must be the solutions. Total cooperation by all nations is the only hope for a dynamic world population living in a finite world with limited amounts of irreplaceable resources. The technological era has brought about worldwide interdependence as well as great advances in the sciences. On the other hand, we are suffering from cultural lag in adapting to the new world order. We are attempting to live in the age of the space ship with a value system and political mentality forged in the horse-and-buggy era.

According to reconstructionism, humanity now lives in a world society in which technological ability can do away with material wants for all people. In this society, a "utopian" existence is possible as the international community cooperatively moves from a preoccupation with producing and fighting over material goods to a phase in which human needs and interests are considered most important. In such a world, people could concentrate on being better human beings as an end in itself.

Formal education can become a major agent in the reconstruction of the social order. Schools that reflect the dominant social values, claim the reconstructionists, will merely transmit the social, economic, and political ills that are currently afflicting human society. The school can and must reverse its traditional role and become a fountainhead of social innovation. The task of reversing the educational role is urgent, due to the fact that humanity now has the capability of self-annihilation.

The critics of social reconstruction argue that Brameld and his colleagues place too much confidence in the power of teachers and other educators to act as primary instruments of social change. The reconstructionists reply that the only alternative to social reconstruction is global chaos and the eventual obliteration of human civilization. From their perspective, either education will be an instrument to obscure the urgent necessity of social transformation and thus thwart change, or it will be enlisted as an agent for effecting society's positive and orderly transition into the future.[28]

The reconstructionists do not see the school as having the power to create social change single-handedly. On the other hand, they do view the school as a major agent of power that touches the life of the entire society, since it reaches its children during their most impressionable age. As such, it can be a primary instigator of insight into social problems and a foremost agitator for social change.

Teaching methods must be based upon democratic principles that rely upon the native intelligence of the majority to recognize and act upon the most valid solution to the world's problems. Reconstructionists, like those in other branches of the progressive movement, are unified in their view of democracy as the best political system. From their perspective, it is imperative that democratic procedures be used in the classroom as students are led into opportunities to choose between varying social, political, and economic options.

Brameld uses the term "defensible partiality" to describe the position of teachers in relation to controversial curricular items. In this posture, teachers allow the open examination of evidence that agrees and disagrees with their position, and they present alternative positions as fairly as possible. On the other hand, teachers should not mask their convictions. They should both express and defend their partialities publicly. Beyond that, teachers must work for the acceptance of their viewpoint by the largest possible majority. It seems to be assumed by reconstructionists that the issues are so clear-cut that the majority will agree about both the problems and the solutions if free and democratic dialog is allowed. Some observers have noted that reconstructionism has a great deal of faith in the intelligence and good will of humanity—what some have called a utopian faith.

If formal education is to be a part of the social solution in the present world crisis, it must actively teach for social change. "Teachers," penned Counts, "should deliberately reach for power and then make the most of their conquest."[29] Education must awaken students' consciousness to social problems and engage them actively in working for a solution. Social consciousness may be awakened if students are encouraged to question the *status quo* and to investigate controversial issues in religion, society, economics, politics, and education.

Critical investigation and discussion will help students see the injustice and nonfunctionality of many aspects of the present system. It also will help them develop alternatives to conventional wisdom.

The social sciences of anthropology, economics, sociology, political science, and psychology form a helpful curricular foundation which reconstructionists utilize to identify major problem areas of controversy, conflict, and inconsistency. The role of education is to expose the problem areas of human culture and to build the widest possible consensus about the primary aims that should govern humanity in the reconstruction of world culture. The ideal world society of reconstructionism would be "under the control of the great majority of the people who are rightly the sovereign determiners of their own destiny."[30]

FUTURISM IN RELATION TO RECONSTRUCTIONISM

In 1970 Alvin Toffler, in response to the ever-accelerating explosion of knowledge and technology, raised a new dimension of educational theory in his best-selling *Future Shock*. "What passes for education today, even in our 'best' schools and colleges," claimed Toffler, "is a hopeless anachronism."[31] He noted that schools are operating on a set of practices and assumptions developed in the industrial era, while society has entered the age of super-industrialism. As a result, schools are educating youth with an emphasis on the past, while they live in a world order undergoing continuing and accelerating change. Toffler claimed that

> our schools face backward toward a dying system, rather than forward to the emerging new society. Their vast energies are applied to cranking out Industrial Men—people tooled for survival in a system that will be dead before they are.
>
> To help avert future shock, we must create a super-industrial educational system. And to do this, we must search for our objectives and methods in the future, rather than the past.[32]

Toffler emphasized the need of the educational system "to generate successive, alternative images of the future," so that students and teachers might have something to direct their attention to in the educational undertaking.[33] Students should examine possible, probable, and preferable futures as they study the future of human society and develop the expertise that will lead, hopefully, to a preferable future.[34]

In the early 1990s Toffler was still urging futurist education, and also reemphasizing the repackaging of delivery systems. As he saw it, in the face of the new information technology

> our mass education systems are largely obsolete. Exactly as in the case of the media, education will require a proliferation of new channels and a vast expansion of program diversity. A high-choice system will have to replace a low-choice system if schools are to prepare people for a decent life in the new Third Wave society, let alone for economically productive roles.[35]

The futurists, unlike the reconstructionists, are not so insistent on claiming that schools can directly initiate social change. The aim of the futurists is to help prepare people to respond to change and make choices in an intelligent manner as humanity moves into a future that has more than one possible configuration. In order to do this, however, the futurist, like the reconstructionist, must critically examine the current social, political, and economic order.

Harold Shane outlined a futurist curriculum that focuses on the injustices, contradictions, and problems in the existing world order.[36] The curricular emphasis and educational activities he suggests are similar to what the reconstructionists have put forth, and the results of both systems would be largely the same—to develop "a preferable future" through education. From this perspective, futurism can be seen as an extension and modification of reconstructionism.

CRITICAL PEDAGOGY IN RELATION TO RECONSTRUCTIONISM

An educational movement closely related to reconstructionism and more loosely related to futurism is what has come to be known as critical pedagogy. In addition to its reconstructionist heritage, critical pedagogy builds upon the ideas of several other theoretical movements. One is the school of social and political thought known as the Frankfurt School or critical theory. Emerging in Germany in the 1930s, the Frankfurt School brought together ideas from social theory and philosophy in the interest of ending all forms of domination through the transformation of society. The critical theorists accepted the Marxist critique of capitalism and remained committed to many of the central concerns of the Enlightenment.

An especially powerful influence on the development of critical pedagogy has been the third-world educational program of liberation and development. That program is built upon a revolutionary educational theory that seeks to bring about changes in worldwide culture in favor of a healthier future through grassroots education of the lower classes concerning their political, social, and economic rights and possibilities. Paulo Freire's *Pedagogy of the Oppressed* (1970) was at the forefront of this movement. A truly revolutionary theory of education, this educational perspective is closely linked to the various movements of liberation theology in the underdeveloped nations and among the disadvantaged minorities in developed countries.[37] Freire has made an enormous impact on critical pedagogy.

Another major influence in the formation of critical pedagogy has been postmodern thought. Its views of the subjectivity of knowledge and knowledge as power have done much to inform the critical pedagogy agenda. With the assumptions of postmodernism in mind, it doesn't take too much imagination to see that for the proponents of critical pedagogy the archenemies of healthy education are the theories set forth by the essentialists, perennialists, and behaviorists.

"Critical pedagogy," Peter McLaren claims, "is fundamentally concerned with understanding the relationship between power and knowledge." That understanding is important because, claim the critical pedagogy theorists, the curriculum represents much more than a program of study. "Rather, it represents the *introduction to a particular form of life; it serves in part to prepare students for dominant or subordinate positions in the existing society*." Thus the curriculum must be viewed as a form of "*cultural politics*."[38]

The traditional function of schools has been social reproduction, the perpetuation and reproduction of the social and economic relationships and attitudes needed to sustain the existing economic and class structure. In the spirit of the reconstructionists, the critical pedagogy theorists propose a revolutionary role for schools. The schools must lead out in creating a more just society. Or, as McLaren puts it, "the tradition of critical pedagogy . . . represents an approach to schooling that is committed to the imperatives of empowering students and transforming the larger social order in the interests of justice and equality."[39]

The neutral school, claim the critical pedagogy theorists, is a destructive myth. That myth ignores the

> social construction of knowledge and cognition. It ignores the fact that one of the most important exercises of power in a postmodern world involves the perogative to define meanings and to specify what knowledge is valuable. Without a critical resistance, knowledge becomes oppression—oppression of nonwhites, the poor, and women.[40]

The need, according to such critical pedagogical theorists as Henry A. Giroux, is for "new forms of knowledge" and "new spaces where knowledge can be produced." He notes that

> critical pedagogy as a cultural politics points to the necessity of inserting the struggle over the production and creation of knowledge into a broader attempt to create a public sphere of citizens who are able to exercise power over their lives and especially over the conditions of knowledge production and acquisition. . . . At stake here is a pedagogy that provides the knowledge, skills, and habits for students and others to read history in ways that enable them to reclaim their identities in the interests of constructing forms of life that are more democratic and more just.[41]

Multiculturalism

Multicultural education found an increasing place in schools in the last half of the twentieth century. While some have thought of multiculturalism as an awareness and appreciation of differences, others have viewed it as a revolutionary tool.

It is in that latter guise that multiculturalism unites with the ideas of the critical pedagogists. The title of Christine E. Sleeter's *Multicultural Education as Social Activism* makes the connection nicely. She argues that multicultural education should be "understood as a form of resistance to dominant modes of schooling, and particularly to white supremacy."[42]

The advocates of multiculturalism point out that in the past minority voices had been silenced by those majority groups who controlled the institutions of cultural reproduction, such as schools, museums, universities, and publishing houses. Minorities in the past spoke largely to one another. But those days are gone. Multiculturalism is a call for minority voices to be unleashed so that their story becomes a part of a shared heritage. Beyond that, multicultural education is a move to correct the social, economic, and political injustices of the past.

Feminism

There is a sense in which educational feminism is also a subset of critical pedagogy. After all, women and their concerns have not had an equal voice in male-dominated societies. Not only has feminism created such curricular innovations as women's studies, but the movement has sought to increase the number of women in the educational power structure.

While feminism in education is concerned with such issues as representation and power, it also has a more complex and subtle side to its agenda. Some advocates, for example, have argued that women's experiences, values, responsibilities, and activities need to be integrated into the curriculum. In a similar vein, Nel Noddings argues in *The Challenge to Care in Schools* for restructuring education on an ethic of caring that flows out of women's maternal practices and feminist consciousness.[43] In short, feminist advocates are acutely aware of the role of personal relationships, aesthetics, and emotion in the construction of knowledge within the context of schooling, and they want to see such concerns receive a larger place in educational experience.

BEHAVIORISM

Background

A major force in education since the middle of the twentieth century has been behaviorism. Behaviorism is in one sense a psychological theory, but in another sense it has burst the bounds of traditional psychological concerns and has developed into a full-blown educational theory. As an approach to education, it has been welcomed among those "modern" individuals who treasure scientific methodology and "objectivity," as well as among a sizable sector of the business community that values visible and immediate results, efficiency, and economy.

Behaviorism has several ideological roots. One of these is philosophical realism. With realism, behaviorism focuses on the laws of nature. Humanity, from the behaviorist perspective, is a part of nature and, as a result, operates according to nature's laws. Reality, for the behaviorist, is independent of the human knower. The task of the behaviorist is to observe living organisms, including humans, in an attempt to discover the laws of behavior. After these laws have been discovered, they will provide a foundation for a technology of behavior.

A second root of behaviorism is positivism.[44] The thrust of the positivists was to arrive at what Auguste Comte (1798-1857) described as "positive" knowledge. Comte divided human history into three epochs, each of which was characterized by a distinct way of thinking. The most primitive epoch is the *theological*, in which things are explained by references to spirits and gods. The middle period is the *metaphysical*, in which events are explained by essences, causes, and inner principles. The highest period is the *positive*. In this last stage, people do not attempt to go beyond observable and measurable fact. Comte was seeking to develop a science of society, and the behaviorists have built upon his platform. Their position represents a rejection of essences, feelings, and inner causes that cannot be measured.[45] Empirical verification is central in behavioral methodology.

A third historical root of behaviorism is materialism. Materialism, reduced to its core, is the theory that reality may be explained by the laws of matter and motion. It represents an explicit rejection of beliefs about mind, spirit, and consciousness. These are claimed to be relics of a prescientific age.

Russian psychologist Ivan Pavlov (1849-1936) set the stage for behaviorist psychology through his study of reflex reaction. Pavlov noted that he could condition dogs to salivate by ringing a bell if the dogs had previously been trained to associate the sound of the bell with the arrival of food.

The father of modern behaviorism, John B. Watson (1878-1958), following the lead of Pavlov, asserted that human behavior is a matter of conditioned reflexes. Watson postulated that psychology should stop studying what people think and feel, and begin to study what people do. For Watson the environment was the primary shaper of behavior. He held that if a child's environment could be controlled, then he could engineer that child into any type of person desired.

The most influential behaviorist has been B. F. Skinner. Skinner's work has been at the forefront of the battle of behaviorism in education in such areas as behavior modification, teaching machines, and programmed learning. Some of Skinner's more influential works have been *Science and Human Behavior* (1953), *Beyond Freedom and Dignity* (1971), and *Walden Two* (1948). Perhaps his utopian novel of a behaviorally engineered society, *Walden Two*, has given his ideas as much publicity as anything he has written.

Skinner has been a storm center of controversy, because he repudiates the freedom and dignity traditionally ascribed to human beings and seems to indicate that some individuals should decide how others will be conditioned. That, for his critics, brings frightful visions of George Orwell's *1984* into view. Skinner, however, notes that we are being conditioned by the environment anyway, and that it makes more sense to use the laws of behavioral technology to condition people in such a way as to maximize the chances of human survival in a technologically complex age than to let those laws operate at random.

It should be plain from this short overview of the foundations of behaviorism that it is deeply embedded in the presuppositions of naturalistic science. Behaviorists hope to develop the "science" of humanity. "Behaviorism," however, notes Skinner, "is not the science of human behavior; it is the philosophy of that science."[46] Skinner's statement highlights the fact that there are no sciences without philosophic assumptions—assumptions which shape and limit their potential discoveries. Since this is the case, it is essential that Christian teachers be aware of the assumptions of any given theory before they seek to apply those theories in their professional practice.

Behaviorist Principles

Human beings are highly developed animals who learn in the same way that other animals learn. For behaviorists, humanity does not stand above and outside of nature. People are not beings who are related to a supernatural Being (God). Humanity is rather a part of nature. According to Skinner, "a small part of the universe is contained within the skin of each of us. There is no reason why it should have any special physical status because it lies within this boundary."[47] Humans do not have any special dignity or freedom. It is true that a person is a complex natural organism, but an individual is still primarily a part of the animal kingdom. Behaviorism is unapologetically evolutionary, and that position sets the framework for its study of psychology.

The task of behavioral psychology is to learn the laws of behavior. These laws are the same for all animals. A scientist can therefore discover many of the laws of human learning by studying the behavior of less complex creatures, such as rats and pigeons. Scientists, likewise, can refine the techniques of teaching through experimentation with animals. These techniques can then be applied to human beings.

Education is a process of behavioral engineering. From the behaviorist perspective, people are programmed to act in certain ways by their environment. They are rewarded for acting some ways and are punished for acting in other ways. Those activities that receive a positive reward tend to be repeated, while those receiving a negative reward tend to be extinguished. This process of positive and negative reward (reinforcement) shapes or programs a person to behave in certain ways. Behavior may be modified, therefore, by manipulating environmental reinforcers. The task of education is to create learning environments that lead to desired behaviors. Schooling and other educative institutions are therefore viewed as ways of designing a culture.

Skinner and other behaviorists claim that environmental conditioning and programming have always been a part of education and schooling. What they are calling for is a more conscious use of the laws of learning to control individuals so that the quality of life and the chances of racial survival will be enhanced.[48]

The teacher's role is to create an effective learning environment. Skinner and other behaviorists have, over the years, advocated a thorough revision of classroom practices. The main ingredient missing in most school environments, claims Skinner, is positive reinforcement. Traditional education has tended to use aversive forms of control, such as corporal punishment, scolding, extra homework, forced labor, the withdrawal of privileges, and examinations designed to show what students do not know. Consequently, students, if they are to be positively reinforced, must learn ways of escaping from the aversive situation of the classroom through such techniques as daydreaming, becoming aggressive, or eventually dropping out of school.

Skinner's contention is that students learn in daily life through the consequences of their acts. The task of the teacher is to arrange a learning environment that will provide positive reinforcement for desired student actions. Unrewarded acts, in a controlled environment, will be extinguished over time.

Harold Ozmon and Sam Craver have summarized the basic procedures for behavior modification in the ordinary classroom in the following way:

> (1) Specify the desired outcome, what needs to be changed, and how it will be evaluated; (2) establish a favorable environment by removing unfavorable stimuli which might complicate learning; (3) choose the proper reinforcers for desired behavioral manifestations; (4) begin shaping desired behavior by utilizing immediate reinforcers for desired behavior; (5) once a pattern of desired behaviors has been begun, slacken the number of times reinforcers are given; (6) evaluate results and reassess for future development.[49]

It can be seen from the above summary that behavioral objectives and the proper use of positive reinforcers are central to the effective learning environment as set forth by behaviorists. To aid the teacher in the complex task of maintaining a rewarding environment, Skinner and others have advocated programmed textbooks and other materials that break up the subject matter into small steps so that students will be rewarded positively as they complete each step successfully. Reinforcement occurs frequently because the successive steps in the learning process are as small as possible. Teaching machines and computerized teaching have been advocated by behaviorists to aid in this process of sequential learning.

Efficiency, economy, precision, and objectivity are central value considerations in education. These values are fostered by both the philosophic orientation of behaviorism and by the objectives of the business community with which the school coexists in modern culture. Behavioral techniques have been applied to such business practices as systems management, advertising, and sales promotion with a great deal of success. This has led a large sector of the business community to join the psychological behaviorists in calling for schools and individual educators to be "accountable." The accountability movement has sought to fix the responsibility for instructional outcomes—what children learn—upon those doing the teaching. That mindset has stimulated an interest in applying business management techniques, objectives, and performance-based measures to school contexts.

It has been felt by the critics of behaviorism that its whole approach to education is based on a simplistic notion of the educative process and a false premise that equates training and manipulation with education. They suggest that what may be successful as an advertising technique may not be sufficient for the education of children.

EDUCATIONAL ANARCHISM:
THE DESCHOOLING PROPOSAL[50]

By 1970 the Western world had witnessed some 2,500 years of periodic attempts at educational reform and 150 years of intensified reform as schooling became available to the masses. The year 1970 saw a proposal that went beyond educational reform to the realm of educational revolution. This movement was initiated by the publication of *Deschooling Society* by Ivan Illich. Illich's approach to the social order is basically that of anti-institutionalism and disestablishment. He opposed institutionalism on the grounds that it monopolized services and opportunities and set rigid and expensive routes as the only way of fulfilling basic human needs.

Illich saw the school system as the archenemy of his vision of the good life, since it taught all youth to look to the institutional model as the ideal.

> The pupil is thereby "schooled" to confuse teaching with learning, grade advancement with education, a diploma with competence, and fluency with the ability to say something new. His imagination is "schooled" to accept service in place of value. Medical treatment is mistaken for health care, social work for the improvement of community life, police protection for safety, military poise for national security, the rat race for productive work.[51]

The deschooling proposal calls for the disestablishment of the school and the repeal of compulsory education laws. In their place, Illich and his colleagues suggest a system of vouchers or tuition grants by which educational funds will be channeled directly to the beneficiaries, who will decide how to spend their funds in an attempt to buy their share of the education of their choice.

A good educational system, according to Illich,

> should have three purposes: it should provide all who want to learn with access to available resources at any time in their lives; empower all who want to share what they know to find those who want to learn it from

them; and, finally, furnish all who want to present an issue to the public with the opportunity to make their challenge known.[52]

To help people become educated in a deschooled society, Illich recommends what he calls four "learning webs," or "educational networks," that would put learners in touch with teachers, other learners, and learning tools. He identifies these networks as reference services to educational objects, skill exchanges, peer-matching, and reference services to educators-at-large.[53]

Illich and his colleagues see the deschooling proposal as the answer to society's educational problems and social injustices. The critics of the proposal tend to see it as a pipe dream and Illich as a mystic.

By the 1990s the deschooling proposal was not receiving much of a hearing. However, it has been retained in our discussion because it still remains a possible option and may at some future date be resurrected.

CRITIQUE AND PERSPECTIVE

The educational theories discussed in this chapter differ from the philosophies studied in Chapters 3 through 5 in the sense that the theories have been stimulated by educational problems rather than philosophic issues. The theorists, therefore, have not communicated to us in the language of philosophy, even though their theories have been built upon metaphysical, epistemological, and axiological beliefs. Part of the function of the study of educational philosophy is to heighten the awareness of educators concerning the philosophic assumptions undergirding the educational theories and to provide educators with the conceptual tools to evaluate those theories. Only through an awareness of the philosophic implications of the theories can Christian educators compare them with the Christian world view and be in a position to use those aspects of the theories that are in harmony with Christianity as building blocks for developing a Christian philosophy of education.

The contemporary educational theories have changed the shape of education over the past century. It is at the level of the theories that the educational battle has been, and is being, fought, both in the literature and in the schools. The theories have generated widespread educational experimentation and a literature aimed at both popular and professional audiences.

Central to the struggle among the theorists has been the progressive position. Alfred North Whitehead once noted that all philosophy was actually a footnote to Plato—philosophers either aligned in some way with Plato or revolted against him. The same sort of statement might be made about the educational theories. Progressivism has served as a stimulant and a catalyst for both those who agree and those who disagree with its basic presuppositions and educational practices. That catalyst has instigated the formulation of contemporary theories in an era in which educational disputes have broken out of the cloistered realm of academia and into the public press. The vital issues faced by the theorists have enlisted both interest and enthusiasm for educational ideas and experimentation among large sectors of the reading public.

This summary will not analyze each of these theories in the light of the Christian world view, since some of that has been done in the critiques of the root philosophies upon which the theories have been built. There is, however, an important observation that must be made: from a Christian perspective, most of the educational theories are built upon an inadequate view of human nature and humanity's social predicament. The behaviorally-oriented theorists see humans as highly evolved and evolving animals, while the many progressive-humanistic approaches to education see human nature as intrinsically good when left to unfold without undue interference from external forces. Neither of these positions accounts for the perversity of human nature, and neither fully accounts for the effects of sin and the fall.

Most of the theories hold that humanity is potentially able to solve its own problems if educators would establish the "proper" social and educational environment. That naturalistic and anthropocentric (human-centered) premise flies in the face of the Christian world view, which holds that God, not people, will solve the problems of this earth.

Perhaps at the root of this problem is the widely believed concept that the current state of society and human nature is normal. By way of contrast, the Christian perspective holds that the current world order and the state of the unrenewed (in Christian terms) person is abnormal and is in need of both transformation and restoration. In short, the Christian view holds, in opposition to most social theorists, that humanity is not able to solve its own problems, no matter how it manipulates its educational and social environment. The Bible holds that God will intervene in human history a second time to save humanity from itself. That insight, along with a more rounded view of social problems and the condition of human nature, must be taken into consideration in both evaluating educational theories and in seeking to develop a Christian perspective.

You have probably observed that each of these theories has captured an aspect of truth concerning humanity, education, and society. It is this realization, along with the fact that many of their ideals and practices correlate with our daily experience, that has made the educational theories powerful forces in the ongoing dialogue about schooling and education. These theories, however, are only as true as their basic assumptions. Insofar as their presuppositions are true, they shed light upon viable practices for Christian education.

It is a part of the task of the Christian educator to evaluate the assumptions underlying these theories in the light of Christian philosophy, and then to build a personal educational theory that utilizes, where helpful, the discoveries of the educational philosophers and theorists. That conclusion does not imply the wholesale adoption of a theory, but rather the building of a theory of Christian education upon a Christian philosophic position. Part III will present one approach to that task. Before moving to Christian education, however, we will first examine the unique role of analytic philosophy in education.

Notes

1. The best history of progressivism in education is found in Lawrence A. Cremin, *The Transformation of the School: Progressivism in American Education,* 1876-1957 (New York: Vintage Books, 1964).

2. Allan C. Ornstein, *An Introduction to the Foundations of Education* (Chicago: Rand McNally College Publishing Co., 1977), p. 204.

3. Kathe Jervis and Carol Montag, eds., *Progressive Education for the 1990s: Transforming Practice* (New York: Teachers College Press, Columbia University, 1991), p. xi.

4. John Dewey, *The School and Society,* rev. ed. (Chicago: University of Chicago Press, 1915), p. 37.

5. John Holt, *Freedom and Beyond* (New York: Dell Publishing Co., Laurel Edition, 1972), p. 10.

6. Herbert R. Kohl, *The Open Classroom: A Practical Guide to a New Way of Teaching* (New York: New York Review, 1969), p. 20.

7. Jonathan Kozol, *Free Schools* (Boston: Houghton Mifflin Co., 1972), p. 14.

8. Bonnie Barrett Stretch, "The Rise of the 'Free School,'" in *Curriculum Quest for Relevance,* 2d ed., ed. William Van Til (Boston: Houghton Mifflin Co., 1974), p. 113.

9. William Glasser, *Schools Without Failure* (New York: Harper & Row, Perennial Library,

1975), pp. 14, 25-26, 232; William Glasser, *Reality Therapy: A New Approach to Psychiatry* (New York: Harper & Row, Perennial Library, 1975), pp. 15-18.

10. A prominent exception to this generalization is Jacques Maritain, a Roman Catholic philosopher, who, in *Education at the Crossroads* (pp. 12-14), commends progressive education for its methodological advances, but faults it on its lack of educational ends. As noted below, Mortimer J. Adler's *Padeia Proposal* (1982) seems to have taken a softer look at Dewey's contribution than did traditional perennialism, but one gets the impression that Adler merely selected those progressive insights that could be utilized to further his own program.

11. Robert M. Hutchins, *The Learning Society* (New York: New American Library, 1968), p. 165.

12. See Mortimer J. Adler, *The Paideia Proposal: An Educational Manifesto* (New York: Macmillan Publishing Co., 1982); Mortimer J. Adler, *Paideia Problems and Possibilities* (New York: Macmillan Publishing Co., 1983); Mortimer J. Adler, ed., The *Paideia Program: An Educational Syllabus* (New York: Macmillan Publishing Co., 1984).

13. Hutchins, *The Learning Society*, p. 114.

14. Robert M. Hutchins, *The Conflict in Education* (New York: Harper and Brothers, 1953), p. 68.

15. Hutchins, *The Higher Learning in America*, p. 66.

16. Mortimer J. Adler, "The Crisis in Contemporary Education," *Social Frontier* 5 (February 1939): 144.

17. Hutchins, *The Higher Learning in America*, pp. 78-79. It should be noted that the thrust of the argument for the use of the great books is aimed at higher education rather than at the elementary level. It seems that even those perennialists most enthusiastic about the great books in high school and college would grant the necessity of using textbooks to gain the tools of learning in such areas as mathematics and grammar. See, e.g., Adler, *Paideia Proposal*, pp. 23, 24.

18. Quoted in Henry J. Perkinson, *The Imperfect Panacea: American Faith in Education, 1865-1976*, 2d ed. (New York: Random House, 1977), p. 93.

19. National Commission on Excellence in Education, *A Nation at Risk: The Imperative for Educational Reform* (Washington, DC: U.S. Government Printing Office, 1983), p. 5.

20. Ibid., p. 24.

21. For treatments of the "excitement" stirred up by this 1980s back-to-the-basics movement, see Beatrice and Ronald Gross, ed., *The Great School Debate: Which Way for American Education?* (New York: Simon & Shuster, 1985); William W. Wayson et al., *Up from Excellence: The Impact of the Excellence Movement on Schools* (Bloomington, IN: Phi Delta Kappa Educational Foundation, 1988).

22. Jerry Falwell, *Listen, America!* (Garden City, NY: Doubleday & Co., 1980); Tim LaHaye, *The Battle for the Mind* (Old Tappan, NJ: Fleming H. Revell, 1980); James C. Carper, "The Christian Day School," in *Religious Schooling in America*, eds. James C. Carper and Thomas C. Hunt (Birmingham, AL: Religious Education Press, 1984), pp. 110-29.

23. E. D. Hirsch, Jr., *The Schools We Need and Why We Don't Have Them* (New York: Doubleday, 1996), pp. 58, 2.

24. E. D. Hirsch, Jr., *Cultural Literacy: What Every American Needs to Know*, updated and expanded ed. (New York: Vintage Books, 1988), p. xiii; Hirsch, *The Schools We Need*, 13.

25. Christopher J. Lucas, ed., *Challenge and Choice in Contemporary Education: Six Major Ideological Perspectives* (New York: Macmillan Publishing Co., 1976), p. 14.

26. George F. Kneller, *Introduction to the Philosophy of Education*, 2d ed. (New York: John Wiley & Sons, 1971), pp. 60-61.

27. George S. Counts, *Dare the School Build a New Social Order?* (New York: John Day Co., 1932), pp. 28-30.

28. Lucas, *Challenge and Choice in Contemporary Education*, p. 326.

29. Counts, *Dare the School Build a New Social Order?*, p. 28.

30. Theodore Brameld, *Education for the Emerging Age* (New York: Harper & Row, 1961), p. 25.

31. Alvin Toffler, *Future Shock* (New York: Random House, 1970), p. 353.

32. Ibid., p. 354.

33. Ibid., p. 357. For more on Toffler's educational ideas, see Alvin Toffler, ed., *Learning for Tomorrow: The Role of the Future in Education* (New York: Vintage Books, 1974).

34. Cf. George R. Knight, "The Transformation of Change and the Future Role of Education," *Philosophic Research and Analysis*, 8 (Early Spring, 1980), pp. 10-11.

35. Alvin Toffler, *Power Shift: Knowledge, Wealth, and Violence at the Edge of the 21st Century* (New York: Bantam Books, 1990), p. 360.

36. Harold G. Shane, *The Educational Significance of the Future* (Bloomington, IN: Phi Delta Kappa, 1973), pp. 83-91.

37. See, e.g., Jose Miguez Bonino, *Doing Theology in a Revolutionary Situation* (Philadelphia: Fortress Press, 1975); Gustavo Gutiérrez, *A Theology of Liberation: History, Politics, and Salvation*, rev. ed. (Maryknoll, NY: Orbis Books, 1988); James H. Cone, *A Black Theology of Liberation*, 2d ed. (Maryknoll, NY: Orbis Books, 1986).

38. Peter McLaren, *Life in Schools: An Introduction to Critical Pedagogy in the Foundations of Education*, 3d ed. (New York: Longman, 1998), pp. 183, 186, 188, 189.

39. Ibid., p. xiii. See also Giroux, *Pedagogy and the Politics of Hope;* Ira Shor, *Empowering Education: Critical Teaching for Social Change* (Chicago: University of Chicago Press, 1992).

40. Kincheloe, *Toward a Critical Politics of Teacher Thinking*, p. 48.

41. Giroux, *Pedagogy and the Politics of Hope*, p. 221.

42. Christine E. Sleeter, *Multicultural Education as Social Activism* (Albany, NY: State University of New York Press, 1996), p. 2.

43. Nel Noddings, *The Challenge to Care in Schools: An Alternative Approach to Education* (New York: Teachers College Press, Columbia University, 1992).

44. This philosophical approach will be more fully discussed in Chapter 7.

45. Some writers have accused behaviorism, on the basis of its demand for positive knowledge, of the error of creating humanity in the image of the techniques by which it is studied.

46. B. F. Skinner, *About Behaviorism* (New York: Vintage Books, 1976), p. 3.

47. Ibid., p. 24.

48. Critics of behaviorism have no doubt regarding the power of behavioral engineering, but they are concerned with the issue of who will control the controllers.

49. Howard Ozmon and Sam Craver, *Philosophical Foundations of Education* (Columbus, OH: Charles E. Merrill Publishing Co., 1976), p. 149.

50. I am indebted to William F. O'Neill for the "educational anarchism" label. "Anarchism," he writes, "is the point of view that advocates the abolition of virtually all institutional restraints over human freedom as a way of providing the fullest expression of liberated human potentialities." (*Educational Ideologies: Contemporary Expressions of Educational Philosophy* [Santa Monica, CA: Goodyear Publishing Co., 1981], p. 287.) Anarchists, contending that external government is the root of evil, argue that harmony will prevail if external controls are abolished. Thus O'Neill's phrase aptly fits Illich's deschooling proposal.

51. Ivan Illich, *Deschooling Society* (New York: Harper & Row, 1970), p. 1.

52. Ibid., p. 75.

53. Ibid., pp. 76-79.

7

Analytic Philosophy and Education

Analytic philosophy in its pure form might best be seen as a revolt against the traditional aims and methods of philosophy. It is not a school of philosophy, but rather an approach to doing philosophy. This approach dominated much of the philosophical work in English-speaking countries in the mid to late decades of the twentieth century. As a result, many educational philosophers in both the United States and Great Britain dealt with philosophic and educational issues from the analytic perspective.

The analytic movement in educational philosophy reached the peak of its influence in the 1960s and 1970s, but in the face of new philosophical trends it began to lose ground in the 1980s. Because of its earlier dominance and the fact that analytic method still finds a large place in the philosophy of education, it is important that students of the field become acquainted with the analytic rationale and methodology as well as the possible uses and misuses of analysis.

The present chapter will first examine analytic philosophy in the light of its historic formulation. It will then take a look at some of the modifications in the field that arose in the 1980s and 1990s.

THE ANALYTIC MOVEMENT IN PHILOSOPHY

The analytic movement in philosophy, unlike such outlooks as idealism and pragmatism, did not attempt to provide a systematic philosophy. It was not interested in making metaphysical, epistemological, or axiological statements. On the contrary, it was quite convinced that the broad, sweeping statements of philosophers have merely added to the confusion. The problems of the past, claimed the analysts, were not really problems concerning ultimate reality, truth, and value, but problems having to do with confusion in language and meaning. Imprecision in the use of language and unclear meanings stand at the center of philosophic confusion. Many of our philosophic problems find their genesis in the "sloppy" use of language.

Analytic philosophers, therefore, turned away from the speculative, prescriptive, and synthesizing roles of philosophy. They refused to develop philosophic theories.[1] The common denominator of the analysts, who have had some serious disagreements among themselves, was the logical criticism of language and the way language can be misleading. Their unifying theme might be seen in the term "clarification." The goal of analytic philosophy has been succinctly described by Ludwig Wittgenstein:

> Philosophy aims at the logical clarification of thoughts.
> Philosophy is not a body of doctrine but an activity.
> A philosophical work consists essentially of elucidations.
> Philosophy does not result in "philosophical propositions," but rather in the clarification of propositions.
> Without philosophy thoughts are, as it were, cloudy and indistinct: its task is to make them clear and to give them sharp boundaries.[2]

Genuine knowledge, claimed most analysts, is the business of science rather than philosophy. The true role of philosophy is critical clarification.

In one sense, analytic philosophy has a history that reaches back to the Greeks. Certainly Socrates was concerned that terms and concepts be properly understood, and Aristotle took an interest in precisely defining the words he used. On the other hand, the movement is a phenomenon of the twentieth century.

Perhaps the difference between the twentieth-century model and the use of analysis in the past might best be seen in terms of means and ends. For philosophers prior to the twentieth century, analysis was a means of clarifying language, so that the implications of their philosophic propositions might be understood. They were most concerned with the precise use of language in order that they might achieve the end of making meaningful statements about reality and truth. Analytic philosophers, by way of contrast, have seen the precise use of language (as far as philosophy is concerned) as an end in itself. They were not attempting to make propositions, but were rather interested in clarifying the exact meaning of the propositions set down by others.

The historical roots of modern philosophic analysis can be traced back to linguistic analysis and positivism. Linguistic analysis developed in early twentieth-century England. It was stimulated by Bertrand Russell and Alfred North Whitehead's *Principia Mathematica*, which was published in three volumes between 1910 and 1914. Russell and Whitehead reduced mathematics to a logical language. Their idea was that mathematics possessed a clarity and logic that was, unfortunately, not found in the general use of language.

George Edward Moore, another Englishman, took a different tack from Whitehead and Russell in claiming that the analysis of ordinary language and common sense, rather than scientific-mathematical language, should be the focal point of linguistic analysis.

Perhaps the person who made the largest impact on the analytic movement was Ludwig Wittgenstein, who published his *Tractatus Logico-Philosophicus* in the early twenties. Wittgenstein, in his early years, was influenced by Russell, his teacher; and his work, in turn, influenced the positivistic philosophers of the Vienna Circle.

A second major root of modern philosophic analysis was positivism. The nineteenth-century French positivists, under the lead of Auguste Comte, held the position that knowledge must be based on sense perceptions and the investigations of objective science. Positivism, therefore, limited knowledge to statements of observable facts and their interrelations, and rejected metaphysical world views or world views that contained elements that could not be empirically verified. That negative attitude toward any reality beyond the human senses has influenced many modern fields of thought, including pragmatism, behaviorism, scientific naturalism, and the analytic movement.

Positivism became the rallying point for a group of twentieth-century scholars known as the Vienna Circle. This group was made up largely of scientists, mathematicians, and symbolic logicians who were interested in philosophy. The Vienna Circle saw philosophy as the logic of science, and their thought form came to be known as logical positivism. A major aim of this group was to find an inclusive terminological and conceptual system common to all the sciences. This led them away from a possible role of criticizing the arguments of traditional philosophy, and toward the study of the language of particular sciences and an analysis of language in general in the hope of finding a universal language of science.

Positivists of all varieties have put a great deal of stock in the assumption that human observers can achieve neutrality in their investigations. As noted previously, they also uplifted the principle of rigorous empirical verification. A crucial weakness in their position developed when, in their zeal for verification, they ruled out any consideration of unverifiable propositions. It was in time realized, to the discomfort and depreciation of positivism, that some of the fundamental assumptions of science itself were unverifiable in the way verification was applied by the positivists.

It should be noted that analytic philosophy is an umbrella term that encompasses a number of somewhat diverse viewpoints that are referred to under such labels as logical positivism, logical empiricism, linguistic analysis, logical atomism, and Oxford analysis.

THE ROLE OF PHILOSOPHIC ANALYSIS
IN EDUCATION

At this point, it should be clear that the role of analytic philosophy in regard to education has been radically different from the relationship between the philosophic "schools" and the educational enterprise. "There was a time," notes R. S. Peters, a leading analytic philosopher, "when it was taken for granted that the philosophy of education consisted in the formulation of high-level directives which would guide educational practice and shape the organization of schools."[3] In other words, the function of educational philosophy has traditionally been (and has been put forth in this book) to develop and prescribe educational aims and practices that are built upon, and are in harmony with, a philosophic outlook based on a particular view concerning the nature of reality, truth, and value. That approach obviously runs into conflict with the stance of Wittgenstein, who in his early career stated that metaphysical statements are "nonsense."

What, then, we might ask, are the value, use, and function of educational philosophy for the analyst? The answer is given to us by Peters, who says that one of the main preoccupations of the analytic philosopher is to lay "high-level directives for education . . . under the analytic guillotine."[4] In essence, Peters and his colleagues were stating that the role of educational philosophy is not to develop some new educational "ism" or ideology, but to help us better understand the meanings of our current ideologies. The benefit to be achieved for students, parents, teachers, administrators, and society from such a clarification will be a more meaningful approach to the educational process. Analysts have contended that many educational problems are essentially language problems. Therefore, if we can solve the language problems, we will be in a better position to disentangle the educational problems.

One charge of the analysts is that many educational statements are nonsense. Samuel Shermis has illustrated this point, as well as analytic methodology, by a simple example.

> Analysts might give attention to such typical statements as, "Teachers should provide real-life experiences for their students" or "The curriculum should be based on lifelike situations." First, these statements should be recognized as prescriptions, statements of what someone ought to do, rather than descriptions. Second, the descriptive terms "real-life experience" and "lifelike" should be examined to determine their meanings. The term "life" is a description of all the activities of human beings. One of the activities of living human beings is conjugating verbs. Yet as this statement is usually employed, conjugating verbs is not what is meant, for grammatical exercises are not considered "lifelike." But if grammar is part of "life," why should it not be included in the prescription?[5]

According to Shermis, the type of statements in the above quotation are examples of the all-too-common substitution of ambiguous emotive slogans for meaningful, precise terms. Education, unfortunately, is riddled with imprecise statements and slogans, and analytic philosophers perform a valuable service in their function as clarifiers of language, concepts, and purposes.

It should be seen from the above illustration that the use of analysis can dissolve some problems through the act of clarification by demonstrating that certain statements or prescriptions are meaningless, or at least misleading, as they are stated. In a certain sense, that is a negative function. On the other hand, dissolving issues that are pseudo problems is an important service if teachers are to have time to deal with meaningful concerns. "To the extent that teachers need not worry about doing the impossible—in this case 'providing' 'lifelike' experiences—to that extent can they ask themselves questions which really make sense."[6]

The simplicity of the above example should not be taken as being typical of analytic procedure. It was chosen specifically for its brevity and simplicity. The "doing" or reading of analytic philosophy is a rigorous, exacting, and tedious business that would tend to bore most people quite rapidly. That may be seen by some as a disadvantage, but not to the analytic philosopher, who claims that no progress has ever come in the scientific and mathematical realms without a great deal of rigorous effort and precision. Those are prerequisites to progress.

Philosophical analysts have been not only interested in clarifying the educator's use of language, but also in clarifying the conceptual devices used by the educator, the processes of using them, their underlying presuppositions, and the purposes involved. A typical introductory textbook in educational philosophy from the analytic position centers around an analysis of the "concept of education," the "concept of training," the "concept of child-centered," and other concepts, including "aims," "culture," "curriculum," "liberal education," "conditioning and indoctrination," "value-judgment," "values," "morals," and "freedom and authority."[7] With the exception of the introductory chapter, this listing exhausts the table of contents for a three-hundred-page book. The above list of contents is given in the hope that the reader will intuit the difference between the approach taken by an analytic introduction to educational philosophy and the survey-type approach utilized by *Philosophy and Education* and many other non-analytic introductions.

Analysts have not only avoided making prescriptive statements about what students and teachers ought to do or ought not to do, but they also have avoided statements of value concerning such activities. For example, let us suppose that the suggestion is put forth by certain school authorities that elementary students should read the Macmillan Basal Readers up through the sixth grade. The traditional function of the analyst, in this case, would not be to attempt to say whether a child should read Macmillan or something else, but to examine the claims made regarding the merits of such activities. Instead of saying that a child should read, think, or learn, the analyst will examine what is meant by "read," "think," or "learn," but will not prescribe or make a value judgment. Analysts have viewed their function as clarifying through analysis.

One area into which the analysts moved in education was in the development of models which helped educators clarify and order concepts. Those models might be thought of in terms of strategies to help educators in specific "language games." Analysts also developed theoretical models to help teachers with particular problems. They noted that scientists often construct a theoretical model before engaging in an activity. It follows, claimed the analysts, that the same would be helpful in teaching. The use of models can help clear up ambiguity and can thereby aid the profession.

EVALUATION OF ANALYTIC PHILOSOPHY

Philosophic analysis has in many ways improved educational philosophy by making it more sensitive to the implications of educational terms and adding rigor and precision to the study of education as a professional field. The analytic critique of education has brought about an awareness and a critical attitude that should help the profession be wary of ready-made answers, slogans, and cliches as solutions to social and educational dilemmas. Clarification of educational ideas and statements has been needed in the past, and will be just as needed in the future if professional education is to make progress rather than being content merely with ill-defined motion.

On the other hand, analytic philosophy as an educational philosophy has some glaring weaknesses if analysis is seen as the *only* meaningful way of doing philosophy. First, there is a widespread criticism that philosophic analysis is too narrow and too limited to meet adequately the complex demands of modern life, society, and education. Abraham Kaplan, speaking to this point, has written:

> But note how great is the preoccupation here with purely intellectual goals and standards—the emphasis is on science, truth, belief, observation, and inference. But art, beauty, morality, politics, and religion apparently lie outside the scope of this powerful method, if not outside the scope of philosophical interest altogether. . . . I cannot help but feel that there is something seriously wrong with a philosophy, in the mid-twen-

tieth century, that takes no notice of war, revolution, nationalism, nuclear energy, the exploration of space, or anything else distinctive of the life of our time save the magnificient sweep of the intellect in the achievements of pure science and mathematics.[8]

Philosophic analysis, in its attempts to achieve clarity and precision, has been seen by some as an escape from the really important problems of life and the perennial issues of philosophy.

A second criticism of analytic philosophy is that it is prone to confuse philosophic means with philosophic ends. In its search for clarification and precision, it often has glorified philosophic techniques, and, to a certain extent, turned the philosopher into a highly-skilled technician. One might seriously ask the analytic philosopher not only where we are to go after we have cleared up our ambiguities, but whether clarification of what we are doing is of much value if we are doing the wrong things at the outset.

One analytic philosopher, sensing this problem, has noted that perhaps "a certain systemic ambiguity is more desirable than an artificial precision."[9] Kaplan also warns us to beware of the implications of any trade-offs made between gains in philosophic precision and losses in philosophic wisdom.[10] In regard to the confusion of ends and means, John Wild has noted that the person who is confused on this point "is like a man who becomes so interested in the cracks and spots of dust upon his glasses that he loses all interest in what he may actually see through them."[11] Analytic philosophy, if seen as the only mode of doing philosophy, could develop into "little more than a new form of scholasticism where, instead of arguing about how many angels can stand on the head of a pin, they debate how the words 'should' and 'ought' may be used."[12]

We must realize that even if philosophers cease to speak on metaphysical and axiological questions, others, such as social and physical scientists, will continue to make grand statements and propositions in regard to life and education. One cannot escape facing humanity's basic questions by merely defining them in such a way that they fall outside the definition of philosophy. If philosophers do not do philosophy, then someone else will. Philosophy in its "grand manner" will continue, and educational prescriptions will therefore continue to be made, with or without the aid of professional philosophers. A myopic confusion of ends and means leads nowhere beyond the ideal of clarification of propositions for the sake of clarification. That is a negative rather than a positive philosophic position.

A third criticism of analytic philosophy as a total way of approaching philosophic issues stems from its seeming blindness to its own metaphysical and epistemological presuppositions. On the one hand, analysts generally eschew *a priori* assumptions. On the other hand, when they insist that every descriptive or factual term must be in the language of science and that propositions must be verifiable by sensory observation, they assume a metaphysical doctrine in harmony with materialism, realism, and positivism. As such, their metaphysics and epistemology, whether consciously or unconsciously selected, are open to the same criticisms as those philosophic positions.

It is in the area of blindness to its presuppositions that analytic philosophy has fallen on especially hard times since the late 1970s. At the forefront of the attack have been analytically-trained scholars such as Richard Rorty, who criticized "the very notion of 'analytic philosophy'" on the basis that the ideas undergirding the movement in effect "mirror" a set of presuppositions concerning the shape of reality.[13]

Related to Rorty's criticism is the deconstructionist approach of postmodernism to language, which unpacks philosophical and literary texts for their several layers of assumptions. The end result is that the very claims of the analysts themselves discredit philosophic analysis. In short, there are no assumption-free ways of doing philosophy.

That conclusion has led to further objections to analysis by critical pedagogists and those concerned with feminist issues, who have viewed the scientific and masculine presuppositions undergirding analytic philosophy as tools by which the powerless are kept in subjection.[14]

THE COMPLEMENTARY ROLES OF ANALYTIC AND COMPREHENSIVE PHILOSOPHY

Even at the height of the movement, not all analytic philosophers took a position that identified analytic philosophy with the total task of philosophy. Many leading analysts realized that they had chosen to specialize in one mode of doing philosophy and that there were other modes that could answer different sorts of questions than those asked by analytic philosophy.[15] Unfortunately, many proponents (especially early advocates) of analytic philosophy did not always reflect that balance.

Perhaps the best way to look at the relationship between the comprehensive and analytic ways of doing philosophy might be to see them in terms of being complementary to one another. Jonas F. Soltis, an analyst, has noted that possibly the phrase "in tandem" could express the relationship between analytic and world-view philosophies.[16] In this relationship the techniques of analysis could be used to clarify and make more precise and intelligible the broad concepts of comprehensive philosophical systems. Soltis illustrates this "in tandem" idea through analogy:

> If we could liken the use of analysis to the use of a microscope (and some also use this instrument well or poorly), then we might also liken the traditional philosophical world-view building to the astronomer's use of the telescope in charting the universe. The instruments are designed for different tasks, and so we should expect different results from their respective uses. But the fruitful use of one does not preclude or deny the validity of the use of the other; nor does it cancel the possibility that they may be used in conjunction or in some other complementary way. Thus I would argue that, although there are certain limits to philosophical analysis, these limits are not as narrow and circumscribed as some contemporary philosophers of education believe. In a word, these two approaches are not necessarily antithetical and can complement each other in the unending philosophical attempt to better conceptualize and understand the complex process of education from every available vantage point.[17]

In the wake of postmodern and other criticisms of philosophic analysis, there has been an effort on the part of some analytical philosophers of education to unify the analytic and comprehensive philosophic approaches into a synthesis of the two. Thus, taking a post-positivist stance, Richard Pratte in his *Philosophy of Education: Two Traditions* notes that

> philosophy of education must be rooted in more than a methodology; it requires a normative base. Hence, though a grounding in methodology is proposed[,] it is our starting point; it is not our goal or purpose. What is needed is a normative dimension.[18]

Pratte also points out that "the analytic and normative [i.e., comprehensive] traditions, although they have been taken as antithetical views, inhabit a social reality in our daily lives that makes a mockery of the dualism."[19]

This turn of events, points out one analytic scholar, is nothing less than revolutionary. He refers to it as "the normative revival in *post-analytic* philosophy of education."[20]

CRITIQUE AND PERSPECTIVE

In conclusion, it may be noted that analytic philosophy, by itself, is incomplete. Certain analytic philosophers may have turned away from the broader concerns of philosophy, but they have not invalidated those concerns. Someone must still make speculative decisions concerning such issues as the nature and destiny of humanity and the nature of truth if civilized life is to continue. Out of these decisions will proceed prescriptions in regard to society and its schools. People still need visions of the good life; and, as a result, the six-fold role of philosophy in its synthetic, speculative, prescriptive, evaluative, analytic, and examining aspects must be integrated. No one function may become the whole of philosophy without distorting the entire quest for answers to humanity's basic questions.

From a Christian perspective, the weaknesses of analytic philosophy as the only mode of doing philosophy are quite obvious. Certainly its naturalistic assumptions concerning the nature of valid knowledge and its stress on the efficacy of empiricism as the foremost way of gaining knowledge run into conflict with a Christianity that is founded upon the supernatural and divine revelation. Another difficulty is the analysts' desire to escape from the speculative, prescriptive, and synthetic functions of philosophy. The Christian message, by its very nature, focuses on speculation, prescription, and synthesis.

On the other hand, Christians have much to learn from the analytic movement. For example, much of the language and many of the concepts used by Christians are unnecessarily imprecise. In addition, there are many emotive slogans and ambiguities that have led to semantic difficulties in Christian thought and communication. The insights and methods of the analysts are needed for building a Christian philosophy of education. Those insights and methods, however, must not be seen as an end in themselves or as a complete approach to philosophy, but rather as a philosophic activity that helps Christians sharpen the speculative, prescriptive, evaluative, and synthetic aspects of their philosophic enterprise. In short, Christians will find themselves more in harmony with post-analytic philosophers than with those earlier in the movement.

SUMMARY OF PART II

Part II surveyed the answers given by selected traditional and modern philosophies to people's most basic questions (What is ultimately real?, What is true?, and What is of value?) and probed the relationship between these philosophies and education. In addition, it examined the major theories developed by educators and surveyed the implications of analytic philosophy and postmodernism for education. Part II built upon the basic concepts of philosophy developed in Part I, and it provides the context for the development of a Christian philosophy of education in Part III.

It was noted that each of the philosophies and theories discussed has some insights that are of value for Christian education, but that perhaps none of them is a sufficient base for that education. A major point of emphasis has been to lead educators to examine the presuppositions of the various philosophies and theories, and then to compare their findings with the Christian world view. Each chapter has made a limited analysis of how these philosophic and educational viewpoints relate to the Christian perspective. Much more could have been done in that line, but the purpose of the present book will have been achieved if it leads the reader to an awareness of the need to critically analyze and evaluate all philosophic and educational proposals in the light of Christianity. That task is ongoing and essential.

Beyond that critical undertaking, however, is the more important task of building a positive philosophy of education. The purpose of Part III is to provide one model for building a philosophy of Christian education. That model should also be examined in an attitude of critical awareness concerning its presuppositions, shortcomings, and contributions. The model is not being presented as a complete philosophy of education, or even as the only Christian approach. It is rather being presented as a stimulus to thought about the possible shape of a Christian philosophy of education.

Notes

1. The reason analytic philosophy has been treated in isolation from the traditional and modern philosophies in this text is that the analysts have separated themselves from the perennial concerns of philosophy by focusing on analysis rather than on the full range of philosophic activity. The separation in this chapter, therefore, is not artificial, but inherent in the world of philosophy itself.

2. Ludwig Wittgenstein, *Tractatus Logico-Philosophicus*, trans. D. F. Pears and B. F. McGuinness (London: Routledge and Kegan Paul, 1961), p. 49 (4.112).

3. R. S. Peters, *Ethics and Education* (London: George Allen & Unwin, 1966), p. 15.

4. Ibid.

5. S. Samuel Shermis, *Philosophic Foundations of Education* (New York: D. Van Nostrand Company, 1967), p. 266.

6. Ibid., p. 267.

7. Harry Schofield, *The Philosophy of Education: An Introduction* (London: George Allen & Unwin, 1972).

8. Abraham Kaplan, *The New World of Philosophy* (New York: Random House, 1961), pp. 89-90.

9. Jonas F. Soltis, *An Introduction to the Analysis of Educational Concepts*, 2d ed. (Reading, MA: Addison-Wesley Publishing Co., 1978), p. 82. This is an excellent introduction to analytic method.

10. Kaplan, *The New World of Philosophy*, p. 58.

11. John Wild, *The Challenge of Existentialism* (Bloomington, IN: Indiana Univ. Press, 1955), p. 10. It is of interest to note that Wild treats analytical philosophy in a chapter entitled "The Breakdown of Modern Philosophy."

12. Ozmon and Craver, *Philosophical Foundations of Education*, p. 216.

13. Rorty, *Philosophy and the Mirror of Nature*, see especially pp. 7, 8, 170-73.

14. See Robert D. Heslep, "Analytic Philosophy," in *Philosophy of Education: An Encyclopedia*, ed. J. J. Chambliss (New York: Garland Publishing, 1996), pp. 23-24.

15. Frederick Copleston, *Contemporary Philosophy: Studies of Logical Positivism and Existentialism*, rev. ed. (London: Search Press, 1972), chap. 1.

16. Soltis, *An Introduction to the Analysis of Educational Concepts*, p. 82.

17. Ibid., 83.

18. Richard Pratte, *Philosophy of Education: Two Traditions* (Springfield, IL: Charles C. Thomas, Publisher, 1992), p. xiv.

19. Ibid., p. xii.

20. H. A. Alexander, "After the Revolution, the Normative Revival in Post-Analytic Philosophy of Education," in *Philosophy of Education 1992: Proceedings of the Forty-Eighth Annual Meeting of the Philosophy of Education Society* (italics supplied).

PART THREE:
PHILOSOPHY AND
CHRISTIAN EDUCATION

8

The Necessity of Building a Personal Philosophy of Education

The stage for the discussion of a Christian philosophy of education has been set in Parts I and II. Part I highlighted the role of philosophy in education, analyzed the basic issues of philosophy, and noted the relationship of philosophic issues to educational goals and practices. Part II examined the various answers that traditional and modern philosophers have given to the basic questions of philosophy, noted the implications of their answers for educational practice, and discussed the theories of education that have been the focal point for much of the educational ferment of the past century.

Part III focuses on Christian education. Chapter 8 highlights the need for Christian educators and Christian educational systems to consciously and deliberately develop a philosophy of education based upon Christian answers to the basic issues of philosophy, Chapter 9 proposes one possible approach to a Christian philosophy, and Chapter 10 develops some of the implications of such a philosophy for educational practice in Christian schools.

A CENTRAL PROBLEM OF CHRISTIAN EDUCATION

In the early 1950s the Association of Lutheran College Faculties, meeting at Augustana College in Illinois, was brought face to face with a perennial problem. One of the principal speakers argued that American Lutheran colleges "operated according to no distinctive Lutheran or even Christian philosophy of education, but had simply imitated secular patterns to which they had added chapel services, religious classes, and a religious 'atmosphere.'"[1]

That insight, although not universally valid, has proven to be all too true of many systems of "Christian" education and of individual institutions within those systems. All too often, Christian education has not been deliberately built upon a distinctive Christian philosophy. As a result, many Christian schools have tended to offer something less than Christian education and have thereby frustrated the purpose of their existence. Gordon Clark has noted that what goes by the name of Christian education is sometimes a program of "pagan education with a chocolate coating of Christianity."[2] He added that it is the pill, not the coating, that works.

What is needed by Christian institutions is a thorough and ongoing examination, evaluation, and correction of their educational practices in the light of their basic philosophic beliefs. Christian educators must come to see their educational systems as unified endeavors built upon a foundation of Christian philosophy. Beyond the philosophic foundation, the entire superstructure of the educational system must be built out of materials and processes that are in harmony with Christianity. That is a difficult task in an overwhelmingly secular world in which even professed Christian institutions are often riddled with an aggressive and all-pervasive secularism and materialism.

The task at hand is to seek to develop a genuinely Christian approach to philosophy and education, rather than to maintain an eclectic relationship to the larger culture, in which Christian educators pick and choose among secular options in their quest for Christian culture. Eclecticism, at its best, is an insufficient base for Christian education.

THE UNSATISFACTORY NATURE OF ECLECTICISM FOR CHRISTIAN EDUCATION

According to Webster, eclecticism is a method whereby persons select from various systems, doctrines, or sources those materials they feel might be useful. Eclecticism in educational philosophy is a smorgasbord method which may be tempting to the beginner (and which may be a necessary starting point in some cases), but is nearly always an inadequate basis for a satisfactory educational system.

After studying the various philosophies and educational theories, a person is almost certain to note that there is something good in each of them. For example, Christian educators generally appreciate the emphasis that existentialism places upon individual responsibility and personal choice, the concern that realism has for natural law, the stress of progressivism on enlisting the interest of the child in the learning process, the accent of idealism on that timeless realm beyond the confines of this world, and the desire for a better social order that is emphasized by reconstructionism, futurism, and critical pedagogy. Each of the philosophies and theories studied has captured a portion of philosophic and educational truth. For that reason they are patronized by significant numbers of educators. The practical and theoretical implications of each philosophy and theory have been extensively developed. These implications may be profitably studied by Christian educators as they seek to enrich their educational programs.

Along with the insight that there is something of value in each of the philosophic positions comes the feeling that if individuals select the best from each of them, they will be able to operate as successful educators. The effect of such a method, however, is to develop a patchwork quilt rather than a seamless tapestry. It is true that patchwork quilts have their own beauty and functionality, but it must be asked whether such an eclectic product is the best that can be done in terms of building a philosophic foundation for the important social enterprise called Christian education.

With the passage of time and with added conceptual maturity comes the realization that eclecticism is generally only a "second best" method of developing an educational position. It soon becomes apparent, for instance, that eclecticism may lead to internal contradictions as a person selects a bit from this philosophy and a piece from that theory. The maturing educator is also bound to realize, sooner or later, that two different philosophic schools can use the same words while implying different meanings, and that they can suggest what are apparently the same methodologies to bring about dissimilar results, since they have different starting points, goals, and directions.

Beyond those problems, an examination of the presuppositions underlying the various philosophies and theories leads to the realization that each has elements that are out of harmony with biblical Christianity. For example, Christian educators have often objected to the naturalistic assumptions undergirding such views as pragmatism, realism, and behaviorism; the anthropocentric humanism of existentialism, progressivism, postmodernism, and reconstructionism; and the overemphasis on intellectualism and rationalism in idealism and neo-scholasticism. Each of the philosophies and theories studied has been found to have significant difficulties as well as a portion of truth. None of them, therefore, provides a totally adequate base for a philosophy of Christian education. Neither, for the reasons listed above, does an eclectic adoption of their true aspects guarantee a sufficient foundation for Christian education.

The better way is for educators and educational systems to individually examine their own basic beliefs in terms of reality, truth, and value, and then consciously to build a personal educational philosophy upon that platform. In performing that task, the Christian educator may choose to utilize the insights of the philosophies and theories where appropriate and valid. Their appropriateness, however, must be determined from the perspective of Christian philosophy. Such an approach can develop an educational outlook that will have internal consistency, offer the promise of external validity, and provide the foundation for educational practices that will be the means for arriving at chosen ends.

The careful reader has probably noticed that the preceding discussion used such words as "useful," "good," and "best" in discussing eclectic choice. The very use of these words implies that eclectics have a philosophical base with a definite axiology that they use to make value judgments. The task for educators is to come to grips with the basic presuppositions which in reality undergird their surface eclecticism. For Christian educators, this means making explicit the philosophical beliefs that have led them to label some things as good and others as useless. John Brubacher has noted that an eclectic philosophy may not be an impossible position for an uncritical relativist, even though it is difficult to justify on close examination.[3] On the other hand, eclecticism certainly seems to be less than satisfactory for an education that claims to be built upon the revealed will of the omniscient God.

It should be noted that philosophy building is an ongoing process. As educators gain new insights, and as their breadth of knowledge grows, they will be continually developing their philosophic system. They will note, also, that their philosophy will guide their practice and that, on the other hand, their practice will tend to modify their theory.

Educational professionals should think of educational philosophy as something they "do" on a continual basis, rather than as something they once studied in a course with those words in the title.

TOWARD A PHILOSOPHY OF CHRISTIAN EDUCATION

Perhaps the greatest need of Christian schools is a philosophical foundation that is truly Christian. The following pages will present one approach to such a philosophy.

It should be realized at the very outset that the statements made in this study in regard to Christian philosophy and the educational extensions of that philosophy should in no way be considered comprehensive. *The approach that has been taken is suggestive rather than exhaustive.* Universal agreement concerning the approach taken to both philosophy and education is not expected, or even desired in many cases. The intention is rather to raise significant questions and issues in relation to the philosophy of Christianity and Christian education. Some of the issues raised should lead to both individual thought and group discussion.

Underlying the argument is a realization of the necessity for the individual Christian educator to make responsible, intelligent choices concerning education in relation to personal factors and unique social contexts. What is needed is not a "philosophic blueprint," but a heightened sensitivity to the challenges of professional responsibility, as educators, both individually and collectively, seek to develop a philosophy and a practice that unites the eternal principles of Christianity with the needs and particulars of their unique time and place. That task calls for thought, sanctified choice, and the responsible use of Christian freedom on the part of Christian educators.

A second point to note in the following chapters is that no attempt is made to compare Christian educational philosophy with the philosophies and theories discussed in Part II. The focus is not on rebuttal or comparison, but, as suggested earlier, on building from the foundation up, while using the insights of other philosophers and theorists where valid. Of course, the individual reader may choose to focus on comparison and/or rebuttal, but such a task is beyond the limits of this presentation.

A third aspect of the following discussion that should be taken into consideration is that a Christian philosophy of education covers a great deal of common ground with what might be considered a theology of education. That is true because of the basic perspective of biblical Christianity, which sees no radical dichotomy between philosophy and theology. From the Christian viewpoint, the Bible sheds light on the issues of metaphysics, epistemology, and axiology. The approach used in the following discussion, after the initial treatment of metaphysics, has been to use an integrated avenue to the philosophical-theological aspects of education.

Last, the section on Christian educational philosophy utilizes the same format as was used to analyze the traditional and modern philosophies in Part II. Building upon an examination of the metaphysics, epistemology, and axiology of Christianity in Chapter 9, the last chapter will develop some of the educational extensions of that philosophic foundation.

Notes

1. Harold H. Ditmanson, Harold V. Hong, and Warren A. Quanbeck, eds., *Christian Faith and the Liberal Arts* (Minneapolis: Augsburg Publishing House, 1960), p. iii.

2. Gordon H. Clark, *A Christian Philosophy of Education* (Grand Rapids, MI: Wm. B. Eerdmans Publishing Co., 1946), p. 210.

3. John Brubacher, *Modern Philosophies of Education*, 4th ed. (New York: McGraw-Hill Co., 1969), pp. 134-35.

9

A Christian Approach to Philosophy

This chapter briefly discusses some of the issues that are important in Christian philosophy. The section on metaphysics is more concerned with building a rationale for the acceptance of the biblical view of reality than it is in a systematic treatment of the four aspects of metaphysics outlined in Chapter 2. As a result, the line of reasoning moves from selected observations concerning reality to humanity's search for meaning, to the self-disclosure of God in Christ, to a summary of the biblical view of reality. Many answers to questions raised by the anthropological,[1] theological, ontological, and cosmological aspects of metaphysics are implicit rather than explicit in the discussion.

The section on epistemology focuses on the central role of the Bible as a source of valid truth, and how this source relates to other knowledge sources, such as science and reason. The discussion of ethics highlights the essence of sin and righteousness, the basis of Christian ethics, the tension between legalism and antinomianism, and some observations for Christian ethics in daily life. Aesthetics is treated in terms of people's aesthetic nature, the relation of the beautiful and the ugly, and Christian aesthetic responsibility.

The selection of material for discussion in this chapter has been somewhat arbitrary. Many other approaches to a Christian philosophy could have been utilized, and many other topics could have been discussed within the existing framework. The goal of this chapter will be fulfilled if it serves as a catalyst for thought about the philosophy undergirding Christian education.

SOME OBSERVATIONS
CONCERNING METAPHYSICS

The most fundamental and inescapable observation facing every individual is the reality and mystery of personal existence in a complex environment. Jean-Paul Sartre, an existentialist of atheistic persuasion, raised this issue when he noted that the basic philosophic problem is that something is there, rather than that nothing is there. Francis Schaeffer, reflecting upon this thought, wrote that "nothing that is worth calling a philosophy can sidestep the question of the fact that things do exist and that they exist in their present form and complexity."[2] People are continually faced with the fact of their being and existence. Even an attempt to deny that existence is, in effect, a confirmation of it as individuals rationalize, postulate, and conjecture.

Reality Has Intelligible, Friendly,
Purposeful, Personal, and Infinite Aspects

As persons examine the universe in which they exist, they make several observations. One is that their environment is intelligible. They do not exist in a universe "gone mad" or one behaving in an erratic fashion. On the contrary, the universe apparently operates according to consistent laws that can be discovered, communicated, and utilized in making trustworthy predictions. Modern science is predicated upon this predictability.

Observant individuals also note that the universe in its most basic nature is friendly to humans and other forms of life. If it were not basically friendly, life would be unable to continue. Life would most certainly be extinguished by the ceaseless warfare of an unfriendly environment upon a relatively feeble existence. People have found that the natural world appears to be made-to-order to meet such needs as food, water, temperature, light, and a host of other necessities that are essential to the continuation of life. The parameters of conditions necessary for the maintenance of life are quite narrow, and even small changes in the supply of life's essentials threaten the existence of life as we know it. The continued existence of life, therefore, points to a basically friendly universe.

Closely related to the observations of cosmic intelligibility and friendliness is the purposefulness of existence. The purposefulness of our environment is attested to by the fact that nearly everything in our daily lives lends itself to purpose. Human beings would cease to exist meaningfully without purpose.[3] Our lives do not exist, either internally or externally, in a state of randomness.

Another aspect of existence that people have noted is that human existence is personal. We each recognize that we differ from other individuals—I am not you, my thoughts are not your thoughts, and my reactions to a situation may differ markedly from yours. People are not interchangeable parts of a universal machine. Individuality is built into human existence. When individuality is separated from human existence, such as in slavery or prostitution, people become less than fully human. Individuals not only differ from other humans; they also differ from other forms of life. Human beings are manipulators of abstract symbols. That gives them the ability to reflect upon the contingencies of life rather than merely to respond to them in the manner of Pavlov's dogs or Skinner's rats and pigeons. It is true, as certain schools of psychology have pointed out, that individuals often (perhaps most often) live on a level less than fully human. Much of the advertising industry is built upon that insight. People, however, living at their fullest as human beings are not tied into some variation of an unalterable stimulus-response reinforcement sequence. In their individuality they make choices, initiate actions, and undergo the results of those choices and actions. My choices and experiences are unique and mold me into the personal, distinctive individual that I am.

Human beings are also aware that they exist in an apparently infinite universe. Their own sun is one of approximately 100 billion flaming stars that make up the Milky Way Galaxy. They realize that it would take at least 100,000 years to cross their galaxy if they could travel at the speed of light—about 186,000 miles per second. And yet their own star cluster is only one of at least one billion known galaxies. People are faced with the mind-boggling problem of apparent infinity in terms of both time and space, and still they find, as they develop more sophisticated scientific instruments, that universal space presents itself as a receding frontier. One is left to wonder what might lie beyond the boundaries of space—except more space.

Humanity's Observations Lead to a Search for Meaning

As people face the inescapability of their own personal existence; the apparent infinity in space, time, and complexity of their universe;

and the orderliness of "what is" and/or "what appears to be," they are also confronted with the problem of meaning for both personal life and the existence of the universe. Humanity throughout time has been unable to escape the quest for meaning. Different people have approached the problem in varying ways. The existentialist claims, in opposition to the underlying rationale of modern science, that there is no external meaning in the universe except absurdity or whatever meaning a person may choose to impute to it; the cosmos of itself has no meaning. The postmodernists hold that knowledge is a social construction. The pragmatist claims that the ultimate meaning of existence is beyond us, and that philosophers must not make factual statements that cannot be validated by the experience of their senses. Meanwhile, the analytic philosopher claims that metaphysical statements are meaningless, and that people must seek to define ever more clearly the words and concepts of their immediate environment.

Others are not satisfied with these evasive and meaningless answers to the problem of meaning. Their minds rebel at a system of thought that sees intelligence flowing out of ignorance, order out of chaos, personality out of impersonality, and something out of nothing. They cannot accept the irrational explanation that existence is the result of infinite time plus infinite chance plus nothing.[4] For them an infinite universe postulates an infinite Creator, an intelligent and orderly universe points to an ultimate Intelligence, a basically friendly universe points to a benevolent Being, and the personality of the individual leads to the concept of a Personality upon which individual personalities are modeled. They refer to this infinite Creator, ultimate Intelligence, benevolent Being, and original Personality as "god," while at the same time realizing that no word is more meaningless than "god" until it is defined.

It should be noted at this juncture that these observations do not "prove" the existence of God. On the other hand, they deliver a telling thrust in favor of His existence. The existence of a Creator-God cannot be proven, but neither can it be disproven. The conclusion of His existence, however, is more reasonable than the opposite conclusion, which leaves us in the hands of chance, necessity, adaptive response, and nothingness. "So," claims Herman Horne, "we accept it on faith, faith in our reason and faith beyond our demonstration."[5]

It was noted in the first half of this book, when we discussed the metaphysical-epistemological dilemma, that all persons (whether they admit it or recognize it or not) live by faith. It remains for each individual to appropriate and focus this faith in design or accident, in plan or chance, in intelligence or ignorance, in purposefulness and meaningfulness or aimlessness and randomness. In his perceptive essay, "The Will to Believe," William James laid down the principle that in the absence of positive proof one is entitled to believe the best.[6] If what is best is partially defined as what is possible and logical, then faith in a Creator-God would be better than faith in time plus chance plus nothing.[7]

The Problem of Pain Confuses Meaning[8]

Credibility in a benevolent Creator-God is lessened for some individuals by the fact that all is not well in their environment. There seems to be a tension in nature. They observe a beautiful creation that appears to be made for life and happiness, but is filled with animosity, deterioration, and killing. Humanity is faced with the seemingly impossible problem of pain and death existing in the midst of orderliness and life. There is a great controversy between the forces of good and the forces of evil, and this is reflected in every phase of life. The universe may be friendly to life; but there is no denying that it is often antagonistic to peace, orderliness, and life. The habitation of humanity is not a place of neutrality. It is often an arena of active conflict. This state of affairs points to the forces of evil within a friendly universe.

Such a paradox raises an important question: If God is both omnipotent (infinite in power) and loving (benevolent), how can evil exist? If God is perfectly loving, He must wish to abolish evil; and if He is all-powerful, He must be able to abolish evil. Why, therefore, if there is a God, does evil continue to exist? Any viable theistic answer to humanity's quest for meaning must take this problem into account in a satisfactory manner.

Human Limitations and the Necessity of God's Self-disclosure

Observant individuals soon become aware of their own mental limitations and those of the race. They not only realize humanity's almost complete ignorance of the intricacies of its immediate environment, but they are also aware of their inability even to begin mentally to cope with the apparent infinity of time, space, and complexity in the universe at large. At this point they also become aware of the fact that if unaided finite minds are incapable of understanding the complexities of creation, they will also be unable to begin to understand the infinite Creator, since of necessity a maker must be more complex than that which is made.

Even after realizing their intellectual limitations, people still have a driving desire to uncover the meaning of life. Humanity, in its search for the meaning of existence, wonders if there is an understandable answer, or whether the response of the universe is total, absolute, and unbearable silence. Is the Creator-God "a maker who went on vacation" after the creation, as the eighteenth-century deists postulated, or is He one who is willing to make a revelation of Himself to finite beings on a level which they can understand?

Many believe it to be incomprehensible that the Creator-God, who put so much intelligent thought into the design of the universe, and so much purposeful care into the development of human personality and the maintenance of life, would leave intelligent life on a spinning ball in the midst of space in silence regarding meaning. In the light of conscious thought, total silence can be held as a possibility but not necessarily a probability. It seems more probable in the context of environmental purposefulness, friendliness, personalness, and intelligibility that the Creator-God would break through to humanity in its finiteness and helplessness by means of a revelation of Himself and universal purpose in a communicative mode and on a level that would be understandable. Individuals have seen this self-revelation in terms of sacred writings that claim to be from a divine source.

Why the Christian Revelation as God's Self-disclosure?

Why should one choose the Christian revelation above that of Hinduism, Buddhism, Islam, or other world religions?[9] Hendrik Kraemer claims that the "liberal" attitude to this question is that one must regard all religions as revelations of God. Kraemer recognizes the positive contributions of the world religions, but points out that the liberals have basically confused a consideration of truth with "big-heartedness." For him, the real problem in the liberal answer is that the full force of the question—the question of truth—is by-passed.[10] In answering this question, Kraemer notes, we must see that "the absolutely distinctive and peculiar and unique element in Christianity is the *fact* of Jesus Christ" and not some set of doctrines.[11] If that is true, one might be led to inquire if the distinctive fact in Buddhism is not Buddha or in Islam the fact of Muhammad? The question, he claims, sounds plausible, but the answer is a definite no.

> Buddhism is a "way" of release from life which consists essentially of suffering, change and impermanence. This way has been discovered and promulgated by the Buddha. He is, as it were, the first successful Pathfinder. His followers can learn the way from him, but the goal they must reach under their own steam.[12]

Islam calls individuals to penitence, conversion, and an unconditional submission to Allah, the One and the Almighty. Muhammad is the envoy of Allah, and as such he occupies a position of prominence in Islam. According to the *Koran*, Muhammad is a "'Messenger' or 'Bearer' of the revelation 'sent down' to him, and not a part of the Revelation, let alone *the* Revelation itself." On the other hand, continues Kraemer, the distinctiveness of Jesus Christ is that He is Himself the Revelation of God in His own Person and is the substance of that Revelation. His position is quite distinct from that of Buddha, Muhammad, or Confucius. He places Himself before human beings as *the* Truth, *the* Way, and *the* Life.[13]

In the light of Christ, all other religions, in their deepest and most essential aspects, are in error, even if they may be noble but misguided attempts to answer the question of meaning on their own terms. Non-Christian religions are found to be self-redemptive and self-justifying. They fail at the very point that Christ highlighted. They fail adequately to account for individual human nature—"[its] greatness and [its] wretchedness, [its] reaching out towards the highest and [its] satanic devilishness, [its] place half-way between angel and ape."[14]

By failing to account for the inability of humankind to save itself, the non-Christian religions have not given sufficient weight to the problem of sin, which is expressed in the tension we find in nature. It is true that the non-Christian religions have not entirely overlooked sin, but it remains "secondary and incidental and is never treated as the central mystery demanding solution." In what they conceive to be their ultimate and fundamental aim, the non-Christian religions are blind to the most vital problem of humanity. Because they refuse to take sin and people's inability to overcome it seriously, they are "bound to be escapist in one way or another."[15]

Why the Christian Revelation as the self-revelation of the Creator-God? Because only Christianity provides a sufficient framework in which to view the predicament of human existence. The Eastern religions are not a sufficient answer, because they are impersonal and fail to account for the personal nature of our lives. They view the ultimate end of humans as the losing of self and personality in nirvana or some other form of mystical impersonality. Their gods are impersonal, and we have already noted that personality is not derived from impersonal sources. On the other hand, such conceptions of god as those set forth by the ancient Greeks and Romans are inadequate, since their own finiteness is in conflict with the infinite nature of the universe.

The Christian Revelation puts itself forth not as a truth but as *the* Truth. C. S. Lewis, commenting on this point, has said that Jesus Christ is either what He claims to be, or a lunatic, or the world's greatest deceiver and the "Devil of Hell." He is either God and Saviour, or He is the archenemy of truthfulness. Separated from His claims, He can never be considered a "great human teacher" of morals. He has made the most astounding assertions. Jesus, notes Lewis, did not leave us any option but to accept or to reject His unparalleled statements.[16]

The Biblical Framework of Reality

Christians accept the Bible as the self-revelation of the Creator-God through Jesus Christ. This revelation allows them to make further observations concerning the nature of reality, and it provides the metaphysical framework in which Christian education takes place. The basic pillars of the biblical world view consist of the following elements: (1) the existence of the living God, the Creator-God; (2) the creation by God of a perfect world and universe; (3) humanity's creation in the image of God; (4) the "invention" of sin by Lucifer, who forgot his own creatureliness and sought to put himself in the place of God; (5) the spread of sin to the earth by Lucifer, and the Fall of humanity, which resulted in the partial loss of God's image; (6) the inability of human beings, without divine aid, to change their own nature, overcome their inherent sinfulness, or restore the lost image of God; (7) the initiative of God for humanity's salvation and its restoration to its original state through the incarnation, life, death, and resurrection of Jesus Christ; (8) the activity of the Holy Spirit in the plan of restoring God's image in fallen humanity and His work in the calling out of the community of believers, the church; (9) the return of Christ at the end of earthly history; and (10) the eventual restoration of our world (and its faithful inhabitants) to its Edenic condition.

Christian Metaphysics and Education

Christian education must be built upon a Christian view of reality. Christianity is a supernatural religion, and it is thoroughly antithetical to all forms of naturalism, to those theistic schemes of thought that do not place God at the center of the human educational experience, and to humanism, which purports that humanity can save itself through its own wisdom and goodness. Christian education, which is Christian education in actuality and not so only in name, must consciously be built upon a biblical metaphysical position.

A Christian view of metaphysics lays the foundation for Christian education. Christian educational systems have been established because God exists. His existence calls for an educational system in which He is the central reality that gives meaning to everything else. Other educational systems have alternative foundations and cannot be substituted for Christian education. Belief in the Christian view of reality motivates people to sacrifice both their time and their means for the establishment of Christian schools.

Christian metaphysics also determines what shall be studied and the contextual framework in which every subject is studied. The Christian view of reality supplies the criteria for curricular selection and emphasis. The Christian curriculum has a unique emphasis because of Christianity's unique metaphysical viewpoint. Christian education, furthermore, treats all subject matter from the perspective of the Christian world view. All subjects are seen in their relationship to the existence and purposes of the Creator-God.

Every aspect of Christian education is determined by the Christian view of reality. Christian metaphysical presuppositions not only justify and determine the existence, curriculum, and social role of Christian education; they also explicate the nature and potential of the learner, suggest the most beneficial types of relationships between teachers and their students, and provide criteria for the selection of teaching methodologies. These topics will be further developed in Chapter 10.

A CHRISTIAN PERSPECTIVE ON EPISTEMOLOGY

Epistemology deals with how a person knows. As such, it has to do with one of the most basic problems in human existence. If our epistemology is incorrect, then it follows that everything else in our knowledge system will be wrong or, at the very least, distorted. In the quest for truth and knowledge every philosophic system develops a hierarchy of epistemological methods in which one method generally serves as an authoritative foundation and acts as a criterion for judging the veracity of conclusions attained by other means. For the past 150 years of Western civilization the most widely accepted criterion of truth has been the empirical findings of science. Scientific findings have carried a great deal of weight. Some people have claimed that nothing can be true unless it agrees with the "facts" of science.

The Bible as the Primary Source of Christian Epistemology

For the Christian, the Bible is the foremost source of knowledge and the most essential epistemological authority. All other sources of knowledge must be tested and verified in the light of scripture. Underlying the authoritative role of the Bible are several assumptions: (1) humans exists in a supernatural universe in which the infinite Creator-God has revealed Himself to finite minds on a level they can comprehend in at least a limited fashion; (2) human beings created in the image of God, even though fallen, are capable of rational thought; (3) communication with other intelligent beings (people and God) is possible in spite of humanity's inherent limitations and the imperfections and imprecision of human language; (4) the God who cared enough to reveal Himself to people also cared enough to protect the essence of that revelation as it was transmitted through succeeding generations; and (5) human beings are able to make sufficiently correct interpretations of the Bible, through the guidance of the Holy Spirit, to arrive at Truth.

The Bible is an authoritative source of Truths that are beyond the possibility of attainment except through revelation. This source of knowledge deals mainly with the "big questions": the meaning of life and death, where the world came from and what its future will be, how the problem of sin arose and how it is being dealt with, and the like.

The purpose of scripture is to make people "wise unto salvation through faith which is in Christ Jesus" and to provide doctrine, reproof, correction, and "instruction in righteousness: That the man of God may be perfect" (2 Tim 3:15-17 KJV). It should be apparent, therefore, that the Bible is not an exhaustive source of knowledge and never was intended to be a "divine encyclopedia." It leaves many questions unanswered. On the other hand, in answering the most basic questions of finite humanity, it provides a perspective and a metaphysical framework that furnish a context in which to explore unanswered questions and to arrive at unified answers.

The Bible does not try to justify its claims. Neither can it be "proven" through other epistemological methods to be what it purports to be. It begins with the statement that "in the beginning God created" (Gen 1:1), and the book of Hebrews claims that we must accept by faith the *ex nihilo* (out of nothing) creation of the universe by God (Heb 11:3). God apparently has not attempted to explain His operations to us because of extreme limitations in our ability to comprehend. He has not given us what our curiosity might desire. Rather, He has given us what we can understand and what we need to know in relation to our lostness and the way of salvation. Even though the Bible cannot be "proved," there are still "evidences" that lead us to have faith in its dependability. Some of those evidences are the discoveries of archaeology, the witness of fulfilled prophecy, and the satisfaction its way of life[17] brings to the human heart and life.

God's Revelation in the Natural World

The source of knowledge next in importance for the Christian is that of nature as people come into contact with it in daily life and through scientific study. The world around us is a revelation of the Creator-God (Ps 19:1-4; Rom 1:20). Theologians have given the term "special revelation" to the scriptures, while they have viewed nature as a "general revelation." Rightly understood, both special and general revelation give the same message, because they have the same Author.

Even casual observers, however, will soon discover problems in interpreting the book of nature. They see not only love and life but also hate and death. The natural world, as seen by fallible humanity, gives a garbled and seemingly contradictory message concerning ultimate reality. The Apostle Paul noted that the whole of creation has been affected by the Fall (Rom 8:22). The effects of the tension between good and evil have made general revelation, by itself, an insufficient source of knowledge concerning God and ultimate reality. The findings of science and the daily experiences of life must be interpreted in the light of the scriptural revelation, which supplies the framework for epistemological interpretation.

The study of nature certainly enriches humanity's understanding of its environment. It also provides answers for some of the many questions not dealt with in the Bible. On the other hand, the investigative power of human science must not be overestimated. As Frank Gaebelein has noted, scientific people have not made the truth of science. They have merely uncovered it and found what is already there. The "hunches" of patient scientific research, Gaebelein continues, that lead to a further grasp of truth are not mere luck. They are a part of God's disclosure of truth in His common grace.[18]

Human beings are the discoverers, not the originators, of truth; and the entire edifice of scientific inquiry is built upon *a priori* principles. "Among these is the confidence that nature is orderly and intelligible and that it is open to human investigation—an odd assumption today, when outside science men declare the utter meaninglessness of existence."[19]

The Role of Reason

A third epistemological source for the Christian is that of rationality. Humans, having been created in the image of God, are rational by nature. Human beings can think abstractly, be reflective, and reason from cause to effect. Through the Genesis Fall, humanity's reasoning powers were lessened but not destroyed. God's plea to sinful individuals is that they might "reason together" with Him concerning the human predicament and its solution (Isa 1:18).

The role of rationalism in Christian epistemology must be clearly seen. The Christian faith is not a rationalistic production. People have not arrived at Christian truth through developing, by themselves, a system of thought that leads to a correct view of God, humanity, and the nature of sin and salvation. Christianity is a revealed religion. Unaided human reason can be deceitful and lead away from truth. Human reason is an insufficient agent of truth. Christians, therefore, are not rationalists in the fullest sense of the word; but they are rational. Bernard Ramm has correctly remarked that reason is not a source of religious authority, but is rather a mode of apprehending truth. As such, "it is the truth apprehended which is authoritative, not reason."[20]

The rational aspect of epistemology is an essential, but not the sole element, in knowing. Its function is to help us understand truth obtained through special and general revelation, and to enable us to extend that knowledge into the unknown. The findings of reason are always checked, in a Christian epistemology, by the truth of scripture. This same principle must be applied to knowledge gained through intuition and from the study of authorities. The all-encompassing epistemological test is to compare all purported truth to the scriptural framework.

Some Additional Epistemological Observations

In concluding our remarks on a Christian approach to epistemology, several observations are in order. First, the biblical perspective is that all truth is God's truth. As such, the distinction between secular and sacred truth is a false dichotomy. All truth finds its source in God as the Creator and Originator.[21]

Second, the truth of Christianity is true to what actually exists in the universe. Upon these two positions is based the Christian concept of academic freedom. If all truth is God's truth, and if Christianity is true to what is actually there, then the Christian can pursue truth without the fear of ultimate contradiction.

Third, there is a great controversy in the area of epistemology just as surely as there is a tension in nature. The forces of evil are continually seeking to undermine the Bible, distort human reasoning, and lead individuals to rely on their own inadequate and fallen selves in the pursuit of truth. Beyond that, undergirding every theory and every school system is an epistemological system that gives shape and interpretive meaning to the larger whole. Such epistemologies may be true or false, but they are always there, even when they are unacknowledged.[22] The epistemological point of attack is crucial, because if humanity can be led astray in the area of epistemology, it can be misled in every other area.

Fourth, there are absolute Truths in the universe, but human beings in their fallen state have only a relative grasp of those absolutes. In other words, while God can know absolutely, Christians can know absolutes only in a relative sense. Thus there is room for Christian humility in the epistemological enterprise.[23]

Fifth, the Bible is not concerned with abstract truth. It always sees truth as related to life. Knowing, in the fullest biblical sense, is applying perceived knowledge to one's daily life. Thus Christian knowing is an active, dynamic experience, rather than one that is merely passive.[24] We therefore find a scriptural difference between knowing about truth as found in Christ and knowing Christ as one's personal Saviour. There is knowledge and saving knowledge. The first is a mere understanding about truth, while the latter is an application of God's truth to our lives.

Sixth, the various sources of knowledge available to the Christian are complementary. All these sources can and should be used by the Christian, and all should be seen in the light of the biblical pattern.

Seventh, the acceptance of a Christian epistemology cannot be separated from the acceptance of a Christian metaphysics, and vice versa. The acceptance, as noted in Chapter 2, of any metaphysical-epistemological configuration is a faith-choice, and it necessitates a total commitment to a way of life.

Christian Epistemology and Education

The Christian view of truth, along with Christian metaphysics, lies at the foundation of the very existence of Christian education. The acceptance of revelation as the basic source of authority places the Bible at the heart of Christian education and provides the knowledge framework in which all subject matters are evaluated. This particularly impacts upon the curriculum. It will be seen in Chapter 10 that the biblical revelation provides both the foundation and the context for all subjects in the curriculum of Christian education. Christian epistemology, since it deals with the way people come to know anything, also directly influences the selection and ultilization of teaching methodologies.

SOME AXIOLOGICAL CONSIDERATIONS

Christian principles in the realm of values are built directly upon a Christian perspective in regard to metaphysics and epistemology. In other words, views of reality and truth lead to a conception of values. The principles of Christian axiology are derived from the Bible, which in its ultimate sense is a revelation of the character and values of God.

An important consideration that influences all forms of value is that Christian metaphysics postulates a position of radical discontinuity from most other world views in terms of the normality of the present world order. While most non-Christians hold that the present condition of humanity and earthly affairs is the normal state of things, the Bible teaches that human beings have fallen from their normal relationship with God, other people, their own selves, and the world around them. From the biblical perspective, sin and its results have altered people's nature and affected their ideals and valuing processes.

As a result of the abnormality of the present world, and the fact that many individuals are not even aware of this abnormality, people often value the wrong things. They are liable to call evil "good" and good "evil" because their frame of reference is faulty. The Christian who has been born again has a radical set of values compared to much of the world around him or her because of a different frame of reference concerning the human predicament.

Perhaps the most radical axiological statement ever penned is the Sermon on the Mount. Its radicalism stems from the fact that Christ believed that humanity's true home is heaven and not earth. He did not imply that the present life is not of value. Rather, He claimed that there is something of more value and that those things of most value should be the foundation for human activity.

One implication of Christ's teaching is that the Christian life will be based upon a different set of values from those of persons who are at home in the abnormal world of sin. To be normal in terms of God's ideals would therefore make one appear abnormal by the standards of the present social order. Christian values must be built upon Christian principles. They are not merely an extension of non-Christian values, even though there are certainly areas of overlap.

Ethics

The essence and antithesis of sin. A Christian might well ask: "What is the great sin? What sin might be seen as the most serious in the sight of a holy God? Is it murder, unchastity, anger, greed, or drunkenness?" The biblical answer is a resounding no! It is pride.

Pride is integrally linked to self-centeredness, self-sufficiency, and an unhealthy self-love—a frame of mind which induces us to trust in our own goodness, strength, and wisdom, rather than to rely upon the Creator-God.

It was through pride and self-sufficiency that Lucifer became the devil, that Eve became the mother of a sinful race, and that Christ's twelve disciples failed to receive His blessings as they continually bickered as to who was the greatest (Isa 14:12-15; Eze 28:13-17; Gen 3; Matt 18:1). C. S. Lewis remarks that "pride leads to every other vice: it is the complete anti-God state of mind."[25] It is an attitude that places the universal center of meaning on the individual self rather than upon God. In pride and self-sufficiency we find the essence of sin. One of the first fruits of that attitude is rebellion against the authority of God.

Since the root of evil is found in self-centeredness, it follows that the antithesis of this would be that good is rooted in other-centeredness. It was upon this basis that Christ answered the question concerning the identity of the "great" commandment.

> You shall love the Lord your God with all your heart, and with all your soul, and with all your mind. This is the great and first commandment. And a second is like it, You shall love your neighbor as yourself. On these two commandments depend all the law and the prophets (Matt 22:37-40).

The essence of Christianity and Christian ethics is a death—crucifixion—of self, pride, self-centeredness, and self-sufficiency, and a new birth in which we act upon a different set of principles because of our new relationship to Jesus Christ (Rom 6:1-6; Matt 16:24; Gal 2:20; John 3:3, 5). The biblical picture is that the natural person is hopeless because of the fixation of his or her love upon self.[26]

What is needed is a transformation (metamorphosis) of our minds, a crucifixion of our selves, and a spiritual rebirth, so that we can become new creatures with God and God's attributes at the center of our existence (Rom 12:2; Phil 2:5-8; 2 Cor 5:17). In this process our desire to rebel against God will be translated into a life of surrender to His will. Paul noted that this renewal is a daily experience, and Jesus remarked that the transformation is accomplished through the power of the Holy Spirit (1 Cor 15:31; John 3:5).

It should be noted that the ethical ideal of Christianity is not a bettering of the self through a secular model of self-improvement. It is rather an ethic interrelating with the converting factor of the Holy Spirit. It cannot be a model based on self-improvement, due to the fact that human nature is such that self-improvement by itself invariably leads a person even deeper into the central problem of pride and self-sufficiency. (Dwight L. Moody once remarked that if anyone ever got to the Kingdom of Heaven through his or her own efforts, we would never hear the end of it.)

It should also be realized that the Christian ethic is, in the end, a positive force. It goes beyond the death of adoration for one's self to a love to God and our fellow human beings that is expressed in an outward life of activity and service.

God's character: the basis of Christian ethics. The absolute basis of Christian ethics is God. There is no standard or law beyond God. Law, as it is revealed in scripture, is based upon God's character. The major attributes of God, as depicted in both the Old and New Testaments, are love and justice (Exod 34:6-7; 1 John 4:8; Rev 16:7; 19:2). Love may be seen as a summary of the law, while justice defines its content.[27] Biblical history is a glimpse of divine love and justice in action, as God relates to a self-willed world in the midst of sin.

The concept of "love," like that of "god," is a meaningless idea until it is defined. The biblical Christian looks to the Bible for a definition of love, because it is there that the God who is love has revealed Himself in a concrete way that is understandable to human minds. Christian love can be studied in 1 Corinthians 13, the actions and attitudes expressed by Jesus (Luke 15 gives a great deal of insight on this point), and in the underlying meaning of the Ten Commandments. Even a short study will reveal that there is a distinct qualitative difference between what humans often refer to as love, and the biblical concept of divine love, which works for the very best good of others, even those generally thought of as enemies. John Powell captured the essence of divine love when he pointed out that love focuses on giving rather than receiving.[28]

Likewise, Anders Nygren, in his important study of human and divine love, concluded that "there cannot be any real synthesis between two forces so completely contrary to one another as Eros [human love that seeks to gain a reward from the object of its attention] and Agape [divine love that finds its joy in giving to the object of its attention]." Eros begins with a sense of poverty and emptiness and seeks God and other people in order to find satisfaction for its own wants, while Agape, "being rich in divine grace, pours itself out in love" toward others.[29] Thus Christian love stands in radical discontinuity from what is generally thought of as human love.

Carl Henry has aptly written that "Christian ethics is an ethics of service."[30] The most basic spelling out of this ethic is found in Christ's two great commandments—love to God and love to humanity (Matt 22:37-40). Some Christians have taken the Ten Commandments to be the basic statement of Christian ethics. In this they err. The New Testament makes it evident that love is the fulfilling of the law (Rom 13:9; Gal 5:14). The Ten Commandments might be seen as a delineation and particularization of the Law of Love. The first four commandments explain a person's duties in regard to love to God, while the last six are an explication of aspects of a person's love to other individuals. In one sense, the Ten Commandments may be seen as a negative explanation of the Law of Love and as an attempt to give people some definite guidelines that they can grasp in a concrete way.

Part of the problem with this negative expression as an ethical base is that people are always seeking to know when they can stop loving their neighbor, when the limit has been reached. Peter's question in regard to the limits of forgiveness is a case in point. Peter, like all "natural" individuals, was more interested in when he could stop loving his neighbors than he was in how he could continue to love them (Matt 18:21-35). Christ's answer is that there is no limit to Christian love. There is never a time when we can stop loving and cut loose and be our "real self." That is the message of the two great commandments.

Positive Christian love is an attitude of mind and heart that can never be shut off in the Christian life. It is an ever-growing relationship with both God and other people. As God seeks out His lost sheep, as Jesus died for us while we were still His enemies, even so must we, in unselfish love, seek to relate to others.

At this point it should be noted that the biblical injunction—"be ye therefore perfect, even as your Father which is in heaven is perfect"—was given in the context of loving one's enemy (Matt 5:43-48 KJV). Perfect love, as God defines love, is the Christian ethical ideal. In this same vein, Jesus implied in His parable of the sheep and the goats that Christian love in action is the sole basis of His final judgment (Matt 25:31-46; see also James 1:27). This should not be interpreted as salvation by works. Christian help to another individual should rather be seen as an outflowing of interest in and care for others because of a personal acceptance of God's love. It is an active response of concrete love to other humans because of our recognition, acceptance, and appropriation of God's love in our life. It is the response of the person who has been justified by faith through grace. In this context we realize that love to God cannot be separated in any way from love to other people.

The legalist-antinomian tension. A most difficult area for many Christians in the realm of ethics is to live the Christian life without succumbing to the polar pitfalls of Christian ethics—legalism and antinomianism. Legalism sees the Bible and the law in much the same way as the Pharisees viewed it in Christ's day. The legalist looks at the Bible as an ethical rule book that offers a maxim for every case that arises. From the perspective of legalism, rules are extremely important and people must come under their jurisdiction in an unbending fashion. ("What is right is right; don't try to explain your actions on the basis of extenuating circumstances.") The opposite extreme is antinomianism, which rejects all moral law and has no place for universal principles.

Arthur Holmes has noted that legalism might be defined as unlimited absolutism, while antinomianism is unlimited relativism.[31] Jesus rejected unlimited absolutism, and His life stood as a continual condemnation of the Pharisees, who followed a thousand laws but loved neither God nor people. An example of this rejection can be found in Christ's relation to the Sabbath. Out of the events of Mark 2 and 3, Jesus enunciated the principles that "the Sabbath was made for man" and "not man for the Sabbath," and that it is lawful to work on the Sabbath if one is doing good for another person (Mark 2:23-3:6). In effect, Jesus is saying that people are more important than rules and that certain situations make it permissible to break the letter of the law. In no way can Jesus be seen as an unlimited absolutist or legalist.

On the other hand, neither can Jesus be classified as an unlimited relativist or an antinomian. He remarked in the Sermon on the Mount that He had not come to destroy the law, and near the end of His earthly career He claimed to have kept His Father's law and that His followers must do likewise (Matt 5:17; John 15:10).

Holmes has labeled one attempt to get between the polar extremes of unlimited absolutism and unlimited relativism as limited relativism.[32] A modern expression of this position is seen in the school of thought espousing situation ethics. The essence of situation ethics, claims Joseph Fletcher, one of its major exponents, is that "anything and everything is right or wrong, according to the situation." The good action, he asserts, would be the most loving and concerned act.[33]

Situation ethics is correct in its repudiation of legalism and in its admission of limited ethical relativity. Its major problem is that it rejects moral principles and rules and consequently extends relativism to every specific moral question.[34] Thus, situation ethics misinterprets Christian love. As noted above, the Bible never separates love from the moral law. On the contrary, it repeatedly unites the two. Love, from Christ's perspective, was a fulfilling and a summing up of the commandments. The biblical position is a rejection of limited relativism, or situation ethics, with its inability to set moral boundaries.

If not all the values and rules of behavior are absolute, it follows that what people need are limited absolutes rather than the unlimited absolutism of the legalist. A fourth ethical position, one which lines up more with the biblical viewpoint, might be called limited absolutism. This position allows love to retain its cognitive content as expressed in the actions and attitudes of God and in the Ten Commandments. It retains the timeless universal principles for the application of law to different situations, while providing for Christian liberty where the law is silent. Limited absolutism, therefore, manages to steer between the dangers of legalism and relativism, and it points toward a solution "in which relativism is limited by laws."

According to Holmes, limited absolutism allows for several types of relativity: (1) relativity in applying universal principles to unique situations (e.g., Christ illustrated that there are times when work could and should be done on the Sabbath); (2) relativity in our understanding of ethical principles and how these principles were applied differently in different historical periods (e.g., the biblical position on slavery and polygamy); and (3) relativity in morals which are due to differences in culture rather than to differences in principle (e.g., biblical courtship practices and marriage rites as compared to our own).

At the same time, Holmes continues, the biblical ethic of limited absolutism also affirms absolute elements: (1) the unchanging character of God, who articulates the law not as an arbitrary code, but as wise guidance for human life; and (2) the moral law as given in the Law of Love and the Ten Commandments, interpreted in the Sermon on the Mount, and applied to historic situations in the prophetic and apostolic writings.[35]

Some additional ethical observations. Before closing our discussion of Christian ethics, there are several more points that should be briefly considered. First, the biblical ethic is internal rather than external. Jesus remarked that harboring thoughts of hate or adultery was just as immoral as the acts themselves. He also claimed that it is out of the abundance of the heart that the mouth speaks (Matt 5:21-28; 12:34). External actions, from the biblical perspective, are the result of a person's mental attitudes. "In relation to morals, *the thought is the thing*. Hate does not just lead to murder; morally it *is* murder."[36] Thus the biblical ethic is much deeper than the model provided by the behaviorist in psychology. The Christian ethic points beyond overt acts and their consequences to the realm of thoughts and motives. In this sense, it is a very demanding ethic.

Second, the Christian ethic is based upon personal relationships to both God and other people. It involves an actual caring for them and cannot be satisfied with a mere legal and/or mechanical relationship. Of necessity, our relationships with others should be legal, but beyond this they must also be personal.

Third, biblical ethics are based upon the fact that every individual is created in the image of God and can reason from cause to effect and make moral decisions. Individuals can therefore live morally within the framework of limited absolutism. Ethical conduct is more than following rules and laws in terms of reward and punishment contingencies (e.g., heaven and hell). It is an intelligent process. Unthinking morality is a contradiction in terms.

Fourth, Christian morality is not just concerned with the good for people. It wants the very best. C. S. Lewis relates the story of the schoolboy who was asked what he thought God was like. "He replied that, as far as he could make out, God was 'the sort of person who is always snooping round to see if anyone is enjoying himself and then trying to stop it.'" Christian ethics, to the contrary, are not something that interfere with the good life. "In reality, moral rules are directions for running the human machine. Every moral rule is there to prevent a breakdown, or a strain, or a friction, in the running of that machine."[37] Christian ethics should be viewed from a positive perspective rather than from that of negativity. A corollary of this position is that the main thing in our Christian life is not that we have died to the old way of life, but that we have been born again for the new way of life. All too often Christians look at morality from the negative viewpoint. Christian growth does not come from what we don't do. It is rather a product of what we actively do in our daily lives. The Christian ethic is a positive ethic, and the Christian life, as an expression of that ethic, is a positive, active existence.

Last, the function of the Christian ethic is redemptive and restorative. In the Fall individuals became alienated from God, other people, their own selves, and their physical environment. The role of the ethical life is to allow people to live in such a way as to restore these relationships and to bring them into the position of wholeness for which they were created.

Christian ethics and education. Christian ethics are rich in implications for Christian education. Teaching methodologies, for example, are impacted upon by ethical considerations. The belief that the teacher (or parent) holds in regard to the tension between legalism and antinomianism will help determine whether classroom discipline will be based on authoritarian control, moral laissez-faire, or individual student responsibility in the context of moral principles.

Likewise, the other-centeredness and service orientation of Christian ethics have important implications for such educational issues as the social function of Christian education and the preferred types of relationships between students, between faculty members, and between students and faculty. In addition, and perhaps most importantly, the ethical implications of the loving character of God are directly related to the character-building role of Christian education. This is central to Christian education, since one of its foremost tasks is to help students develop a Christlike life. In summary, a Christian view of ethics provides another major pillar in the philosophic foundation of Christian education. As such, it influences every aspect of that education.

Aesthetics

Humans are aesthetic beings. Individuals not only appreciate beauty, but they seem to be compulsive creators in their own right.

People in all ages have sought to beautify their environment through works of art. From the biblical point of view, this is a result of humanity's being created in the image of the Creator-God. God not only created, but He created things of beauty. He could have created the earth in dull colors, destitute of the songs of birds, and without the sweet scent of a flower. Human beings and other forms of life could have existed without these delightful refinements. The existence of beauty in nature says something about the Creator and about those created in His likeness. Humans are lovers of beauty; they seek to create because of their unique relationship to God. One major difference between the creatorship of people and the creatorship of God, however, is that God creates out of nothing (Heb 11:3), while humans in their finiteness fashion and mold that which already exists.

The beautiful and the ugly in Christian art. Creativity in itself is good. That statement, however, does not imply that all that people create is good, beautiful, or edifying. That is true because even though human beings were created in the image of God, they have fallen and are now alienated from God and have a distorted view of reality, truth, and value. In the present age people are in various states of separation, alienation, and spiritual death or spiritual life. Art forms, therefore, not only show forth truth, beauty, and goodness; but they can also represent the unnatural, the erroneous, and the perverted. The planet earth is in the midst of a great controversy, and this affects every aspect of human life. This great controversy is especially evident and powerful in the arts, due to their emotional impact and their in-depth involvement in the intricacies of human existence.

A leading question in the area of Christian aesthetics involves the issue of whether the subject matter of artistic forms should deal only with the good life or whether it should also include the ugly and grotesque. If we take the Bible as a model, we could hardly say that it deals with only the good and the beautiful. It deals with both the good and the evil, and it puts each in proper perspective. To emphasize only the good and beautiful is less than biblical. Such a practice would be a romantic aesthetic, but it would certainly not be true to life in the sense that the Bible is true to life. Francis Schaeffer has pointed out that the Christian world view can be divided into a major and a minor theme.[38] The minor theme deals with the abnormality of a world in revolt, with the fact that humanity has rebelled, has become separated from God, and has come to see its own meaninglessness. The minor theme is the defeated and sinful side of human life. The major theme is the opposite of the minor. Metaphysically it uplifts the fact that God exists, all is not lost, and life is not absurd. People have significance due to the fact that they are made in God's image.

If art exclusively emphasizes the major theme, it is both unbiblical and unreal.[39] It would be less than Christian art. It would be romanticism, and by its shallowness and lack of insight into "real-life problems" would have to be rejected rightfully as genuine art in the biblical sense. On the other hand, it is equally unbiblical for art to emphasize exclusively the minor theme of human lostness, degradation, and abnormality.

The Bible deals with both the major and the minor themes. It is a very realistic, true-to-life book that does not hesitate to show humanity in all its degeneration. It does not, however, exhibit human foulness as an end in itself. Rather, sin, evil, and ugliness are exhibited to point up humanity's desperate need of a Saviour and the efficacy of God's grace in the sinner's life. The relationship of the beautiful and the ugly in the Bible is treated realistically, so that the Christian can, with the eyes of faith, come to hate the ugly because he or she has come to know the God who is beauty, truth, and goodness.

The whole problem of the relationship between the beautiful and the ugly in art forms is vital to Christian aesthetics because of the principle, laid down by Paul, that by beholding we become changed (2 Cor 3:18). Aesthetics has a bearing on ethics. What we read, see, hear, and touch has an effect upon our daily lives. Aesthetics, therefore, lies at the very center of the Christian life. This aesthetic impact is central, because the ultimate work and end of Christian art is the fully developed Christian life in all of its beauty and symmetry.

Art and Christian responsibility. Hans Rookmaaker has written that

> art has its own meaning as God's creation, it does not need justification. Its justification is its being a God-given possibility. Nevertheless it can fulfill many functions. This is a proof of the richness and unity of God's creation. It can be used to communicate, to stand for high values, to decorate our environment or just to be a thing of beauty. It can be used in the church. We make a fine baptismal font; we use good silverware for our communion service and so on. But its use is much wider than that.

Its uses are manifold. Yet, all these possibilities together do not "justify" art.[40]

Rookmaaker is certainly correct in claiming that art needs no ultimate justification outside the aesthetic dimension. Much of God's creation in terms of beauty has no functionality beyond the realm of aesthetics, and we find in His relationship to the Jews that He instructed them to develop certain works of art in His sanctuary just "for beauty" (2 Chr 3:6 KJV; Exod 28:2).

On the other hand, Rookmaaker is also quite right when he says that art may serve a functional purpose. One of those potential purposes is communication. He also notes that "artists, almost without exception, strive to express something in their art, and only rarely are happy with the aesthetic element alone." Art, he claims, is not necessarily a copy of reality, but it "always gives an interpretation of reality."[41] Both the subject matters and the techniques used by painters, poets, musicians, and other artists are indicators of their world view—of what they think is meaningful, expressive, important, and so on. Some approaches to art reflect alienation, meaninglessness, absurdity, and lostness, while other artistic expressions may voice alternative points of view.

It is true that some artistic creations have more clarity as expressions of the world view of their creators than others. The point is, however, that there is no neutrality[42] in either artistic creation or in the consumer's selection of literature, music, or visual art. People select and create in a cultural, philosophic, and perceptual context. Calvin Seeveld writes:

> In short, art tells what lies in a man's heart and with what vision he views the world. Art always tell-tales in whose service a person stands, because art itself is always a consecrated offering, a disconcertingly undogmatic yet terribly moving attempt to bring honor and glory and power to something.[43]

An understanding of this fact is crucial in Christian education if people are to glean the important message that the arts have for contemporary culture and personal life.

Nicholas Wolterstorff views the Christian artist from the biblical point of view as a "responsible servant" to both God and other people.[44] That characterization certainly fits with Christ's teaching of the talents and other biblical indicators that each of us has a responsibility for the health and happiness of other people.

From that viewpoint, it might be said that Christian love is the basis of aesthetics and art as well as the foundation of ethical conduct. If love means helping our neighbor by making his or her world more beautiful, harmonious, and suitable for human living, then the artist, notes Rookmaaker, has a special gift and a wonderful calling. The calling and the responsibility of the Christian artist are "to make life better, more worthwhile, to create the sound, the shape, the tale, the decoration, the environment that is meaningful and lovely and a joy to mankind."[45] In doing this the artist is witnessing to the love of the Creator-God, who went beyond the necessity of mere existence when He developed humanity's sensory (aesthetic) receptors. Part of the role of aesthetics and art in our lives is to aid us in becoming more fully human through a heightened sense of perception, an elevation of feeling, and the ability to apprehend new meanings. Humans are aesthetic beings, and that side of their life and education may not be neglected without unfavorable consequences.

Additional aesthetic considerations. A Christian aesthetic does not imply that all Christian art must dwell upon religious subjects in the narrow sense of "religious," which denotes that some things are religious while others are secular. On the contrary, everything that exists was created by God and holds aesthetic implications. Certainly, however, each Christian creator and consumer of aesthetic objects has a system of beliefs that will lead him or her to hold that certain subject matters and techniques are a better witness to the love of God and the beauty of His world than others. In part, the creation and consumption of art is a matter of taste. Beyond taste, however, is the realization that aesthetic value is not in an isolated realm, but is directly related to one's beliefs in regard to metaphysics, epistemology, and ethics. These other aspects of people's philosophy condition their tastes and help them arrive at aesthetic criteria.

A scriptural view of aesthetics does not see any particular style of art as "Christian." Biblical art forms were carried on in the format of the larger contemporary culture. Art forms change, and art may be expressed in various cultural and technical modes and still uplift the unchanging message of the love of God. Nor does a biblical view of aesthetics imply a dichotomy between "high art," as found in poetry or classical music, and the objects of daily life. To the contrary, the biblical perspective seems to indicate that God is interested in people's aesthetic experience in every aspect of their lives.

Perhaps that which is most beautiful, from a Christian viewpoint, is that which contributes toward restoring individuals to a right relationship with their Maker, other people, and their own selves. That which is evil, ugly, and unbeautiful is that which obstructs the restorative process. The ultimate end of Christian aesthetics is the beautiful character. The challenge to Christians in general, and Christian artists in particular, is to develop art forms and aesthetic environments that are capable of being agents in the process of restoring humanity to its lost estate.

Christian aesthetics and education. Aesthetic value is more closely tied to education than most people at first recognize. The beliefs, for example, that a person holds on such issues as the relationship of the beautiful and the ugly in art forms and the relation of aesthetics to ethics act as evaluative criteria for the curricular inclusion (or exclusion) of certain types of visual art, music, and literature. These beliefs also help determine how these artistic creations will be treated and evaluated in the educational context. Outside of formal schooling, these beliefs provide criteria for the selection and understanding of such leisure-time activities as watching television and personal reading.

The fact that God created a world of beauty suggests that the total educational environment has aesthetic implications. Therefore, such items as the architecture of the school plant, student dress, and even the neatness of homework are within the realm of the school's aesthetic concern. Christian education should help students become aware of the role of aesthetics, both in their daily lives and in the realm of "higher culture." Beyond awareness, the Christian ethic implies that Christian education will aid people in realizing their responsibility to contribute to the aesthetic quality of their environment. For Christian educators to slight or ignore the importance of aesthetics is to neglect a crucial aspect of education, since that neglect implies a view of both humanity and God that is less than adequate from the biblical perspective.

CHRISTIAN PHILOSOPHY AND EDUCATION

Chapter 9 holds an important place in the structure of Part III, since an underlying assumption of this study is that philosophic beliefs provide the basic boundaries for preferred educational practices for any group in society. We noted earlier, however, that philosophic beliefs are not the sole determinant of educational practices. Political, social, economic, and other forces modify the impact of philosophy in daily practice.

The very existence of Christian schools as an alternative to public systems indicates a different set of philosophic assumptions and educational boundaries from those of the larger culture. A belief in the reality of Jesus as Lord and Saviour and the trustworthiness of the Bible as the primary source of dependable knowledge, for example, has led people to sacrifice largely of their time and material goods to establish schools in which the Christian metaphysical and epistemological stance will be central.

Those beliefs not only account for the existence of Christian schools; they also provide criteria for curriculum selection and emphasis, teaching methodologies, and the type of relationship that teachers will seek to build with students. Philosophic beliefs in regard to ethics and aesthetics also influence nearly every aspect of Christian education, including such diverse areas as the choice of music and literature to be studied, the process of developing and enforcing rules, the arrangement of the classroom, and the role of competition both in the classroom and on the playing field.

Educational practices are conditioned by philosophic beliefs. Teachers, parents, and other educators develop unnecessary difficulties when their practices conflict with the world view that they are seeking to transmit to the youth in their charge. A healthy educational program is one that is in as close a harmony with its philosophic beliefs as external circumstances permit.

Since the circumstances of the educational environment may change with time and location, it is important that individual educators consciously understand the beliefs that govern their actions, so that they will remain flexible in applying the educational principles that grow out of their world view. There is both freedom of choice and individual responsibility in applying philosophic beliefs in educational practice. That responsibility and freedom are part of the professional aspect of teaching.

Teaching is not learning a formula for relating to people or following a blueprint for the development of Christian character. It is rather an art which demands responsible thought and action on the part of the educator. In order to practice this art, the educator must have an understanding of the psychological and sociological, as well as the philosophical, implications of human interaction. These understandings lie at the foundation of the crucial role of both parent and professional educator.

Notes

1. The fullest discussion of the anthropological aspect of Christian metaphysics is found in the section on the nature of the student in Chapter 10.

2. Francis A. Schaeffer, *He Is There and He Is Not Silent* (Wheaton, IL: Tyndale House, 1972), p. 1.

3. See Viktor E. Frankl, *Man's Search for Meaning: An Introduction to Logotherapy* (New York: Washington Square Press, 1963) for an existentialist's revealing recognition of this problem in the context of a Nazi concentration camp.

4. Perhaps the cautions put forth by Harold Titus are in order at this point. He noted that the truth or falsity of a belief is not established by the wishes of people, since wishful thinking leads a person to read in what is not there. "Yet ignoring what does exist is equally dangerous." *Living Issues in Philosophy*, p. 335.

5. Herman Harrell Horne, *The Philosophy of Christian Education* (New York: Fleming H. Revell Co., 1937), p. 163.

6. James, *Essays in Pragmatism*, p. 109.

7. This chapter does not have space to examine the fundamental problem underlying the theistic answer to meaning. If the basic problem underlying naturalistic evolution is how something came from nothing, then the basic problem at the foundation of supernaturalism must be related to the cause of the First Cause—in other words, Where did God come from? I have dealt somewhat with an answer to this question in "How Did the Galaxies Come into Existence?," *These Times*, September 1, 1978, pp. 8-12.

8. Helpful discussions of the problem of evil and its results are found in Norman L. Geisler, *The Roots of Evil* (Grand Rapids, MI: Zondervan Publishing House, 1978); John Hick, *Evil and the God of Love*, rev. ed. (New York: Harper & Row, 1978); John W. Wenham, *The Enigma of Evil: Can We Believe in the Goodness of God?* (Grand Rapids, MI: Zondervan Publishing House, 1985); John S. Feinberg, *The Many Faces of Evil: Theological Systems and the Problem of Evil* (Grand Rapids, MI: Zondervan Publishing House, 1994).

9. An informative discussion of this topic is found in Hendrik Kraemer, *Why Christianity of All Religions?*, trans. Hubert Hoskins (Philadelphia: The Westminster Press, 1962). See also the discussion of "Revelation Outside Christianity" in Leon Morris, *I Believe in Revelation* (Grand Rapids, MI: Wm. B. Eerdmans Publishing Co., 1976), pp. 148-59.

10. Kraemer, *Why Christianity of All Religions?*, p. 39. At this point the reader has probably observed that we are beginning to pass from metaphysical concerns to those of epistemology. That is because, as noted earlier, epistemology and metaphysics cannot be studied in isolation from each other. You cannot have a view of reality without a conception of truth and how to arrive at truth, and vice versa.

11. Ibid., p. 80.

12. Ibid., pp. 81-82.

13. Ibid., pp. 82-83.

14. Ibid., pp. 94, 99.

15. Ibid., p. 99. For a comparative analysis of the various world religions' conceptions of sin, see Bernard Ramm, *Offense to Reason: The Theology of Sin* (San Francisco: Harper & Row, 1985), pp. 58-61.

16. C. S. Lewis, *Mere Christianity* (New York: The Macmillan Company, 1960), p. 56.

17. Not necessarily to be confused with the actual life of professed Christians or ecclesiastical organizations.

18. Frank E. Gaebelein, "Toward a Philosophy of Christian Education," in *An Introduction to Evangelical Christian Education*, ed., J. Edward Hakes (Chicago: Moody Press, 1964), p. 44.

19. Arthur F. Holmes, *Faith Seeks Understanding: A Christian Approach to Knowledge* (Grand Rapids, MI: Wm. B. Eerdmans Publishing Co., 1971), p. 32.

20. Bernard Ramm, *The Pattern of Religious Authority* (Grand Rapids, MI: Wm. B. Eerdmans Publishing Co., 1959), p. 44.

21. Arthur F. Holmes, *All Truth is God's Truth* (Grand Rapids, MI: Wm. B. Eerdmans Publishing Co., 1977), pp. 8-15.

22. Roy A. Clouser, *The Myth of Religious Neutrality: An Essay on the Hidden Role of Religious Belief in Theories* (Notre Dame, IN: University of Notre Dame Press, 1991); Richard J. Edlin, *The Cause of Christian Education*, 2d ed. (Newport, AL: Vision Press, 1998), pp. 41-54.

23. H. Richard Niebuhr, *Christ and Culture* (New York: Harper & Brothers, Torchbook Edition, 1956), pp. 238, 234.

24. Donald Oppewal, *Biblical Knowing and Teaching*, Calvin College Monograph Series (Grand Rapids, MI: Calvin College, 1985), pp. 7-9.

25. Lewis, *Mere Christianity*, p. 109.

26. The genuine and the counterfeit are often close neighbors in life. This is true with healthy and unhealthy versions of self-love. Jesus uplifted a healthy self-love. It is, in fact, at the root of the Golden Rule and the second great commandment (Matt 7:12; 22:39; Luke 6:31). I cannot love my neighbor unless I first love my self. Healthy self-love, however, is founded upon God's love for me rather than my intrinsic goodness. I have significance and value *only* because God loves me. Without God I am nothing and have no meaning. God loves my neighbor just as he loves me. I, therefore, hope the best and do the best for my neighbor, who is just as valuable (and helpless) in God's eyes as I am. Distorted self-love leaves God out of the center of the picture and puts my lost self at the focal point. This self-centeredness becomes the foundation of pride and selfishness rather than the basis of love and service.

27. Holmes, *Faith Seeks Understanding*, p. 97.

28. John Powell, *The Secret of Staying in Love* (Niles, IL: Argus Communications, 1974), pp. 44, 48.

29. Anders Nygren, *Agape and Eros*, trans. Philip S. Watson (Philadelphia: Westminster Press, 1953), p. 232.

30. Carl F. H. Henry, *Christian Personal Ethics* (Grand Rapids, MI: Wm. B. Eerdmans Publishing Co., 1957), p. 219.

31. Holmes, *Faith Seeks Understanding*, p. 93.

32. Ibid.

33. Joseph Fletcher, *Situation Ethics: The New Morality* (Philadelphia: The Westminster Press, 1966), p. 124.

34. Holmes, *Faith Seeks Understanding*, p. 94.

35. Ibid., pp. 97-98.

36. Francis A. Schaeffer, *True Spirituality* (Wheaton, IL: Tyndale House, 1971), p. 111.

37. C. S. Lewis, *Mere Christianity*, p. 69.

38. Francis A. Schaeffer, *Art & the Bible: Two Essays* (Downers Grove, IL: InterVarsity Press, 1973), p. 56. The terms minor and major, in this discussion, have no relationship to their use in music.

39. See Leland Ryken, *Culture in Christian Perspective: A Door to Understanding and Enjoying the Arts* (Portland, OR: Multnomah Press, 1986), pp. 264, 15.

40. H. R. Rookmaaker, *Art Needs No Justification* (Downers Grove, IL: InterVarsity Press, 1978), p. 38.

41. H. R. Rookmaaker, *Modern Art and the Death of a Culture* (Downers Grove, IL: Inter-Varsity Press, 1973), pp. 231, 236.

42. Rookmaaker, *Art Needs No Justification*, p. 45.

43. Calvin Seeveld, "Christian Art," in *The Christian Imagination: Essays on Literature and the Arts*, ed., Leland Ryken (Grand Rapids, MI: Baker Book House, 1981), p. 390.

44. Nicholas Wolterstorff, *Art In Action: Toward a Christian Aesthetic* (Grand Rapids, MI: Wm. B. Eerdmans Publishing Co., 1980), pp. 67-91.

45. Rookmaaker, *Modern Art and the Death of a Culture*, p. 243.

10

A Christian Approach to Education

Christianity is based upon a distinctive and unique view of reality, truth, and value. The educational configuration stemming from that world view grows out of those beliefs. Christian education that is Christian in fact, rather than merely in word, must view the nature and potential of the student, the role of the teacher, the content of the curriculum, the methodological emphasis, and the social function of the school in the light of its philosophic undergirding.

The present chapter is not an exhaustive treatment of Christian education. Neither is it a detailed explication of methodologies for practical application. Its purpose is to examine some of the educational principles that grow out of the assumptions of the Christian world view. These principles can be viewed as guidelines for the selection and utilization of specific techniques and emphases for practical application within a particular educational context.

This chapter has not attempted to separate the different educational roles found in society. It focuses on the school, but much of what is said can be interpreted within the framework of the home and church, since parents and church workers are also teachers. The home, the church, and the school each deal with the same children—children who have the same nature and needs in their various contexts. The home and church have a curriculum and teaching style, and both home and church certainly have a social function akin to that of the school. There is a great need for parents, church workers, and school teachers to gain greater insight into the interdependent nature of their educative functions and to develop effective channels of appreciation and communication. A cooperative stance is important between the Christian teacher in the school and Christian teachers in the home and church, because Christian education is more than Christian schooling. The home, church, and school are working with the most valuable objects on earth, God's children, and each is ideally founded upon the same principles.

THE NATURE OF THE STUDENT AND THE GOAL OF CHRISTIAN EDUCATION

"Today," writes G. C. Berkouwer, "more than at any time, the question 'What is man?' is at the center of theological and philosophical concern."[1] That question is also at the center of educational thought. The most important component of the school is the learner. Who are these learners? What is their essential nature, their reason for being, their positive aspects, and their negative attributes? Are they good, evil, or neutral? What are their needs, and how should the school relate to those needs? Answers to such questions form pivotal points for various social and educational theories. As D. Elton Trueblood put it, "Until we are clear on what man is we shall not be clear about much else."[2]

Human Nature and the Image of God

Reinhold Niebuhr has pointed out that a major characteristic of the "Christian view of man is that he is understood primarily from the standpoint of God, rather than the uniqueness of his rational faculties or his relation to nature."[3] The essential thing about human beings from the biblical perspective is that "God created man in his own image" (Gen 1:27). Humanity stands in a singular relationship to the Creator-God. Due to the fact of being created in God's likeness, there is a gulf between people and the animal world. Human beings are not merely highly developed bipeds. They are individuals created in the likeness of God, and, as a result, they are partakers of the divine nature. Love and rationality are universal human traits, because they are a part of God's characteristics.

Human uniqueness centers around the fact that God singled humanity out at the creation as being the one creature among earthlings that is responsible and accountable (Gen 1:28). Humankind had the holy calling of the stewardship of God's creation laid upon it. Only humanity acts as God's viceregent, prophet, and priest upon the earth.

Humans were also endowed with an extended ability to live the life of the mind through internal thought and external verbalization, and given the capability of transcending their world and their own being through both consciousness and self-conciousness. Human beings, claims the Bible, were created with the ability to communicate and develop personal relationships with their Creator. The image extends to every part of an individual. Human beings were created in the likeness of God mentally, spiritually, and physically. "Scripture," remarks Berkouwer, "gives no warrant for considering only a part of man as partaking of the image."[4]

Humans at the creation are pictured as beings of love, goodness, trustworthiness, rationality, and righteousness. It does not take a great deal of insight to realize that people are no longer completely lovely, good, responsible, rational, or righteous. Both human society at large and individual personal relationships are honeycombed with aggression, alienation, brutality, and selfishness.

Humanity has changed, and this change is the result of the Fall outlined in Genesis 3. Humanity rejected God and chose its own way. As a result, people became alienated and separated from God (Gen 3:8-10), their fellow beings (Gen 3:11, 12), their own selves (Gen 3:13), and the natural world (Gen 3:17-19). The image was corrupted in all of its aspects. Humanity had chosen to separate itself from the source of life; and, as a result, it became subject to death (Gen 2:17; 3:19).

It is important to note that even though the image has been fractured and grossly distorted, it has not been destroyed (Gen 9:6; 1 Cor 11:7; Jas 3:9). As John Calvin put it, a "residue" of the image continued to exist in humanity after the Fall, "some sparks still gleam" in the "degenerate nature."[5] Therefore, although people are twisted and lost as a result of the Fall, they are still human. They still have godlike potentials and characteristics. Schaeffer has remarked that "man's achievements demonstrate that he is not junk, though the ends to which he often puts them show how lost he is."[6]

Since the Fall there has been a great controversy within human nature, as there is in the world at large, between the forces of good and evil. People are torn between their desire for goodness and an inclination toward evil, and they are often drawn toward good even though their natural propensities lead them to choose evil. This dilemma of humanity cannot be understood apart from the Fall.

People's potential for both good and evil is explained by the biblical revelation of humanity's original position in relation to God and its loss of that position. Individuals now live in an abnormal world in which they are divided against one another and separated from God. Fallen humanity is in active rebellion against its Creator. Humanity's natural tendency is to put itself in the place of God and to rebel against the laws of the universe (Rom 8:7). Its goal is to become autonomous. Unfortunately, humanity's rebellion and its desire to be its own god are the source of its destruction.

Within themselves, fallen individuals cannot realize their own predicament because of the deceptiveness of human nature (Jer 17:9). The most delusive part of humanity's current situation is its ignorance of its ignorance in regard to its true condition and its possibilities for unaided betterment. The Bible presents fallen individuals as rebels who are incapable of finding the Creator-God on their own.

The Restoration of the Image and the Redemptive and Reconciling Role of Education

Fortunately, lost humanity is not left to its own helplessness. God has taken the initiative to help individuals out of their lostness and to renew and restore His image to its fulness in them (Col 3:10). This is the reason Christ came into the world. The first promise of this restoration and reconciliation may be glimpsed in Genesis 3:15, where Adam and Eve were granted the initial vision of the Redeemer. This promise is viewed in a fuller way in the sacrificial services of the Old Testament. It is seen in its fullness in the incarnation of Jesus Christ, who came to save fallen humanity from the results of sin (John 3:16, 17).

The work of Christ might best be seen in terms of atonement (at-one-ment) and reconciliation. His work is to reverse the effects of the Fall by making it possible for persons to become at-one (in harmony) with God, with others, with their deceptive selves, and with the natural creation.[7]

In this light, the two great commandments of love may be seen as emphasizing the restoration of the broken relationships between individuals and God and individuals and their neighbors. Beyond that, Christ's teaching on the necessity of self-examination, confession of sin, and a reliance upon His righteousness can be seen as a means of restoring people to a correct view of their selves. These restored relationships will make possible the restoration of the earth to its edenic condition at the end of time. The Bible is built around a teleological message that points to the time when humanity will be restored to harmony with the realm of nature (Isa 11:6-9). If the entrance of sin brought alienation and the deterioration of relationships, then the essence of the gospel is rebuilding those relationships. The entire process entails a restoration of the image of God in individuals through the agency of the Holy Spirit. Education is one arm of God's restorative and reconciling effort. It may therefore be seen as a redemptive activity.

The nature, condition, and needs of the student provide the focal point for Christian educational philosophy and direct educators toward the goals of Christian education. All students must be seen as individuals who have infinite potential, since they are God's children. They are also individuals whose greatest need is to know Jesus Christ as Lord and Saviour. The redemptive, restorative, and reconciling goal of Christian education provides a focus for the evaluation of all other aspects of Christian education, including the role of the teacher, curricular emphases, proper instructional methodologies, and the reason for establishing Christian alternatives to public education.

Jim Wilhoit points out that the biblical "view of human nature has no parallel in secular theories of education and is [therefore] the main obstacle to the Christian's adopting any such theory wholesale."[8] The elements of a Christian approach to education must always be consciously developed in the light of human need and the human condition. We will return to the goals of Christian education in our examination of the work of the teacher.

Some Educational Considerations
Related to Student Nature

Beyond the central position of the *imago Dei* (image of God) in humanity, there are several other points about the student that the Christian educator should note. First, the Bible treats individuals as holistic units. The Bible does not picture human beings in a dualistic or pluralistic fashion. Thus there is not the idealistic straining to separate body and soul, such as we find in Plato. Adam became a living being (soul) when God united all his parts with the life force at creation (Gen 2:7). The biblical emphasis is on the resurrection of the body at the end of time rather than on "bodyless spirits" (John 5:28,

29; 1 Thess 4:16, 17; 1 Cor 15:51-54).

The whole person is important to God. The body is not more important than the spirit, or vice versa. Whatever affects one part of an individual affects the whole. Balance among the spiritual, social, physical, and mental aspects of a person is the ideal as it is seen in the development of Jesus (Luke 2:52). Part of humanity's present dilemma is that since the Fall people have suffered from a lack of health in each of these areas as well as in their interrelationship. As a result, part of the educative function of redemption is to restore individuals to health in each of these aspects and in their total beings. Restoration of the image, therefore, has social, spiritual, mental, and physical ramifications, as does education.

Second, if persons are to be fully human, they must be controlled by their minds rather than by their animal appetites and propensities. Being in the image of God, people can reason from cause to effect and make responsible choices and spiritual decisions. According to the Bible, humans have genuine freedom of choice and can therefore make moral decisions through the use of their rationality as it is aided by special revelation and the guidance of the Holy Spirit. This freedom of choice is not absolute in the sense that people can be autonomous and live without God, but it is genuine in the sense that individuals can choose Jesus Christ as Lord and live by His principles, or choose Satan as master and be subject to the law of sin and death (Rom 6:12-23).

C. S. Lewis remarked that God made free will possible not because it was not frought with danger, but because even though it makes evil possible, it also is the only thing that "makes possible any love or goodness or joy worth having."[9] For individuals to be controlled by their appetites or sexual desires is less than human from the biblical viewpoint, since it is less than divine. Humans are much more than animals or machines whose activities and choices are determined. Unfortunately, however, people often choose to live on the level of the animal and machine.

Third, the Christian educator must recognize and respect the individuality, uniqueness, and personal worth of each person. The life of Jesus was a constant lesson in regard to the individuality and worth of persons in His relationships both with His disciples and with the population at large. By way of contrast, the mentality of the Pharisees,

Sadducees, and even the disciples was to see "others" in terms of "the herd." Part of the problem with idealism and romanticism is that they obscure personal uniqueness and individuality.[10] A distinctively Christian philosophy can never lose sight of the importance of human individuality as it seeks to relate education to the learner.

That recognition does not mean that a respect for individuality must negate the importance of the group. Paul, in writing to the Corinthians concerning spiritual gifts, uplifted the value of the social whole as well as the unique value of each person (1 Cor 12:12-31). One of his points is that the body (social group) has health when the importance and uniqueness of the individual members of the social whole are respected. That holds true for educational institutions as well as for churches. The wholesome classroom, from this perspective, is not one of unlimited individualism, but rather one in which the respect for individuality is seen in the context of respect for the group.

Fourth, since the Fall the problems of the human race have not changed. Humanity since that time has found itself subject to the struggle of the forces of good and evil. There have been two basic humanities since the race's introduction to sin—those individuals who are still in revolt and those who have accepted Christ as Saviour. It is true that the particulars of the human predicament have changed from time to time, but the underlying principles of the great controversy between good and evil have remained constant. It is therefore true that people today face the same basic temptations and challenges that confronted Moses and Paul. It is because of the unchanging nature of the human problem through both time and space (geographical location) that the scriptures are timeless and speak a universal message to people. The value of the Bible in education is that it speaks to the heart of the problem of sin and its solution—issues which all persons must face.

Students, in Christian perspective, may be seen as children of God. Each is a repository of God's image and one for whom Christ died. Each one, therefore, has infinite and eternal possibilities. The worth of each individual student can only be assessed in terms of the price paid for his or her restoration at the Cross of Calvary.

The Christian educator, understanding the conflict taking place within each human being, realizes that each student is a candidate for God's kingdom and therefore deserves the very best education that can be offered. The Christian educator sees beneath the veneer of outward conduct and is able to get at the core of the human problem—sin, separation from the life and character of God. In the fullest sense of the words, Christian education is redemption and reconciliation. As a result, Christian education seeks a balanced development between the social, spiritual, mental, and physical aspects of the student in all of its activities and through its total program. The purpose and goal of Christian education are the restoration of the image of God in each student and the reconciliation of students with God, their fellow students, their own selves, and the natural world.

THE ROLE OF THE CHRISTIAN TEACHER

Teaching is a Form of Ministry

Since the function of Christian education is one of reconciliation and restoring the balanced image of God in students, education should be seen primarily as a redemptive act. If education is viewed in that manner, then the role of the teacher is ministerial and pastoral in the sense that the teacher is an agent of reconciliation.

The New Testament clearly specifies teaching as a divine calling (Eph 4:11; 1 Cor 12:28; Rom 12:6-8).[11] Furthermore, the scriptures do not seek to separate the functions of teaching and pastoring. On the contrary, Paul wrote to Timothy that a bishop (pastor) must be "an apt teacher" (1 Tim 3:2). In writing to the Ephesians, Paul used a Greek construction that indicates that the offices of pastor and teacher were held by the same person when he noted that "some should be apostles, some prophets, some evangelists, some pastors and teachers" (Eph 4:11). F. F. Bruce, in commenting on this passage, has remarked that "the two terms 'pastors (shepherds) and teachers' denote one and the same class of men."[12] On the other hand, the other gifts are listed separately. The significance of this point is that these two gifts should not be divided if they are to remain functional. Pastors must not only care for the souls of their flock, but they must be persons who teach by precept and example to both individuals and the corporate body of the church. Teachers, likewise, are not merely expounders of truth but persons who have an abiding care for the individuals under their tutelage. A Christian teacher functions in a pastoral role.

The major difference between the roles of pastors and teachers today has to do with the current division of labor. In twentieth-century society, the Christian teacher may be seen as one who pastors in a "school" context, while the pastor is one who teaches in the "larger religious community." It should and must consciously be realized that their function is essentially the same, even though, by today's definitions, they are in charge of different divisions of the Lord's vineyard.

The clearest and fullest integration of the gift of teacher-pastor is seen in the ministry of Christ. One of the terms by which He was most often addressed was that of "master." In the Greek text this word is nearly always *didaskalos*, which is most accurately translated as "teacher."[13] Christ may be seen as the best example of teaching in terms of methodology and meaningful interpersonal relationships.[14] A study of the gospels from the perspective of Christ as teacher will contribute a great deal to our knowledge of how to operate in the classroom. In addition, such a study will put us in direct contact with the aims and goals of Christian education.

The Christian Teacher as an Agent of Reconciliation

The Primary Goal of a Christian Teacher. The foremost goal of Christian education is illustrated with particular clarity in the Gospel of Luke. Luke 15, which records the parables of the lost sheep, the lost coin, and the lost son, is especially pertinent to the role of the Christian teacher. The teacher is one who seeks out and attempts to help those lost and caught in the realm of sin, whether they are (1) like the sheep (those who know they are lost but do not know how to get home); (2) like the coin and older son (those who have not enough spiritual sense to realize their own lostness); or (3) like the younger son (those who know they are lost, know how to get home, but do not want to go home until they have expended their rebellion). The teacher is a searcher and a seeker after that which is lost. In relation to the experience of Zacchaeus, Jesus enunciated the central principle underlying His teaching ministry: "The Son of man came to seek and save the lost" (Luke 19:10).

To those passages may be added Jesus' experience with the ungrateful and inhospitable Samaritans when they refused to provide Him with a place to stay because they perceived He was on His way to Jerusalem. On that occasion, James and John were incensed with the ingratitude of the Samaritans and sought Jesus' permission to destroy the guilty ones by calling down fire from heaven. The reply of Jesus was that "the Son of man is not come to destroy men's lives, but to save them" (Luke 9:51-56 KJV).

The primary goal of Christ's life and of Christian education can also be found in the keynote verse of the Gospel of Matthew, which claims that Mary would bear a son who would "save his people from their sins" (Matt 1:21). The same thought is brought out by John when he claimed that "God so loved the world that He gave His only Son, that whosoever believes in Him should not perish but have eternal life. For God sent the Son into the world, not to condemn the world, but that the world might be saved through him" (John 3:16, 17).

Christian teachers are agents of reconciliation. They are individuals who are out to "seek and to save that which is lost." They are persons willing to work in the spirit of Christ, so that their students might be brought into harmony with God through the sacrifice of Jesus and be restored to God's image.

Teaching is much more than the passing on of information and filling students' heads with knowledge.[15] It is more than helping them prepare for the world of work. The primary function of the teacher is to relate to the Master Teacher in such a way that he or she becomes God's agent in the plan of redemption.

Edwin Rian caught the point when he noted that most writers in educational philosophy, regardless of their philosophical and religious perspectives, "agree on considering the problem of 'sin and death,' which is the problem of man, according to Pauline and Reformed Protestant theology, as irrelevant to the questions of the aims and process of education." Such a position, he indicated, cannot help producing "miseducation and frustration for the individual and for the community." From the perspective of fallen people's predicament, Rian uplifted *"education as conversion."* Herbert Welch, president of Ohio Wesleyan University early in the twentieth century, made the same point when he claimed that "to win its students from sin to righteousness is . . . the highest achievement of the Christian college."[16] The same, of course, can be said for elementary and secondary education. In short, it is the redemptive and reconciliatory aim of Christian education that makes it Christian.

Some secondary aims of Christian teaching. The healing of people's alienation from God sets the stage for the healing of their other alienations and thereby implies the secondary purposes of Christian education. We have repeatedly noted that education is a part of God's plan of reconciliation or atonement. The role of Christian education is to help bring people back to "at-one-ness" with God, other people, their own selves, and the natural world.

Within that context, the focal point of Christian teaching is the healing of broken relationships. The healing of the broken relationships between an individual and God, others, and his or her own self prepares the way for the successful accomplishment of education's secondary purposes, such as the character development, the acquisition of knowledge, job preparation, and the development of students who are socially and physically healthy.

The development of Christian character in students stands as a major goal of Christian teachers. C. B. Eavey related character development to the primary purpose of education when he stated that "the foundational aim in Christian education is the bringing of the individual to Christ for salvation. Before a man of God can be perfected, there must be a man of God to perfect; without the new birth there is no man of God."[17] In other words, true character can develop only in the born-again Christian. Character development outside of that experience may be good humanism or even good pharisaism, but it is not congruent with the Christian model.

God wants to use Christian teachers through the dynamic power of the Holy Spirit in the reproduction of the fruit of the Spirit—love, joy, peace, patience, kindness, goodness, faithfulness, gentleness, and self-control (Gal. 5:22-24)—in the life of each student. God wants teachers to help students to be more like Him, to internalize the essentials of His character into their individual lives. The teacher as a role model is crucial in the area of character development.[18]

Another secondary goal of Christian education that involves the teacher is the development of a Christian mind. Christian educators are not nearly as concerned with passing on information as they are in helping students develop a Christian way of viewing reality and organizing knowledge within the framework of the Christian world view. Gene Garrick pointed out the secondary nature of knowledge acquisition when he wrote that "there can be no truly Christian mind without the new birth since spiritual truth is apprehended and applied spiritually (1 Cor. 2:1-16)."[19]

We will return to the discussion of developing the Christian mind at greater length in the section of this chapter that deals with curriculum; but before leaving the topic we need to realize that the Christian never views gaining knowledge—even Christian knowledge—as an end in itself. In the acquisition of knowledge and in the development of a Christian mind, Christian teachers never lose sight of the fact that their ultimate goal is better service to both God and their fellow beings.

Other secondary educational aims include helping students learn how to develop and retain physical health and how to maintain wholesome relationships with other people. The wholesome-relationship goal is especially closely tied to the concept of education as reconciliation. The Bible is quite explicit on the fact that a person cannot truly love God without loving and caring for one's neighbor. The two go hand in hand (Matt 22:36-40).

 A final secondary aim of Christian education is preparing students for the world of work. Occupational preparation, however, like every other aspect of Christian life, cannot be separated from the issues of the new birth, character development, the development of a Christian mind, the achievement of physical well-being, and the development of a sense of social responsibility. The Christian life is a unit, and each aspect of it interacts with the others and the total person. Christian teachers will strive to enable their students to see so-called secular occupations within the context of an individual's wider vocation as a servant of God. That idea brings us to what we might consider the ultimate and final goal of Christian education.

The ultimate aim of Christian teaching. The life of Jesus was one of service for humanity. He came to our planet to give Himself for the betterment of others. His followers have the same function, and the ultimate end (i.e., final outcome) of education is to prepare or disciple students for that task. Along that line, Herbert Welch concluded that "education for its own sake is as bad as art for art's sake; but culture held in trust to empower one better to serve one's fellow men, the wise for the ignorant, the strong for the weak," is education's highest aim. "The Christian character," he postulated, "which does not find expression in service is scarcely worthy of the name."[20]

Figure 5 indicates that conversion, character development, acquiring a mature Christian mind and good health, and occupational preparation are not ends in themselves. Each is rather an essential element

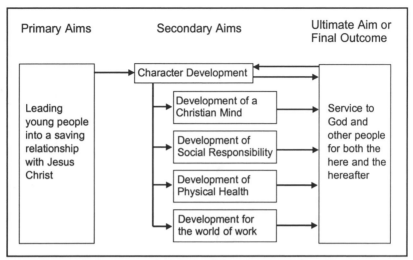

Figure 5. Purposes of Christian Education that Inform Teaching

in an individual's preparation for service to his or her fellow humans as God seeks to heal the alienation between people that developed at the Fall. The essence of Christian love and the Christlike character is service to others.

Teachers should help their students realize that people generally have gotten their educational priorities backward. How often have we heard the following sentiments? "Society owes me a living because of all the years I spent getting an education." "I deserve more of the good life because of what I have accomplished." Even those who claim to be Christians often make—or at least imply—such sentiments. Unfortunately they express the antithesis of the ultimate aim of Christianity.

It is morally wrong for individuals to use society's educational gifts for self-aggrandizement. George S. Counts wrote from a humanistic perspective that

> at every turn the social obligation which the advantages of a college education impose must be stressed: too often have we preached the monetary value of a college education; too widely have we bred the conviction that the training is advantageous because it enables the individual to get ahead; too insidiously have we spread the doctrine that the college opens up avenues to the exploitation of less capable men. *Higher educa-*

tion involves higher responsibility . . . ; this cardinal truth must be impressed upon every recipient of its advantages. In season and out of season, social service, and not individual advancement, must be made the motif of college training.[21]

If Counts from his secular perspective can so recognize this fact, then the committed Christian should see it even more distinctly.

The message of the parable of the talents is that the greater a person's natural endowments and the greater his or her opportunities for their development, the more responsibility he or she has to image Christ in faithful service to those who have mental, spiritual, social, emotional, or physical needs (Matt 25:14-26).

The Christian teacher not only has the responsibility to teach the ideal of service but also to model it. In that context the insight of Gloria Stronks, Doug Blomberg, and their colleagues is helpful. They suggest that a major task of Christian schools is to "help students unwrap their God-given gifts" so that they can find their place in service to others.[22]

In conclusion, it should be emphasized that Christian service is a response to God's love rather than an altruistic humanitarianism that still allows people to congratulate themselves for their personal goodness. The Christian's gratitude toward God for salvation inspires him or her to become a channel of God's love to others in His ministry of reconciliation.

In one sense, as we noted in Figure 5, character development lays the foundation for service. Yet it is also true that such service further develops character (thus the two-way arrow between character development and service). From this perspective, we might visualize the two as working in tandem, each contributing to the other. It is a truism that character development cannot occur without service.

Teachers should seek to instill in their students the fact that Christian service is not something that begins after graduation. Rather, it is an integral part of a Christian's life from the time of conversion. Teachers in the church, home, and school need to introduce their students to opportunities for serving others both inside and outside of their respective communities. In short, a crucial function of Christian teaching is to help students not only internalize God's love but also to externalize it. Teachers as agents of reconciliation need to help their students discover their own roles in God's plan of reconciliation and restoration.

The Primacy of Teaching

Teaching young people is not only a ministerial act, but it is one of the most effective forms of ministry. It affects the entire youth population at its most impressionable age.[23]

It is important to note that of all teaching functions, that of parents is the most important and most influential.[24] On this point, Frank Gaebelein has written that of all the educational forces in society, none is more potent than the home. "The most influential teachers, whether they recognize it or not, are parents." He goes on to point out the paradox of the modern home, where there is greater leisure than ever before but less quality home life than in previous eras. "What this may mean was put in one sentence by Carle Zimmerman, when he said, 'If there were no A-bomb or H-bomb, we would have to recognize the fact that no civilization has ever survived the disintegration of its home life.'"[25]

Our society, both Christian and non-Christian, needs to recognize the fact that the home is the primary educational institution and that parents are the most important teachers. The school and church must therefore be seen as auxiliary educational agencies whose role is to support the work of the home. The home, church, and school working together may greatly multiply their effect for the good of the child.

Within the formal schooling system the teacher is the most influential educational professional in terms of impact upon maturing young people. It is the teacher—and not the superintendent, principal, curriculum specialist, or counselor—who stands at the place where the adult world and the world of the child meet. The non-teaching position, ideal curriculum, latest teaching tools, and flawless organizational pyramid are marginal unless there are quality human relationships at the point where students encounter a school's teachers.

It is unfortunate that the crucial role of the teacher has not been appreciated by Western society. What other group of adults has the powerful role of meeting with the entire youth population for thirty hours per week for one hundred and eighty days every year? And yet any position outside the classroom is generally treated as a promotion. In fact, the further one moves from the scene of classroom education, the larger the social and financial rewards. As a result, a great deal of maturing talent is removed from the classroom, and the Peter Principle[26] is furthered.

This whole situation should be reversed, and the very best human talent that society and the educational system can provide should be at the point where impressionable young minds meet the representatives of the adult world. From this perspective, perhaps a specialist in charge of curriculum or an assistant superintendent in charge of finance might be "promoted" to the classroom where he or she is actually given the responsibility of being entrusted with the care of the Lord's children. A corollary to this revised role of professional values is that the most crucial role in teaching is at the first-grade level, where the students are most impressionable and where they are developing their initial (and generally lasting) attitude toward school and learning. The very best talent and the most ideal teaching conditions should be found at the primary level.

If teaching were actually valued for what it is, it is probable that many current educational problems could be avoided. The centrality of the role of the teacher in education does not do away with the necessity of administration. The role of the principal could be performed by one who is a teacher among teachers, a master teacher, one who truly understands and has succeeded in the teaching field. Such a person could become a head teacher-principal and would not lose touch with the challenges and problems of the classroom context. Other non-educative functions that we often classify under educational administration might be given to technicians and professionals at the periphery of the educational world.[27]

Perhaps the best way to destroy the potential of the educational system as an agent of reconciliation in restoring the image of God in students is first to undermine and downplay the role of parents, and then to make teaching—especially elementary teaching—a second-class professional activity. With these two strokes the true function of education can be stymied. The challenge in Christian education is to value teaching for its true potential as a powerful and crucial form of ministry.

Qualifications of the Christian Teacher

If the teacher stands at the center of the educational process, then it is equally true that the Christian teacher maintains a position of centrality in the Christian school. With this in mind, Gaebelein wrote that there can be "no Christian education without Christian teachers."[28]

What is a Christian teacher? What are the qualifications of such a teacher? These questions are not as easily answered as might be expected, since only God can read the innermost thoughts of individuals, and matters of Christian belief are essentially a concern of internal conviction and commitment. As previously noted, however, the outward life does give some indications as to what people truly believe and hold as their most precious values.

The qualifications of the Christian teacher might be viewed in terms of the categories that we earlier discussed in relation to the balanced nature of each individual. From that perspective, there are spiritual, mental, social, and physical characteristics that are important qualifications for Christian teachers.

First in importance for the Christian teacher is the spiritual qualification. That is true because the essence of the human problem (sin) is of a spiritual nature. Furthermore, the "natural man" is suffering from a form of spiritual death (Gen 3), and his or her greatest need is a spiritual rebirth (John 3:3, 5). C. B. Eavey has written that "only one who has been made a new creature in Christ can mediate to others God's grace or nurture others in that grace." As a result, those who minister in Christian education

> must have in themselves the life of Christ and be possessed by the Spirit of God. Christian education is no matter of mere human activity but one of individuals meeting God in Christ. It is Christ being experienced by persons who, as a consequence, are born again and grow into the likeness of the Person they meet.[29]

Thus qualification number one for Christian teachers is that they have a personal saving relationship with Jesus. If their spiritual life is in harmony with God's revealed will, they will have a reverence for the sacred, and their daily example will be one from which their students can profit.

Christian teachers will also be students who are continually growing in their own mental development. Their literary qualifications are no less important than those of their counterparts in the public sector. On the contrary, because they are inspired by broader goals and higher motives, they may even have gone beyond the average of their profession, and they will undoubtedly strive to move above the minimums established by accrediting agencies. Christian teachers will be individuals who are able both to view and to communicate the subject matter of their specialty in the context of the Christian world view. They will be individuals who are able to lead their students beyond the narrow realm of their field of study as they stimulate genuine thought concerning the relation of their academic specialty to the ultimate meaning of human existence. The literary and the mental are important even though they are not the most important qualifications for a Christian teacher.

A third area of development that should be looked for in Christian teachers is their social qualifications. The social relationships of Christ with His "pupils" in the gospels makes an interesting and profitable study. Christ did not seek to isolate Himself from those He was teaching. He mixed with them and engaged in their social events.

This social mixing is no less essential today. One of the most beneficial gifts teachers can offer their students is the gift of companionship in work and play. It is important to build relationships outside the classroom if teachers are to be successful inside of it. Personal relationships with students lead to understanding on the part of both parties.

Some of the social characteristics found in the life of Christ that are of special importance to teachers at all levels are tactfulness, patience, sympathy, insight into the problems of others, the ability to convey a sense of personal concern to them, ability to gain their respect and confidence, firmness when needed, flexibility, and impartiality. In the realm of social qualifications, teachers must be students of human nature—both their own and that of others.

A fourth sphere of teacher qualification is the physical. Christian teachers will be greatly benefited by good health, because their task is a trying one. Without a good physical constitution it is well-nigh impossible to maintain the sunny disposition and even temper that are a reflection of the image of Christ. Christian teachers should, therefore, be individuals who seek physical health and balance in their own lives through following the laws of health that God has built into the natural world and revealed in His Word.

That which Christian teachers are striving for in the continual improvement of their personal qualifications is the same as the goal that they are seeking for their students—a restoration of the image of God physically, mentally, spiritually, and socially. This balance, as it was found in the life of Christ, will form the base for their professional activity.

Teachers, whether in the home, church, or school, will find their task challenging, demanding, and rewarding. It is a very special work that takes extraordinary dedication for its successful accomplishment. From the Christian perspective, teaching might be viewed as the art of loving God's children.

CURRICULAR CONSIDERATIONS

What Knowledge Is of Most Worth?

One of the most enlightening and coherent essays ever published on the relationship of philosophic beliefs to the content of the curriculum was developed by Herbert Spencer in 1854. "What Knowledge Is of Most Worth?"[30] was both the title and the central question of his essay. To Spencer this was the "question of questions" in the realm of education. "Before there can be a rational *curriculum*, we must settle which things it most concerns us to know; . . . we must determine the relative value of knowledges."[31]

Spencer, in seeking to answer his question, classified the leading kinds of human activity in a hierarchical order based on their importance. He noted the following stratification in terms of descending consequence: (1) those activities relating directly to self-preservation, (2) those activities which indirectly minister to self-preservation, (3) those activities having to do with the rearing of offspring, (4) those activities pertaining to political and social relations, (5) those activities which make up the leisure part of life and are devoted to the tastes and appetites.[32]

His essay then proceeded to analyze human affairs from a naturalistic-evolutionary perspective, and it eventually provided an unequivocal reply to his leading question: "What knowledge is of most worth?—the uniform reply is—Science. This is the verdict on all the counts." Spencer's explanation of his answer relates Science (broadly conceived to include the social and practical sciences as well as the physical and life sciences) to his five-point hierarchy of life's most important activities.[33] His answer is built upon the principle that those activities that occupy the peripheral aspects of life should also occupy marginal places in the curriculum, while those activities which are most important in life should have the most important place in the course of studies.[34]

Biblically based Christians will of necessity reject Spencer's conclusions, which are built upon a naturalistic metaphysics and epistemology, but they must not fail to see the larger issue underlying his argument. It is crucial that Christians understand the rationale for the curriculum in their institutions of learning. Mark Van Doren noted that "the college is meaningless without a curriculum, but it is more so when it has one that is meaningless."[35]

The Christian educator must, with Spencer, settle the issue of "which things it most concerns us to know." The answer to that question, as Spencer noted, leads directly to an understanding of the relative values of knowledge in the curriculum. Christian educators can study Spencer's essay and the methodology included therein and gain some substantial insights into the important task of curriculum development in the light of a distinctive world view.

Authentic and viable curricula must be developed out of, and must be consistent with, their metaphysical and epistemological bases. It is therefore a foundational truth that different philosophic approaches will emphasize different curricula. One implication of that fact is that the curriculum of Christian schools will not be a readjustment or an adaptation of the secular curriculum of the larger society. Biblical Christianity is unique. Therefore the curricular stance of Christian education will be unique.

Another major issue in curriculum development is to find the pattern which holds the curriculum together. Alfred North Whitehead claimed that curricular programs generally suffer from the lack of an integrating principle.

> Instead of this single unity, we offer children—Algebra, from which nothing follows; Geometry, from which nothing follows; Science, from which nothing follows; History, from which nothing follows; a Couple of Languages, never mastered; and lastly, most dreary of all, Literature, represented by plays of Shakespeare, with philological notes and short analyses of plot and character to be in substance committed to memory. Can such a list be said to represent Life, as it is known in the midst of the living of it? The best that can be said of it is, that it is a rapid table of contents which a deity might run over in his mind while he was thinking of creating a world, and has not yet determined how to put it together.[36]

The crux of the problem has not been to realize the need for some overall pattern in which to fit the various subjects of the curriculum together in such a way that they make sense, but to discover that pattern. We live in a world that has fragmented knowledge to the extent that it is very difficult to see how our individual realms of expertise relate to the whole. It is in this context that C. P. Snow's "Two Cultures" takes on significance and meaning.[37]

Our world is one in which subject-area scholars have lost the ability to communicate with each other because they have lost the significance of their subject matter in relation to the whole of the truth. To complicate matters, we find the existentialists and postmodernists denying external meaning, and the analytic philosophers suggesting that since we can't discover meaning, we should continue to focus on defining our words and refining our syntax.

The search for meaning in the curriculum and in the total educational experience has been a major quest of the twentieth century. Some have seen the integrating center in the unity of the classics, while others have seen it in the needs of society, vocationalism, or science. None of these approaches, however, have been broad enough, and their claims have usually been divisive rather than unifying. We seem to live in a schizophrenic world in which many claim that there is no external meaning, while others base their scientific research on postulates which point to an overall meaning. Modern secular people have thrown out Christianity as a unifying force and have tended to concentrate on the parts of their knowledge rather than on the whole. As a result, intellectual fragmentation continues to be a large problem as individuals seek to determine what knowledge is of most worth.

For Christian educators the problem is quite different. They know what knowledge is of most worth, because they realize humanity's greatest needs. They know that the Bible is a cosmic revelation that transcends the limited realm of humanity, and that it not only reveals the human condition but also the remedy for that condition. They further realize that all subject matter becomes meaningful when seen in the light of the Bible. The problem for Christian educators has not been to find the pattern of knowledge in relation to its center; their problem has been to apply what they know.

All too often the curriculum of the Christian school has been "a patchwork of naturalistic ideas mixed with Biblical truth." This has led, claims Gaebelein, to a form of "scholastic schizophrenia in which a highly orthodox theology coexists uneasily with a teaching of non-religious subjects that differs little from that in secular institutions."[38] The challenge confronting the curriculum developer in a Christian school is to move beyond a curricular view focused on the bits and pieces, and to move into a position which clearly and purposefully integrates the details of knowledge into the biblical framework.

The Unity of Truth

A basic postulate underlying the Christian curriculum is that "all truth is God's truth."[39] From the biblical viewpoint, God is the Creator of everything. Therefore, truth in all fields stems from Him. Failing to see this point clearly has led many to develop a false dichotomy between the secular and the religious. That dichotomy implies that the religious has to do with God, while the secular is divorced from Him. From this point of view, the study of science, history, and mathematics is seen as basically secular, while the study of religion, church history, and ethics is viewed as religious.

That is not the biblical perspective. In the Bible, God is seen as the Creator of the objects and patterns of science and math and the Director of historical events. In essence, there is no such thing as "secular" aspects of the curriculum. John Henry Newman pointed to this truth when he wrote that "it is easy enough" on the level of thought "to divide Knowledge into human and divine, secular and religious, and to lay down that we will address ourselves to the one without interfering with the other; but it is impossible in fact."[40]

All truth in the Christian curriculum, whether it deals with nature, humanity, society, or the arts, must be seen in proper relationship to Jesus Christ as Creator and Redeemer. It is true that all truth is not treated in the scriptures. For example, nuclear physics is not explained in the Bible. That, however, does not mean that nuclear physics is not connected with God's natural laws[41] and that it does not have moral and ethical implications as its applications affect the lives of people. Christ was the Creator of all things—not just those things people have chosen to call religious (John 1:1-3; Col 1:16).

All truth, if it be truth indeed, is God's truth, no matter where it is found. As a result, the curriculum of the Christian school must be seen as a unified whole, rather than as a fragmented and rather loosely connected "gang" of topics. Once this viewpoint is recognized, education will have taken a major step forward in its aim of creating an atmosphere in which the "Christian mind" can develop—an educational context in which young people can be taught to think "Christianly" about every aspect of reality.[42]

The Strategic Role of the Bible
in the Curriculum

A second postulate follows that of the unity of all truth: the Bible is the foundational and contextual document for all curricular items in the Christian school. This postulate is a natural outcome of a bibliocentric, revelational epistemology. Just as special revelation forms the basis of epistemological authority, so it must also be the foundation of the curriculum. Our discussion of epistemology noted that the Bible is not an exhaustive source of truth. Much truth exists outside of the Bible, but it is important to note that no truth exists outside the metaphysical framework of the Bible. "The teaching authority of Scripture," writes Arthur Holmes, "commits the believer at certain focal points and so provides an interpretive framework, an overall glimpse of how everything relates to God."[43]

Special revelation is not the whole of knowledge, but it cannot be too firmly emphasized that it does provide the pattern for all truth. Truth is not in conflict, even though it may appear to be so, given the present incomplete state of human knowledge. The Bible provides a frame of reference within which individuals may guide and correct their judgments. Revelation, seen from this perspective, does not rule out reason and human understanding. Its function is to guide and give purpose, meaning, and direction to human activity and thought.

For Christianity, the Bible is both foundational and contextual. It provides a pattern for thinking in all areas. This line of thought has led many Christian educators to see the Bible as the integrating point at which all knowledge comes together for a contextual interpretation. The Bible is the focus of integration for all knowledge, because it provides a unifying perspective that comes from God, the source of all truth.

It will come as no surprise to those familiar with Christian education that the Bible often has not been used to its fullest potential in the Christian curriculum. The Bible has most often been seen as the source for a set of curricular constituents that we find grouped in the "Department of Religion" and as a guidebook for certain aspects of student conduct. The curricular model for such an approach looks something like Figure 6.

In this model, Bible study or religion is seen as one topic among many—an important topic, to be sure, but basically one among several. The model, furthermore, is built upon the widely accepted division between the religious and the secular. At best, the Bible may be seen in this model as the "first among equals." At worst, we may have what Gordon Clark referred to as a "pagan education with a chocolate coating of Christianity."[44] It was with this basic model in mind that Gaebelein noted that there is

> a vast difference between education in which devotional exercises and the study of Scripture have a place, and education in which the Christianity of the Bible is the matrix of the whole program or, to change the figure, the bed in which the river of teaching and learning flows.[45]

In an attempt to correct the above problem, some Christian educators have gone to the other extreme and developed a model which is illustrated in Figure 7. This model seeks to make the Bible into the whole, and, as a result, also misses the mark, since the Bible never claims to be an exhaustive source of truth. It sets the framework for the study of history and science and touches upon those topics, but it is not a "textbook" in all areas that students need to understand. It is a "textbook" in the science of salvation and an enlightener concerning the abnormality of our present world, but it never makes the claim of being a sufficient authority in all areas of possible truth.

A third model might be developed as shown in Figure 8. This model implies that the Bible and its world view provide a foundation

Figure 6. Curriculum Model: Self-contained Subject Matter Areas

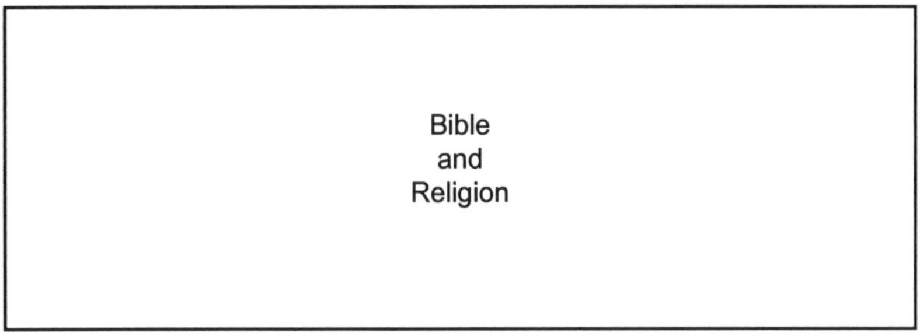

```
                    Bible
                    and
                    Religion
```

Figure 7. Curriculum Model: The Bible as the Whole

and a context for all human knowledge, and that its overall meaning enters into every area of the curriculum and adds significance to each topic. This is in line with what Richard Edlin helpfully refers to as the *"permeative* function of the Bible." "The Bible," he notes, "is not frosting on an otherwise unaltered humanist cake. It needs to be the leaven in the educational loaf, shaping the entire curriculum from its base up as it permeates the whole school program."[46] Figure 8 sets forth an integration model; it indicates that we must approach every subject in the light of the biblical perspective if we are to understand it in its fullest meaning.

The broken lines in Figure 8 signify that there are no hard and fast divisions between the various subjects, let alone a false dichotomy between the sacred and the secular. The two-headed arrows indicate not only the fact that the Bible helps us understand every topic in the curriculum, but also that the study of history, science, and so on also

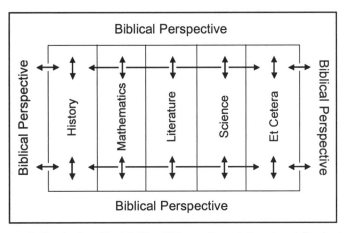

Figure 8. Curriculum Model: The Bible as Foundational and Contextual

sheds light on the meaning of scripture. God has revealed Himself through the Bible in a special revelation and through the world of nature in a general revelation. We can grasp the significance of the latter only in the light of the former, but both shed light on each other, since all truth has its origin in God. Every topic in the curriculum impacts upon every other, and all become the most meaningful when integrated within the biblical context.

An Illustration of the Role of the Bible in the Curriculum

Perhaps at this point we should take a look at the integration of a so-called "secular" aspect of the curriculum with the biblical perspective. One of the areas that most easily lends itself to such an analysis is that of literature. The study of literature holds a crucial position in all school systems, because literature faces and seeks to answer people's greatest questions; reveals humanity's basic desires, wishes, and frustrations; and develops insight into the human experience. Beyond aesthetic sensitivity, the study of literature leads to inductive insights in such areas as psychology, philosophy, history, and sociology; and it provides data on such topics as human nature, sin, and the meaning and purpose of human existence.

The impact of literary study is all the more powerful because it is delivered in a package with which we emotionally identify—that is, it reaches us at the affective and cognitive levels simultaneously. In the fullest sense of the words, literary content is philosophical and religious because it deals with philosophical and religious issues, problems, and answers. Literary study, therefore, holds a position of centrality in curricular structures, and it is perhaps one of the most powerful educational tools for the teaching of religious values.

Because of the overlap of literature and religion, literary study presents itself as a good example for the integration of Christian thought and a traditional subject in the curriculum. A major question in literary study in Christian schools is "What type of literature should we study?" The central issue at this point does not seem to be whether a particular selection is true or fictional in the sense of whether it actually took place in an individual's space-time existence. There are many true events which are written in such a way that their study leads to degradation; and, on the other hand, Jesus at times used fictional events to express a spiritual lesson (e.g., Luke 16:19-31). The criteria of selection seems to revolve more around the interpretive framework in which a literary piece is studied. At this point someone is apt to put forth Philippians 4:8 as a criterion for the study of literature.

> Finally, brethren, whatever is true, whatever is honorable, whatever is just, whatever is pure, whatever is lovely, whatever is gracious, if there is any excellence, if there is anything worthy of praise, think about these things.

The natural rejoinder to a shallow usage of this text is to ask, "What does the Bible mean by 'true,' 'honorable,' 'just,' 'pure,' 'lovely,' 'gracious,' 'excellent,' and 'worthy of praise?'" For example, what is to be done with certain parts of the Old Testament that bring out stories that are sordid in the extreme and that add details about sin that do not seem to be necessary for the understanding of the story?

A case in point is Judges 19-21, which is filled with the evil story of the basest passions of humanity in terms of sexual immorality and mass murder. Or what can be said of the story of David and Bathsheba, or of the genealogy of Matthew 1, which lists only four women—three with very sinful backgrounds and one who merely happened to be a Gentile? Why select Tamar, Rahab, and Bathsheba instead of the many virtuous female ancestors of the Lord? It is furthermore interesting to note that Bathsheba is not even named in Matthew 1. Rather, she is referred to as the wife of Uriah the Hittite. By that one seemingly unnecessary stroke, Matthew not only uplifts the whole story of adultery but also that of murder.

It might be asked, since the Bible is our literary pattern, why such sinful stories were included and at times emphasized. The answer seems to lie in the fact that the Bible always places such stories in an interpretive framework that gives insight into human nature, the results of sin, and the struggle between the forces of good and evil. Such stories are often used to show, first, the degradation that stems from sinful lives, and, second, God's willingness and ability to save. It is with this in mind that it is written, after the genealogy of Matthew 1, that Jesus came to save His people from their sins (Matt 1:21). This text is the keynote of the Gospel of Matthew, and it sets forth God's ability to save in terms of who "His people" are—Rahab, Tamar, the wife of Uriah the Hittite, and Ruth the Moabitess. God can save murderers, adulterers, prostitutes, and Gentiles through Christ—He can save to the uttermost.

In a similar manner, the Bible does not present the story of the multiple sin of David and Bathsheba to fascinate the sinful mind. Rather, it couches the story in the tragic results of the influence of that sin in the lives and deaths of David's children and the events that eventually led to David's repentance (2 Sam 11:1-18:33), his penentential prayer (Ps 51), and God's saving power.

Along that same line, the story of Judges 19-21 provides insight into the nature of sinful humanity left on its own. The major lesson of the book of Judges is that people are not naturally good, and that life would soon degenerate to a chaotic existence without the leadership of the divinely appointed institution of government (Judges 21:25).

It is the responsibility of the literature teacher in a Christian school to help the young learn to read critically, so that they can perceive the meaning of what they read in terms of the great controversy between the forces of good and evil.[47] Literary study is not merely a relaxing diversion into the realm of art. T. S. Eliot observed that what we read affects "the whole of what we are. . . . Though we may read literature merely for pleasure, of 'entertainment' or of 'aesthetic enjoyment,' this reading never affects simply a sort of special sense: it affects our moral and religious existence."[48]

There is no such thing as artistic neutrality. Those items in life which may appear to be neutral are in effect harmful in the sense that their impact is diversionary and they lead us away from the great axiological issues of life in the conflict between Christ and Satan. Anything that keeps us from facing the problem of our condition before God and from confronting ourselves in the light of Christ as Saviour is a tactical victory for the forces of evil. The function of literary study in a Christian school is not to help us become "learned" in the great writers of the past and present, but to help us through some of their writings to view the issues at stake in the great controversy with more clarity and sensitivity.

For Christian educators the question is not a matter of how close we can come to what might be defined as objectionable, but rather how to select the very best literature to accomplish the aim of our schools (restoring the image of God in our students) in the light of our metaphysical, epistemological, and axiological foundation.

In summary, there are at least two basic points of responsibility in the presentation and study of literature in the Christian school—selection and interpretation. Both of these are important as we seek to integrate the religious viewpoint with a particular aspect of the curriculum.

The interpretive function of literary study has traditionally been approached in two different ways, which may be illustrated by drawings A and B in Figure 9. Drawing A represents a classroom approach in which the major emphasis is on the literary qualities of the material, and in which the Bible or ideas from the Bible may be used from time to time as asides. From this point of view, literature may be studied largely as it is in non-Christian institutions, with the biblical insight as an added enrichment.

Drawing B, on the other hand, represents the study of literature in the context of the biblical perspective and what the message means in terms of humanity's universal and personal dilemma. As such, it views literature from the distinctive vantage point of Christianity, including the context of the abnormality of the present world and God's activity in that world. From this position, the study of literature in a Christian institution can be richer than similar study in non-Christian institutions, since non-Christians are handicapped by a lack of the all-important (in terms of insight and interpretation) biblical view of sin and salvation. This does not mean that such literary elements as plot and style are unimportant, but rather that they are not, within the context of Christianity, the most important aspects of literary study.

In retrospect, it appears that what Philippians 4:8 means by such adjectives as "good," "true," and "honest"—in the context of the Bible

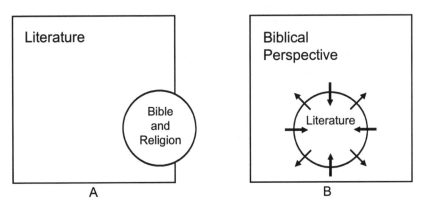

Figure 9. The Contextual Role of the Biblical Perspective

as literature—is that the problems of humanity are put in the context of the great controversy as it is revealed by God. It was noted in the study of Christian aesthetics that the extremes that ignore evil at one end of the spectrum and glorify evil at the other are neither true nor honest, and they certainly leave no room for a viable concept of justice. The challenge for the Christian teacher is to approach literary study in such a way that it leads the youth to see human reality and the world as it actually is—sinful and suffering, but not beyond hope and the redeeming grace of a caring God.

Christian education must help students move beyond the story to the meaning of its insights for daily life. The function of literary study in a Christian institution, writes Virginia Graybill, is to aid students in learning how to "think" about the issues of life—their identity and purpose, the presence of good and evil, justice and forgiveness, the beautiful and the ugly, sexuality and spirituality, ambition and humility, joy and suffering, purity and guilt, and so on.[49]

C. S. Lewis made a similar point when he wrote that "one of the minor rewards of conversion is to be able at last to see the real point of all the literature we were brought up to read with the point left out."[50] The essential thing in literary study is not the passing on of a body of knowledge, but the development of a skill—the ability to think critically and to interpret literary insights within the biblical world view.

Christianity and the Radical
Reorientation of the Curriculum

We have spent considerable time discussing the integration of literary study in the Christian curriculum in order to give some insight into what is meant when we state that in the Christian curriculum the Bible is both foundational and contextual. We might take any other topic in the curriculum and perform the same task.

The point that the Christian educator must grasp is that *the teaching of any topic in a Christian school is not a modification of the approach used in non-Christian schools. It is rather a radical reorientation of that topic within the philosophical framework of Christianity.* Therefore, history in the Christian school is viewed in the light of the biblical message as God seeks to work out His purposes in human affairs as events move toward their prophetic end. The Bible is seen as providing the interpretive framework for events between the Fall of Adam and the second coming of Jesus. The Bible is not treated as a comprehensive history, but it is seen as an account that centers on the history of salvation. There are also points of intersection between general history and the Bible in terms of prophecy and archaeology. The Christian historian realizes, however, that the specific points of intersection are in the minority, and that the major function of the Bible in history teaching is to provide a context for understanding.

The same might be said of the life, physical, and social sciences, or physical education, or agriculture in the curriculum of a Christian school. The Bible provides the framework of a troubled world, while the disciplines bring forth the bits and pieces. The Bible provides the pattern which gives interpretive meaning to the otherwise meaningless details uncovered by the scholar. It is from this perspective that the Bible is seen as the focal point of integration for all of our knowledges.

Gaebelein, in discussing the topic of developing correlations between Christian concepts and the subject matter of the various fields of study, points out that there are some necessary cautions in curricular integration. A major pitfall, as he sees it, is the danger

> of a false integration through forced correlations that are not truly indigenous to the subject in question. Such lugging in of stilted correlations, even though motivated by Christian zeal, is liable to do more harm than good through giving the impression that integration of specific subjects with God's truth is a put-up job.
>
> What may be needed is a more relaxed attack upon the problem and a clearer realization of the limits under which we are working. Here a suggestion of Emil Brunner is useful. Speaking of the distortion brought into our thinking through sin, he sees it at its greatest in such areas as theology, philosophy, and literature, because these are nearest man's relation to God and have thus been most radically altered through the fall. They therefore stand most in need of correction, and in them correlation with Christianity is at its highest. But as we move from the humanities to the sciences and mathematics, the disturbance through sin diminishes almost to the vanishing point. Thus the Christian teacher of the more objective subjects, mathematics in particular, ought not to seek for the detailed and systematic correlations that his colleagues in psychology, literature, or history might validly make.[51]

Gaebelein does not mean that there are no points of contact between a topic such as mathematics and Christianity, but rather that they are fewer.[52] Christian teachers will utilize these points, but they will not seek to force integration in an unnatural manner.

From one point of view, the integration of mathematics and the physical sciences with Christian belief is even more important than the integration of literature and the social sciences with Christianity. This aspect of curricular integration is important because of the uncritical understanding many students bring to these fields that implies that they are "objective," neutral, and functional and have no philosophical presuppositions, biases about reality, or cosmological implications. On the contrary, the study of mathematics and the "hard" sciences is totally embedded in bias and assumption.

Mathematics, for example, like Christianity, is built upon unprovable postulates. Beyond this, assumptions such as the orderliness of the universe and the validity of empirical observation are metaphysical and epistemological presuppositions that undergird science but are rejected by many modern people in both Western and Eastern cultures. It is essential that these assumptions be made evident to students because they are often taken as facts and are "invisible" to the average student who has been raised in an age that has placed its uncritical faith in science and mathematics rather than in the Creator of scientific and mathematical reality. This integration is most natural at the elementary, secondary, and introductory college levels, since courses at these levels provide the intellectual context for such advanced courses as theoretical mechanics and advanced calculus.

Christian math and science teachers will also creatively utilize the natural points of integration between their subject matter and their religion. Mathematics, for example, certainly has contact points with the Christian faith when it deals with such areas as infinity and the existence of number in other parts of daily life, from music to crystallography and astronomy. The world of mathematical precision is God's world, and mathematics is not outside the pattern of God's truth.[53]

The Balanced Curriculum

Beyond the realm of specific subject matter integration in the Christian school is the larger issue of the integration of the curricular program in a manner that provides balance for the development of the various aspects of students as they are being restored to their original position as beings created in the image and likeness of God. In the section on the nature of the student we noted that humanity at the Fall, to a large extent, experienced a fracturing of that image. It was fractured spiritually, socially, mentally, and physically. We also saw that education is basically an agent of redemption and restoration as God seeks to use human teachers to restore fallen individuals to their original estate.

The curriculum must, therefore, bring in an integrated balance that will facilitate that restoration. It cannot focus merely on the mental or any other part. It must develop the whole person. As a result, the physical, social, and spiritual must be considered as well as the mental aspect of each student. In Christian schools the spiritual and social have generally received development as well as the mental. Unfortunately, however, the physical has more often been neglected.

A neglect of balance between physical and mental development finds its roots deep in the history of the past—particularly in Greek idealism. Greek philosophic thought not only brought to the Western educational world an anti-physical bias, but also a bias against the recognition of useful vocations as valid educational endeavors. In the early centuries of the Christian church there was an amalgamation of Greek thought and Christianity with some very non-Christian results that have become traditional in Western education.

The biblical position is not anti-vocational. Jesus was educated as a carpenter, and the wealthy Saul (Paul) acquired the art of tent making, even though in his early life it appeared that he would not have to rely upon his trade for a living. Likewise, the Bible is not anti-physical. God created the physical world and claimed it was "very good" (Gen 1:31). In neither testament is there a straining to separate soul and body. On the other hand, both set forth the concept of bodily resurrection (Dan 12:2; 1 Thess 4:13-18). Paul notes definitely that the body is indeed the temple of God and that what people do with their bodies should glorify their Maker (1 Cor 6:19, 20; 10:31).

If individuals are to be restored to their wholeness, Christian education cannot neglect the balance between the physical and mental. Modern science has shed much light on this issue. The condition of the physical body is important to young Christians, because it is the body that houses the brain, and it is with their brains that they make responsible spiritual decisions. Whatever affects one part of a person affects the total being. Individuals are wholistic units, and the curriculum of the Christian school must meet all their needs if they are to have wholeness and operate at their peak of efficiency. As a part of this balanced wholeness, Christian education must fulfill its role in the vocational development of every person.

The Informal and Null Curricula

The educational experience of the Christian school is obviously wider than the subject matter developed in the formal curriculum and taught by teachers in the classroom. The school also has an informal curriculum with a significant impact. This informal curriculum is sometimes referred to as the extracurricular program. Falling within the informal area are a multiplicity of organizations and activities, such as clubs, musical groups, athletics, work experiences, school publications, and so on. These informal curricular aspects of the Christian school must be brought into harmony with the purposes of the institution and integrated with the Christian message, just as is the formal curriculum, if the school is not to give a dichotomous message to its students, constituency, and onlookers.

Just as all activities in the Christian life fall under the reign of Christian principles, so must every aspect of Christian education be in harmony with the biblical message. There is no time when Christians can be, or even want to be, set free from the obligations of the law of love and the reign of Christ in their lives. They never come to the place where they can say: "I have fulfilled my quota of Christianity for the week; now I can relax and be my natural self." Christianity postulates the entire possession of the individual by the Holy Spirit. In the Christian educational system, likewise, Christ is ever to be in control, and the principles of the Bible are integrated into every activity, so that the result is uplifting, restorative, and re-creative.

The Christian school has two major tasks in regard to the informal curriculum—the selection of activities and the creation of guidelines for the implementation of the activities selected. The problem of selection is basic in Christian education. There are undoubtedly activities that are appropriate for public schools that are out of place in a Christian institution.

The selection principles for Christian extracurricular programs are found in the scriptures. One such principle has been enunciated by the Apostle Paul: "Whatever you do, in word or deed, do everything in the name of the Lord Jesus, giving thanks to God the Father through him" (Col 3:17). This rule is quite general. It allows everything that is wholesome, and rules out only those things that cannot be pursued to the glory of Christ and with thanksgiving to God.[54] Gaebelein noted that the validity and universality of the Bible as a guide in the area of extracurricular Christian activities are enhanced by the fact that it gives principles of selection rather than hidebound rules.

> It is because it is a book that gives principles rather than lists of "borderline" practices that the Bible never wears out. To be sure, it speaks in no uncertain tones against downright sins, but in respect to doubtful questions, things that are permissible in one time or place and not sanctioned in another, it sets down no rigid rules but rather gives abiding principles. The fourteenth chapter of Romans well illustrates this point.[55]

In the realm of the informal curriculum, the task of both faculty and student body is to search the scriptures sincerely and responsibly for those principles that give guidance and then to apply those principles to both the selection and implementation of all programs and activities in the Christian school. Such an approach will enrich the informal curriculum and, in turn, enhance our individual lives and schools as we move closer to an attitude and practice of integrating all that we do with the message of salvation.

From the Christian viewpoint, we must realize that there is nothing neutral in our activity program. All our activities are either re-creative and restorative or diversionary and destructive. The Bible is the primary criterion to help us make wise decisions in all aspects of Christian education. The question should not be, "Is this or that activity wrong?" but "What is the effect of this activity on Christian character? Will it lead its participants to be more sharing, polite, helpful, and generous to others, or will it lead them to be more self-centered and contentious? Will it lead to a better relationship with God, other people, our selves, and our environment, or will it promote a deterioration of relationships? Will it contribute to social, mental, physical, and spiritual balance in the re-creative process, or will it encourage its participants to become one-sided and overdeveloped in one area?" These and other questions are central as we evaluate both the formal and informal curricular aspects of the Christian school and the Christian life.

Beyond the formal and informal aspects of the curriculum are what Robert Pazmiño and Maria Harris call the null curriculum. As Harris sees it, the null curriculum is "what is left out" of a school program. It is important, she holds, because the

> ignorance or the absence of something is not neutral. It skews the balance of options we might consider, alternatives from which we might choose, or perspectives that help us see. The null curriculum includes areas left out (content, themes, points of view) and procedures left unused (the arts, play, critical analysis). The implicit [informal] curriculum, in contrast, does not leave out areas and procedures. It simply does not call them to attention. They are there, operative in the situation but left unnoticed.[56]

The null curriculum is important because it contributes its effect to the total educational program. What is left out or avoided and the significance of that absence need to be understood by educators in relation to both their aims and their total philosophy of education. Everything in a Christian educational program should be done for justifiable reasons.

A Note on Values Education

Earlier in this chapter we spent a great deal of time on explicitly discussing the cognitive aspects of the curriculum. Even though the affective realm of values was implicit in that discussion and undergirded it, it is important to bring the issue of values and moral education to the forefront of our thinking. After all, the entire educational experience is value laden. As Arthur Holmes puts it, "education has to do with the transmission of values."[57]

Whereas Holmes's insight should be obvious to Christians, all too often it is not. The positivist culture that has done so much to shape twentieth-century thinking has set forth the idea that education is value free. Building upon the positivist platform, the advocates of the values clarification movement relativized values while such theorists as Lawrence Kohlberg humanized them. The upshot has been an ethical relativism that goes against the very core of biblical teaching.

When modern culture lost the concept of the God who is "out

there," it also lost the idea that there are universal values "out there" that apply across time, individuals, and cultures. Ronald Nash is correct when he asserts that "America's educational crisis is not exclusively a crisis of the mind," but also a crisis of the "heart," a values crisis.[58]

Christian educators must constantly keep in mind both the crucial nature of values education and the atmosphere of ethical relativism in which their schools exist at the beginning of the twenty-first century. It would be bad enough if students were faced merely with the so-called neutral value concepts of the values clarifiers, but beyond that they are daily confronted by the mass media which all too often has a value message that moves beyond neutrality to being non-Christian and even anti-Christian.

Christian educators don't stand alone in seeing the need to emphasize values. For example, many critical pedagogists, following the lead of Paulo Freire, uplift the need for both critical reflection upon values and acting upon the implications of those reflections. But Christian educators operating within the biblical framework have a strategic advantage over those with a humanistic orientation in the sense that they have an epistemological and metaphysical grounding for their value system that is not available to others. As Pazmiño puts it,

> the Christian educator can propose higher values because he or she can answer such questions as: What are persons and their ultimate end? What is the meaning and purpose of human activity? What, or rather, who is God? These questions can be answered with a certainty and surety which is not possible outside of a revealed faith.[59]

Pazmiño also points out the existence of a hierarchy of values, with spiritual values providing the context for valuing options in such areas as ethics, aesthetics, and the scientific, political, and technical realms.[60] That being the case, Christian educators must purposefully develop formal and informal curricula in the light of biblical values. The biblical value system stands at the very heart of Christian education.

The values taught in a biblically-based school system will not relate exclusively to individual valuing but will also reflect upon the social whole. At times Christian schools will critically examine such issues as the way government uses power, the self-interest motivation of big business and labor, and the plight of the poor. In line with the Old Testament prophets, Christian education will raise significant issues related to social justice in an unjust world because biblical valuing is concerned with the public as well as the private world of believers.[61]

Maintaining a Christian Focus

If any activity in the Christian school comes to the place where it holds the center stage instead of Christ, we may be sure, according to both the first great commandment and the Ten Commandments (Matt 22:37; Exod 20:3), that we have lost our Christian perspective. Paul noted that there are things that are lawful but not helpful for Christian growth (1 Cor 10:23). It is possible for a Christian institution, in either its formal or informal curriculum, to develop problems as it loses the focus of its integration.

Francis Schaeffer noted this issue in terms of the individual life, but the principle also extends to Christian schools and colleges.

> There are many points of false peace and integration, and it is well to recognize them. Entertainment is one. Do we understand that even right entertainment can be the wrong integration point and be just as wicked and just as destructive as wrong entertainment if I put it in the place of God? There is nothing wrong with sport. Many sports are beautiful, but if sport becomes my integration point and my whole life turns upon knocking one second off my time on a downhill race, I am destroyed.[62]

He goes on to remark that intellectual pursuits also offer false integration points. Even the search for correct doctrine and a unified theology can become a game that shuts us away from God.[63] The only integration point for the Christian individual and the Christian school is Jesus Christ.

As we view the Christian curriculum in all of its complexity, we must never forget the great controversy between the forces of good and powers of evil within our epistemology, metaphysics, axiology, and our individual lives. This conflict between Christ and Satan is also evident in the curriculum. The Christian school is, in one sense, a battlefield in which the forces of Christ are being challenged by the legions of Satan. The outcome will, to a large extent, be determined by the position that the Bible holds in the Christian school. If our schools are to be truly Christian, then the biblical perspective must be the foundation and context of all that is done.

METHODOLOGICAL CONSIDERATIONS

A major determinant of the teaching and learning methodologies of any philosophy of education is the goals of that philosophy and the epistemological-metaphysical framework in which those goals are couched. The first part of this study noted that some of the traditional philosophies of education put reading, lecturing, and other forms of symbolic manipulation at the center of methodology, since their goal was to transfer cognitive knowledge. On the other hand, the more modern philosophies of education emphasize experiential methodologies, which allow students to obtain firsthand information in regard to both themselves and their environment through personal experience.

The goals of Christian education go beyond the accumulation of cognitive knowledge, self-awareness, and coping successfully with the environment. To be sure, Christian education includes those aspects of learning, but beyond that it has the more far-reaching goals of reconciling fallen individuals to God and one another and restoring the image of God in them. The methodologies utilized by the Christian educator must take those preeminent purposes into consideration.

That does not mean that somehow Christian teachers will come up with unique and original ways of teaching in the same sense that Christianity is a unique religion and Christ is a unique person. Obviously, Christian educators will use many, if not all, of the same methods as other teachers. They will, however, select and emphasize those methodologies that best aid them in helping their students to develop Christlike characters.

Education, Thinking, and Self-control

Central to the issue of the development of Christian character is the realization that human beings are not simply highly developed animals that operate merely on the reflexive level and are determined by environmental stimuli.[64] The biblical picture is that humans were created in the image of God and have, even in their fallen state, the ability to think reflectively.

Because humans can think reflectively, they can make meaningful decisions in regard to their own courses of action and destinies. Students in the Christian school must be educated to think for themselves rather than merely be trained to respond to environmental cues. As was explained in the first section of this book, animals are trained, while human beings created in God's image are educated. It is true that there are some training aspects in the human learning process. Those training phases, however, generally take place when the person is very young or mentally impaired. The ideal is to move as rapidly as possible, with any given student, from the training process to the more reflective educative process.

The essence of Christian education is to enable students to think and act reflectively for themselves, rather than just to respond to the word or will of an authority figure. This is necessary in terms of both mental and ethical development. Self-control, rather than externally imposed control, is central in Christian education and discipline. Individuals must be brought to the place where they can make their own decisions and be responsible for those decisions without continually being coaxed, directed, and/or forced by a powerful authority. When this goal is achieved, and the power to think and act upon that thought is internalized, then individuals have reached moral maturity. They are not under the control of another, but are making their own moral decisions toward both God and other people.

If the aim of Christian education is the restoration of the image of God in fallen humanity, then the aim of Christian discipline—both in mind and conduct—is self-control rather than control by others. God is not seeking the development of automatons, anymore than He Himself is an automaton. He is rather seeking the development of human beings who can relate to Him because they see the beauty of His way and have therefore consciously chosen to unite their wills with His will. They have experienced the world, have reasoned from cause to effect in regard to the direction of their lives, and have consciously chosen to respond to His love.

One possible model that can be used to illustrate the relation of external manipulation to internal control is shown in Figure 10. This model[65] illustrates in a general way the relationship between internal and external control and the weaning process that is a goal of Christian education. Self-control is the goal to be reached, so that when young people leave the mediatorial guidance of parents and teachers, they will be able to live the Christian life because they have internalized the principles, relationships, and values of Christianity.

This discussion of self control as it relates to the restoration of the image of God has serious implications for the selection of appropriate

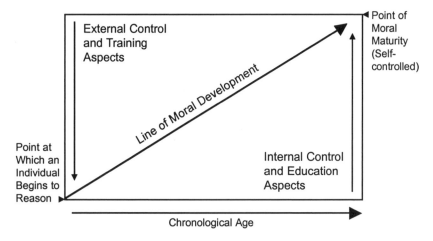

Figure 10. A Developmental Model of Discipline

methodologies for the Christian school. This concept should act as a screening device for Christian teachers as they select learning and teaching strategies for their classrooms. They obviously want to utilize those methodologies that will forward the ends of Christian education as they seek to develop what Harro Van Brummelen refers to as *"responsible* disciples."[66]

Beyond Cognition to Commitment and Responsible Action

Closely related to the above discussion is the fact that Christian knowing is not merely passive. We noted in our discussion of epistemology that Christian knowing is an active, dynamic experience. Thus, instructional methodology in a Christian context must move beyond strategies for passing on information. Nicholas Wolterstorff forcefully argues that Christian education "must aim at producing alterations in what students tend (are disposed, are inclined) to do. It must aim at tendency learning." He points out that Christian schools must move beyond techniques for merely teaching the knowledge and abilities required for acting responsibly, since students can assimilate those entities without developing a "tendency to engage in such action." Thus "a program of Christian education will take that further step of cultivating the appropriate *tendencies* in the child. It will have tendency learning as one of its fundamental goals."[67]

Donald Oppewal has set forth a teaching methodology explicitly based upon the dynamic epistemology of scripture. While noting that actual practice is the ideal, Oppewal suggests a three-stage instructional methodology aimed at a dynamic learning experience. In the *consider* stage the learner is presented with the new material. During the second phase—the *choose* phase—"the options for response are clarified and their implications better understood. . . . If the first phase dramatizes what it *is* that the learner faces, the second phase highlights whatever *oughts* are involved." In the third stage—the *commit* phase— students move "beyond intellectual understanding, beyond exposure of the moral and other considerations, and toward commitment to act on both the is and the ought." Commitment to a form of action, claims Oppewal, is the very minimum that can be aimed at in the context of biblical knowing and teaching.[68] Actual opportunity for acting on those commitments, whenever possible, is also fundamental to a Christian approach to instruction.

The Bible and Instructional Methodology

Beyond these considerations, the central epistemological source for the Christian, the Bible, provides a wealth of information in both the Old and New Testaments in regard to methodologies used by the Lord in the process of education. Even a casual reading of the Old Testament reveals that ancient Israel was immersed in a total educational environment that was consciously constructed to aid in the spiritual, intellectual, social, and physical development of its citizens. It was an educational environment that was structured to provide lifelong learning experiences from birth to death through holidays, sabbatical years, worship, historic memorials, the arts, home instruction, public and private reading of the Torah, and a host of other devices.

The Bible makes it plain that this educational environment was to be used in such a way as to awaken inquiry and develop curiosity in the minds of the young. The interest developed was to be followed by deliberate instruction. Note, for example, the instructions given for the highly symbolic keeping of the Passover. Moses wrote that this service would lead the young to ask, "What do you mean by this service?" and that the family elders would then have a natural opportunity to engage the minds of the youth in a meaningful learning experience (Exod 12:25-27; see also Exod 13:3-16; Deut 6:20-25).

A major principle underlying Old Testament pedagogy is that instruction should not be forced upon unready minds. Rather, the Old Testament illustrates instructional methods whereby the natural interest in a topic was capitalized upon so that minds could be engaged in a dynamic interchange. Central to the whole educational complex of ancient Israel was the sacrificial system, which pointed forward to the life, death, and work of Jesus. This system, with its pagentry, beauty, and life-taking awesomeness, stood as one of the major object lessons of the ancient world. It was undoubtedly an educational device that taught through both the senses and the curiosity it generated.

Methods Used by Jesus

At the center of learning and teaching methodology in the New Testament is the educational work of Jesus. We can learn a great deal about appropriate methods for conveying the Christian message, both in and out of schools, through an examination of the specific techniques of teaching He used and how He related to people. This short discussion, at best, is a mere introduction to the methods of Jesus. The Christian educator can learn much through an inductive and analytical study of His methods in the gospels.

Roy Zuck has noted that "Jesus succeeded as a masterful Teacher" largely because of "his remarkable ability to capture the interest of his audience." He aroused "their desire to learn what he was teaching."[69] That was especially true in His use of parables, object lessons, and provocative questions.

Perhaps the most obvious teaching method of Jesus was His use of illustrations. Two of His most frequent illustrative formats were the parable and the object lesson. Parables form a large portion of the teachings of Jesus recorded in the New Testament—about 25 percent of the words recorded by Mark and 50 percent reported by Luke are in the form of parables. The parable has the advantage of being concrete, appealing to the imagination, and having intrinsic interest. John Price has written that "people who turn away from facts and arguments will listen readily to stories. Not only that, but they will remember them and be influenced by them."[70]

Part of the power of Christ's parables is that they were drawn from the experiences of the everyday life of His hearers. When He dealt with the lost sheep, the sowing of the seeds, and the good Samaritan

(Luke 10:25-37), He was touching the people where they were in their daily experience. This aroused their interest, engaged their minds, and helped them remember the story and its lesson as they interacted with the subjects of His parables in their daily business.

Jesus was one of the world's master storytellers. His parables not only taught didactic lessons, but they were devices that allowed His hearers to inductively draw out their own conclusions. For example, the parable of the good Samaritan (Luke 10:25-37) was given in response to a question concerning the identification of one's neighbor. Christ told the story and let His "student" draw out the lesson. Parables, as used by Jesus, stimulated the process of active thought among His hearers.

A second illustrative method used by Jesus was the object lesson. One can imagine Him standing on the hillside as He talked on the topic of anxiety. While talking, He reached down and plucked a lily, noted its beauty, and gave the lesson that if God so clothed "the grass of the field, which today is alive and tomorrow is thrown into the oven, will he not much more clothe you . . ." (Matt 6:30). Certainly His use of the coin in His discussion with the scribes and Pharisees in regard to the paying of taxes made His accompanying words more effective (Matt 22:15-22).

Another teaching method used repeatedly by Jesus was that of thought-compelling questions. A study of the gospels reveals that Jesus used two hundred and thirteen separate questions, after duplication has been accounted for.[71] This number is remarkable when we consider how few of His words have been preserved. He used questions to drive home spiritual truths, to draw out responses of commitment, and to combat His detractors. His use of questions, therefore, can be seen by the classroom teacher as teaching devices, counseling techniques, and instruments to help maintain classroom control.

Regarding that last point, we teachers at times have students who would like to put us "on the spot." Jesus faced the same problem, and He often answered His detractors' questions by asking questions. By that strategy He was able to maneuver them into the place where they answered their own questions. His success in the disciplinary use of questions can be seen from the fact that the gospels record, at the close of a series of questions engineered to trap Him, that "after that no one dared to ask him any question" (Mark 12:34).

In regard to the use of questions as a learning device, John A.

Marquis has written that "teaching is not telling, because a great deal of our telling elicits no mental response. So our Lord had a habit of throwing in a question now and then that broke up the serenity of his class and made them sit up and think."[72] The aim of the Christian teacher is not to control minds, but to develop them. The use of questions can be a major instrument in that developmental process.

Jesus' teaching methodology utilized both theory and practice. For example, the periods of instruction devoted to the disciples were punctuated by periods when they were sent out to apply what they had learned (Matt 10:5-15; Luke 10:1-20). This undoubtedly helped them realize their need for further instruction, fixed the successful lessons in their minds, and kept them from separating the theoretical from the facts of the everyday world of experience. The practical side of education is usually good for the prevention of intellectual smugness and pride. Beyond that, it is a most effective teaching-learning device. Jesus was more interested in teaching knowledge that would help men and women in their daily lives than He was in conveying knowledge as an abstraction. In the process, He united theoretical knowledge with both daily life and the eternal realities of the Kingdom of God and the great controversy between good and evil.

A strategic factor underlying all methods of learning and teaching is the attitude of teachers toward their students. In this we have much to learn from Christ. His attitude was positive toward even those who were apparently most hopeless. He could therefore reach the woman caught in the act of adultery, the publicans, the common sinners, and even at times the Pharisees.

People sensed that Jesus respected them as individuals and that He saw hope for each of them. That realization, in turn, motivated them to devote their lives to better ends. His hope and trust in them inspired them to new and more worthwhile lives. He utilized the positive power of the self-fulfilling prophecy.[73]

That does not mean that He overlooked sin. On the contrary, He met sin head-on. He did so, however, in a way that indicated that He was against sin while being for sinners. His hearers sensed the love He had for them, and because He cared about them, they began to care more about themselves. That made them responsive to His teaching and teaching methods. The manner in which Jesus related to His "students" is an object lesson from which all can profit and one which, if practiced, will help modern teachers draw out and develop the very best in their pupils.

Healthy relationships, in fact, stand at the heart of both Christ's teaching ministry and Christian teaching methodology. After all, if one of the primary aims of education is reconciliation, then helping students learn how to build Christian, principle-based relationships through modeling and didactic instruction is central to teaching. Just as Jesus was our model, we are models to our students in the discipling process.

In conclusion, it may be noted once again that the methodology of Christian teachers is not distinct from the methodologies utilized by other educators. Christian educators should keep several contexts in mind while selecting their teaching strategies: (1) the redemptive/reconciling nature of their task, (2) the needs of their students, and (3) the strengths and weaknesses of their personal individuality as teachers. Within that milieu, an ongoing study of the methods used by the Master Teacher is imperative for every teacher if Christian education is to fulfill its worldwide role.

THE SOCIAL FUNCTION OF CHRISTIAN EDUCATION

The Centrality of Education in
Cultural Transmission

Central to the messages of both the Old and New Testaments is the importance of education. Abraham was chosen because God saw that he would be faithful in teaching his household (Gen 18:19). God, through Moses, gave Israel an educational system that touched every phase of their lives, and the parting words of Jesus were "teach all nations" (Matt 28:19, 20 KJV).

Education is an important function in any society, because all youth must pass through some type of educational experience before they are ready to take over the society's responsible positions. The future of any society is therefore determined by its current youth. Furthermore, the direction that the youth will carry that society will, to a large extent, be determined by their education. The control of educational institutions and the content to be taught in those institutions has therefore been a perennial social issue. George S. Counts, in writing on this topic, has noted that to shape educational policy is to guard the path that leads from the present to the future. . . . Throughout the centuries since special educational agencies were first established, the strategic position of the school has been appreciated by kings, emperors, and popes, by rebels, reformers, and prophets. Hence, among those opposing forces found in all complex societies, a struggle for the control of the school is always evident. Every group or sect endeavors to pass on to its own children and to the children of others that culture which it happens to esteem; and every privileged class seeks to perpetuate its favored position in society by means of education.[74]

Likewise, observed Counts in discussing the challenge of Soviet education, the failure of revolutions has been a record of the failure to bring education into the service of the revolutionary cause. Revolutionary bodies will possess no more permanence than the small bands of idealists who conceived them if the children of the next generation cannot be persuaded to leave the footsteps of their parents. Therefore, the history of both the Soviets and the National Socialists has demonstrated that one of the first measures taken by modern revolutionary governments is to place all educational agencies under the direct control of the state and to give the schools a central hand in building the new society.[75]

The Conservative and Revolutionary
Roles of Christian Education

The Christian Church, in its biblical form, may be seen as both a conservative social force and an agent of social change. It is conservative in the sense that it seeks to transmit the unchanging truths of Christianity across time, but it is reforming in that it sees itself as the agent of a righteous God in a world of sin.

In this latter posture, it seeks to change the *status quo* through the conversion of men and women from their old way of life to the Christian way. Seen in this light, Christianity is a revolutionary force that has something better to offer both individuals and entire societies. Transformation, metamorphosis, conversion, and death and rebirth are some of the words that have been applied to the dynamics of Christianity as it impacts upon the life of individuals and, through them, the social order in which they live. Christian education and the Christian school must therefore be seen in terms of both the conservative and revolutionary roles of Christianity.

The conservative function of Christian education is twofold: (1) to pass on the legacy of Christian truth, and (2) to provide a protected atmosphere for the young in which this transmission can take place and in which Christian values may be imparted to the young in their formative years through both the formal curriculum and the more informal aspects of the educational context, such as the peer group and extracurricular activities.

The Christian church and Christian believers have the unique role of being in the world, without being of the world (John 17:14-18). How to relate to this seemingly contradictory position has remained a challenge to the church since the time of Christ. At one extreme we historically find the hermits and ascetics, who divorce themselves from contemporary society, while at the other extreme are those who have so accepted the norms of the non-Christian culture that they are indistinguishable from that culture. Neither extreme fulfills the implications of Jesus' paradoxical statement. Both sides of the paradox, however, find support in scripture.

On the side of segregation from the world is the Old Testament thrust for the Jews to remain distinct from the immoral cultures of their time, Paul's injunction not to be unequally yoked with unbelievers (2 Cor 6:14), and Revelation's call for separation from the confusion of the world (Rev 18:4). On the other hand, we see Jesus mixing with people on social occasions (John 2:1-12; Mark 14:3-9), and we are enjoined not to hide our light or to become worthless salt (Matt 5:13-16). Too often Christian groups have sought to follow one subset of the above statements or the other, when in actuality the biblical pattern should lead us to accept both subsets and the tension between them into our lives.

The separatist strand of the paradox has led the church to establish protective atmospheres for its youth during their formative years. These atmospheres can be seen in the church's development of religious schools and Christian youth groups. These agencies act as refuges in which youth from Christian families can learn skills, attitudes, values, and knowledge without being overwhelmed by the world view of the larger culture. The atmosphere in which these activities take place is conducive to the transferring of Christian culture to the upcoming generation. Parents and church members are willing to support such programs financially, because they philosophically recognize that these programs differ from the cultural milieu of the larger society, and they believe that the Christian world view is the correct one in terms of metaphysics, epistemology, and axiology.

Seen from such a viewpoint, the function of the Christian school is not to be an evangelistic agency to convert unbelievers (even though this may be a side result), but it is to be an agency that helps young people from Christian homes meet Jesus Christ and surrender their lives to Him. Implicit in this function is a distinct realization that if the majority of the student peer group in a given school does not espouse Christian values, then the effect of the school in terms of Christianity will be largely blunted. The conservative function of Christian education is therefore to provide a protected atmosphere for the nurturing of Christian youth, and an atmosphere in which all values, skills, and aspects of knowledge can be taught from the perspective of Christian philosophy.

Beyond the conservative function of Christian education is its revolutionary role. Christ's great gospel commission was for Christians to go into all the world, to make disciples of all nations, and to teach other people to observe all that He had commanded (Matt 28:19, 20). The preaching of the gospel changes people's lives, and this in turn disrupts social and private relationships (Matt 10:34-39) as people seek to live lives in line with the gospel imperatives and the Christian philosophic outlook.

The Christian churches have too often been viewed as conservative bastions in society, when in actuality they should be seen as agents for recreating both individuals and societies in terms of the spiritual values of Christianity. Both the church and its schools, in the lineage of the prophets, will stand for social justice and the appropriate forms of activity for maximizing the chances of that justice becoming a reality.

The life of Jesus can best be seen from the perspective of change rather than conservation. He was the Reformer of reformers, and His lever for reform was the revelation of God's plan for humanity, which we find in the Bible. That book is described as a sword (Heb 4:12; Eph 6:17), and it is quite evident that Christians are to use their philosophic "weapon" in an aggressive manner. Christianity, as presented and lived by Jesus, is a faith that is continually on the offensive as it seeks to lead persons to a better way of life. In short, Christianity is a revolutionary belief that seeks not only to change the world, but eventually to bring the present world order to an end with the arrival of Jesus at His second advent (Matt 24:14; John 14:1-3).

The Christian school has a role to play in Christianity's revolutionary task. It is to prepare the youth to become evangelistic workers. That does not mean, it should be emphasized, that they all will be educated for church employment. All will, however, be educated to be witnesses to the love of God, regardless of who may employ them.

As such, the Christian school can be seen as a staging ground for Christian activism and missionary work. It provides, ideally, not only the knowledge underlying the evangelistic imperative of the church, but also practical, guided activities in the larger community that allow students to develop the skills necessary to meet people with the message of Jesus and to perform their individual roles in the context of God's church on earth (1 Cor 12:14-31). Edward Sutherland has written that in God's plan

> the Christian school should be the nursery in which reformers are born and reared—reformers who would go forth from the school burning with practical zeal and enthusiasm to take their places as leaders in these reforms.[76]

In summary, it can be said that the social function of the Christian school has both a conservative and a revolutionary aspect. The mixture of those two roles helps the developing Christian to become one who is able to be in the world but not of the world. In essence, the function of the Christian school is to educate the young of the church for service to God and their neighbors, rather than to train them for self-service through the acquisition of a "good position" and a comfortable income. These, it is true, may be by-products of Christian education, but they are not central to its purpose.

Service to others was the essence of Christ's life, and it is therefore the ultimate aim in Christian education. Seen in the context of the biblical role of the believer, Christian education will develop Christians who will be able to relate well to others in this world. But even more important, Christian schools will educate students for citizenship in the Kingdom of Heaven.

SUMMARY OF PART III

Part III has outlined one possible approach to Christian philosophy and the implications of that philosophy for education. It was noted that today's Christianity is based on supernatural assumptions, even though it exists in a social context permeated with naturalistic premises.

It was suggested that one of the essential needs of Christian education is that it build upon a Christian view of reality, truth, and value. That means that Christian educators must have a clear understanding of both their basic beliefs and how those beliefs affect their educational practice.

In addition, we noted that philosophy is a major, but not the sole, determinant of educational practice. The social, economic, and political context modifies possible and preferred educational goals and calls for wisdom as educators apply their basic beliefs to the everyday world. Individual choice and personal responsibility are therefore important constituents for both parents and educational professionals as they seek to develop educational environments that will meet the needs of the children with whom they are working.

Central to Christian philosophy is the existence of the Creator-God, the great controversy between good and evil, the human predicament, the reliability of God's self-disclosure in the Bible, and God's loving character. A belief in these elements stimulates the need for a distinctively Christian education and forms the basis for a set of criteria concerning what is "most important" in that education.

Students and their needs provide a focal point for Christian educational philosophy and direct educators toward the goals of Christian education. Every student is, in Christian perspective, an individual with infinite potential. The human race was created in the image of God, it fell from that position, and God is seeking to restore each individual to his or her original state through the plan of redemption. Christian education is one agent that God seeks to use in this restorative process.

From the Christian viewpoint, the goal of education is the restoration of God's image in each person. Humanity's greatest need is to know Jesus Christ as Lord and Saviour. Beyond that, individuals need to be restored to a right relationship with their fellow humans and their own selves. Only when these relationships are restored will people escape from the lostness, meaninglessness, and alienation inherent in their fallen condition.

The redemptive, restorative, and reconciling goal of Christian education provides a focus for the evaluation of the role of the teacher, the curricular emphasis, and the social function of the school. The teacher's central task, in this context, is to "seek and to save the lost" by building caring relationships with students and by helping them discover both their personal needs and that better way which is found in Jesus Christ. The curriculum, with this goal in mind, will be seen from the perspective of God's truth, will focus on humanity's greatest need, and will integrate all subject matters within the scriptural framework. Such a curricular format will uplift the unity of all truth in God, highlight the Christian world view, and help students see the unified meaning of all their studies. All aspects of the curriculum in Christian education find their meaning in Jesus Christ; without Him there is no meaning for education or for life.

Teaching methodologies also focus on the restorative goal, and they will be selected on the basis of their effectiveness in implementing that goal. Central to methodology in the Christian educational environment is the caring relationship of teachers toward their pupils. This was central in the method of Jesus, and it is at the heart of the work of His underteachers.

The social function of the Christian school is likewise founded upon its restorative and reconciling goal. That social function is reflected in its conservative aspect as it seeks to provide a protected atmosphere for the young in which they can come to know Christ without undue interference from the non-Christian assumptions of the larger society. The Christian school's social function is also reflected in its revolutionary role, which seeks to provide young Christians with the knowledge and abilities that will enable them to share their Christian experience with the world at large. Christianity is a religion of transformation and change for both individuals and societies. Christian schools are established to help facilitate change.

Christian education has other goals besides reconciliation and the restoration of the image of God in its students. For example, it seeks to transmit information and to prepare people for the world of work. Those goals, however, are subordinate to its primary goal. The very existence of Christian educational institutions is due to the Christian belief that life is meaningless outside of Christ, and that people profit nothing if they gain the whole world, obtain all wisdom, and have a respectable vocation, but lose their souls. From this perspective, Christian educational goals are broader than those of secularized education, since Christian education seeks to prepare the young for both the present world and the world to come.

Notes

1. G. C. Berkouwer, *Man: The Image of God* (Grand Rapids, MI: Wm. B. Eerdmans Publishing Co., 1962), p. 9.

2. Trueblood, *Philosophy of Religion,* p. xiv.

3. Reinhold Niebuhr, *The Nature and Destiny of Man: A Christian Interpretation,* vol. 1 (New York: Charles Scribner's Sons, 1964), p. 13.

4. Berkouwer, *Man: The Image of God,* p. 63; see also pp. 75-77.

5. John Calvin, *Institutes of the Christian Religion,* book 2, chap. 2:12.

6. Francis A. Schaeffer, *Escape From Reason* (Downers Grove, IL: InterVarsity Press, 1968), p. 90.

7. A helpful discussion of Christian education in terms of reconciliation is found in Ronald Habermas and Klaus Issler, *Teaching for Reconciliation: Foundations and Practice of Christian Educational Ministry* (Grand Rapids, MI: Baker Book House, 1992), see especially pp. 33-46.

8. Jim Wilhoit, *Christian Education and the Search for Meaning,* 2d ed. (Grand Rapids, MI: Baker Book House, 1991), p. 61.

9. Lewis, *Mere Christianity,* p. 52.

10. Niebuhr, *The Nature and Destiny of Man,* vol. 1, pp. 74-92.

11. For a thoughtful treatment of issues related to the teacher's calling, see Robert W. Pazmiño, *By What Authority Do We Teach? Sources for Empowering Christian Educators* (Grand Rapids, MI: Baker Book House, 1994).

12. F. F. Bruce, *The Epistle to the Ephesians* (Westwood, NJ: Fleming H. Revell Co., 1961), p. 85.

13. The King James Version renders *didaskalos* as "master" some 47 times. The Revised Standard Version renders this word as "teacher" in each case.

14. For a brief discussion of Jesus' teaching methodologies, refer to the section of this chapter entitled "Methodological Considerations."

15. "For what is a man profited, if he shall gain the whole world, and lose his own soul?" (Matt 16:26 KJV).

16. Edwin H. Rian, "The Need: A World View," in John Paul von Grueningen, ed., *Toward a Christian Philosophy of Higher Education* (Philadelphia: Westminster Press, 1957), pp. 30, 31; Herbert Welch, "The Ideals and Aims of the Christian College," in *The Christian College* (New York: Methodist Book Concern, 1916), p. 21.

17. C. B. Eavey, "Aims and Objectives of Christian Education," in J. Edward Hakes, ed., *An Introduction to Evangelical Christian Education* (Chicago: Moody Press, 1964), p. 62.

18. For a helpful treatment of the teacher as a role model, see Edlin, *The Cause of Christian Education,* 2d ed., pp. 120-35.

19. Gene Garrick, "Developing Educational Objectives for the Christian School," in Paul A. Kienel, ed., *The Philosophy of Christian School Education,* 2d ed. (Whittier, CA: Association of Christian Schools International, 1978), p. 73.

20. Welch, "The Ideals and Aims of the Christian College," pp. 23, 22.

21. J. Crosby Chapman and George S. Counts, *Principles of Education* (Boston: Houghton Mifflin Co., 1924), p. 498. (Italics supplied.)

22. Gloria Goris Stronks and Doug Blomberg, eds., *A Vision with a Task: Christian School-*

ing for Responsive Discipleship (Grand Rapids, MI: Baker Books, 1993), p. 25.

23. Martin Luther's comments on teaching are of interest at this point. "If I had to give up preaching and my other duties," wrote Luther, "there is no office I would rather have than that of school-teacher [sic]. For I know that next to the [pastoral] ministry it is the most useful, greatest, and best; and I am not sure which of the two is to be preferred. For it is hard to make old dogs docile and old rogues pious, yet that is what the ministry works at, and must work at, in great part, in vain; but young trees, though some may break in the process, are more easily bent and trained. Therefore let it be considered one of the highest virtues on earth faithfully to train the children of others, which duty very few parents attend to themselves." Martin Luther, "Sermon on the Duty of Sending Children to School," in *Luther on Education*, by F. V. N. Painter (Philadelphia: Lutheran Publication Society, 1889), p. 264.

24. For the biblical position on the teaching responsibility of the home, see Gen 18:19; Deut 4:9, 10; 6:6, 7; and Eph 6:4.

25. Frank E. Gaebelein, "The Greatest Educational Force," *Christianity Today*, 8 (August 28, 1964), pp. 28-29.

26. Successful people are often promoted to the next higher position in an organizational hierarchy, where they may be incompetent. See Laurence J. Peter and Raymond Hull, *The Peter Principle* (New York: William Morrow & Co., 1969).

27. A fuller discussion of the primacy of teaching can be found in my article, "Reschooling Society: A New Road to Utopia," *Phi Delta Kappan*, 60 (December, 1978), pp. 289-91.

28. Frank E. Gaebelein, *The Pattern of God's Truth: Problems of Integration in Christian Education* (Chicago: Moody Press, 1968), p. 35.

29. Eavey, "Aims and Objectives of Christian Education," p. 61.

30. Herbert Spencer, *Education: Intellectual, Moral, and Physical* (New York: D. Appleton and Company, 1909), pp. 1-87.

31. Ibid., pp. 10-11.

32. Ibid., pp. 13-14.

33. Ibid., pp. 84-86.

34. Ibid., p. 63.

35. Mark Van Doren, *Liberal Education* (Boston: Beacon Press, 1959), p. 108.

36. Alfred North Whitehead, *The Aims of Education and Other Essays* (New York: The Free Press, 1967), p. 7.

37. C. P. Snow, *The Two Cultures and the Scientific Revolution* (New York: Cambridge University Press, 1959).

38. Gaebelein, "Toward a Philosophy of Christian Education," p. 41.

39. Gaebelein, *The Pattern of God's Truth*, p. 20.

40. John Henry Newman, *The Idea of a University* (Notre Dame, IN: University of Notre Dame Press, 1982), p. 19. "Admit a God," wrote Newman, "and you introduce among the subjects of your knowledge, a fact encompassing, closing in upon, absorbing every other fact conceivable." Ibid.

41. Readers interested in an enlightening discussion of the interface between science and religion will find the following books helpful: Richard H. Bube, *The Human Quest: A New Look at Science and the Christian Faith* (Waco, TX: Word Books, 1971), especially pp. 11-131; Charles E. Hummel, *The Galileo Connection: Resolving Conflicts between Science & the Bible* (Downers Grove, IL: InterVarsity Press, 1986).

42. Harry Blamires, *The Christian Mind* (London: S.P.C.K., 1963); Holmes, *All Truth is God's Truth*, p. 125. On the topic of helping students think "worldviewishly" from a Christian perspective, see Arthur F. Holmes, *Contours of a World View* (Grand Rapids, MI: Wm. B. Eerdmans Publishing Co., 1983); James W. Sire, *Discipleship of the Mind: Learning to Love God in the Ways We Think* (Downers Grove, IL: InterVarsity Press, 1990).

43. Arthur F. Holmes, *The Idea of a Christian College* (Grand Rapids, MI: Wm. B. Eerdmans Publishing Co., 1975), p. 26.

44. Clark, *A Christian Philosophy of Education*, p. 210.

45. Gaebelein, "Toward a Philosophy of Christian Education," p. 37.

46. Edlin, *The Cause of Christian Education*, pp. 64-66.

47. A helpful aid to reading in Christian perspective is James W. Sire, *How to Read Slowly: A Christian Guide to Reading with the Mind* (Downers Grove, IL: InterVarsity, 1978).

48. T. S. Eliot, "Religion and Literature," in *The Christian Imagination*, ed. Leland Ryken (Grand Rapids, MI: Baker Book House, 1981), pp. 148-50.

49. Virginia Lowell Graybill, "English Literature," in *Christ and the Modern Mind*, ed. Robert W. Smith (Downers Grove, IL: InterVarsity Press, 1972), p. 21.

50. Quoted in Frank E. Gaebelein, *The Christian, the Arts, and Truth: Regaining the Vision of Greatness* (Portland, OR: Multnomah Press, 1985), pp. 91-92. For an informed treatment of the interface between Christianity and the entertainment arts, see William D. Romanowski, *Pop Culture Wars: Religion and the Role of Entertainment in American Life* (Downers Grove, IL: InterVarsity Press, 1996).

51. Gaebelein, "Toward a Philosophy of Christian Education," pp. 47-48. Cf. Newman, *The Idea of a University*, p. 54. For Brunner's insight on the topic, see Emil Brunner, *Man in Revolt: A Christian Anthropology* (Philadelphia: Westminster Press, 1947), p. 255.

52. For Gaebelein's discussion of the integration of Christianity and mathematics, see *The Pattern of God's Truth*, pp. 57-64.

53. For one of the most sophisticated treatments of the practical aspects of the integration of the sciences, mathematics, and other fields with Christianity, see Harold Heie and David L. Wolfe, *The Reality of Christian Learning: Strategies for Faith-Discipline Integration* (Grand Rapids, MI: Christian University Press and Wm. B. Eerdmans Publishing Co., 1987). In addition to the natural points of integration in science and mathematics, teachers will have opportunity to integrate their faith with their academic specialty on the personality level as they relate, in the spirit of Jesus, to their students and answer their questions in regard to the subject matter at hand, religious meaning, and personal difficulties.

54. Gaebelein, *The Pattern of God's Truth*, p. 87.

55. Ibid., pp. 86-87n.

56. Maria Harris, *Fashion Me A People: Curriculum in the Church* (Louisville: Westminster/John Knox, 1989), p. 69, quoted in Robert W. Pazmiño, *Principles and Practices of Christian Education: An Evangelical Perspective* (Grand Rapids, MI: Baker Book House, 1992), p. 112.

57. Arthur F. Holmes, *Shaping Character: Moral Education in the Christian College* (Grand Rapids, MI: Wm. B. Eerdmans Publishing Co., 1991), p. vii.

58. Ronald H. Nash, *The Closing of the American Heart: What's Really Wrong with America's Schools* ([Dallas]: Probe Books, 1990), pp. 29-30.

59. Robert W. Pazmiño, *Foundational Issues in Christian Education: An Introduction in Evangelical Perspective*, 2d ed. (Grand Rapids, MI: Baker Books, 1997), p. 99.

60. Ibid., p. 101.

61. Stronks and Blomberg, eds., *A Vision with a Task*, pp. 15-38.

62. Schaeffer, *True Spirituality*, p. 143.

63. Ibid., p. 144.

64. This does not mean that humans do not often act on the animal level. Unfortunately, it is probably true that most people live most of the time on the level of their animal propensities (e.g., appetites and passions) and can thus be controlled by reinforcement contingencies. The point is, however, that individuals, if they so choose, may rise above this level through a willingness to accept the power of the Holy Spirit in their lives.

65. Two points should be considered when contemplating this model: (1) chronological age is not necessarily correlated with moral maturity, and (2) the line of moral development is not straight—it has its ups and downs that vary with individuals and the skill and dedication of the significant adults in their lives.

66. Harro Van Brummelen, *Walking With God in the Classroom* (Burlington, Ontario: Welch Publishing, 1988), p. 34.

67. Nicholas Wolterstorff, *Educating for Responsible Action* (Grand Rapids, MI: Wm. B. Eerdmans Publishing Co., 1980), pp. 15, 14. This book lays the theoretical groundwork for a tendency-learning methodology.

68. Oppewal, *Biblical Knowing and Teaching*, pp. 13-17.

69. Roy B. Zuck, *Teaching as Jesus Taught* (Grand Rapids, MI: Baker Books, 1995), p. 158. This volume and its companion, *Teaching as Paul Taught* (Grand Rapids, MI: Baker Books, 1998), provide the most comprehensive analyses of biblical teaching available in the contemporary literature on the subject.

70. J. M. Price, *Jesus the Teacher* (Nashville: The Sunday School Board of the Southern Baptist Convention, 1946), p. 101.

71. John Sutherland Bonnell, *Psychology for Pastor and People*, rev. ed. (New York: Harper & Brothers, 1960), pp. 71-72.

72. John A. Marquis, *Learning to Teach from the Master Teacher* (Philadelphia: The Westminster Press, 1925), p. 29.

73. A self-fulfilling prophecy is a prophecy that causes its own fulfillment and has as its base an expectation. This theory holds that in many, if not most, situations people tend to do what is expected of them.

74. Chapman and Counts, *Principles of Education*, pp. 601-2.

75. George S. Counts, *The Soviet Challenge to America* (New York: John Day Co., 1931), pp. 66-67.

76. E. A. Sutherland, *Studies in Christian Education* (Leominster, MA: The Eusey Press, 1952), p. 72.

Another Word to
the Reader

You have reached the end of this book, but it is hoped that this accomplishment will be the beginning of your personal philosophy building. The building of a personal philosophy for both life and education is an ongoing process of thought and practice that becomes richer, deeper, and more meaningful as you continue to grow in the knowledge of Jesus Christ and as you seek to develop more effective ways of transmitting His ways, knowledge, and values to others. The living Christian is a thinking Christian.

You must not pretend that you now understand philosophy and education and can therefore move on to more important things. Your philosophy is an integral part of who you are and everything you do. Your growth in this area, as well as in other areas of human endeavor, will not stop throughout God's ceaseless eternity. There is no end for the Christian. The greatness of the Creator-God will continue to challenge you as you gain new insights into reality, truth, and value, and as you continue to educate people in the light of their greatest need—Jesus Christ.

Bibliography

Adler, Mortimer J. "The Crisis in Contemporary Education." *Social Frontier* 5 (February 1939): 140-45.

_____. "In Defense of the Philosophy of Education." In *Philosophies of Education*. National Society for the Study of Education, Forty-first Yearbook, Part I. Chicago: University of Chicago Press, 1942.

_____. *Paideia Problems and Possibilities*. New York: Macmillan Publishing Co., 1983.

_____. *The Paideia Proposal: An Educational Manifesto*. New York: Macmillan Publishing Co., 1982.

_____, ed. *The Paideia Program: An Educational Syllabus*. New York: Macmillan Publishing Co., 1984.

Alexander, H. A. "After the Revolution, the Normative Revival in Post-Analytic Philosophy of Education," in *Philosophy of Education 1992: Proceedings of the Forty-Eighth Annual Meeting of the Philosophy of Education Society*.

Aquinas, Thomas. *Summa Theologica*. 3 vols. Translated by Fathers of the English Dominican Province. New York: Benziger Bros., 1947.

Barrett, William. *Irrational Man: A Study in Existential Philosophy*. Garden City, NY: Anchor Books, 1962.

Berkouwer, G. C. *Man: The Image of God*. Grand Rapids, MI: Wm. B. Eerdmans Publishing Co., 1962.

Bernstein, Richard J. "The Resurgence of Pragmatism." *Social Research* 59 (Winter 1992): 813-40.

Bestor, Arthur E. *Educational Wastelands: The Retreat from Learning in Our Public Schools*. Urbana, IL: The University of Illinois Press, 1953.

_____. *The Restoration of Learning: A Program for Redeeming the Unfulfilled Promise of American Education*. New York: Alfred A. Knopf, 1955.

Blamires, Harry. *The Christian Mind*. London: S.P.C.K., 1963.

_____. *Recovering the Christian Mind: Meeting the Challenge of Secularism*. Downers Grove, IL: InterVarsity Press, 1988.

Bloom, Allan. *The Closing of the American Mind*. New York: Simon & Schuster, 1987.

Bonino, Jose Miguez. *Doing Theology in a Revolutionary Situation*. Philadelphia: Fortress Press, 1975.

Bonnell, John Sutherland. *Psychology for Pastor and People*. Rev. ed. New York: Harper & Brothers, 1960.

Bowers, C. A. *Elements of a Post-Liberal Theory of Education*. New York: Teachers College Press, Columbia University, 1987.

Brameld, Theodore. *Education as Power*. New York: Holt, Reinhart and Winston, 1965.

_____. *Education for the Emerging Age*. New York: Harper & Row, 1961.

_____. *Patterns of Educational Philosophy*. New York: Harcourt, Brace & World, 1950.

_____. *Toward a Reconstructed Philosophy of Education*. New York: Holt, Rinehart and Winston, 1956.

Broudy, Harry S. *Building a Philosophy of Education*. 2d ed. Englewood Cliffs, NJ: Prentice Hall, 1961.

_____. *The Uses of Schooling*. New York: Routledge, 1988.

_____. "What Schools Should and Should Not Teach," *Peabody Journal of Education*, October 1976, pp. 31-38.

Brubacher, John S. *Modern Philosophies of Education*. 4th ed. New York: McGraw-Hill Co., 1969.

Bruce, F. F. *The Epistle to the Ephesians*. Westwood, NJ: Fleming H. Revell, 1961.

Brunner, Emile. *Man in Revolt: A Christian Anthropology*. Philadelphia: Westminster Press, 1947.

Bube, Richard H. *The Human Quest: A New Look at Science and the Christian Faith*. Waco, TX: Word Books, 1971.

Buber, Martin. *Between Man and Man*. London: Kegan Paul, 1947.

Burt, Edwin A. *In Search of Philosophic Understanding*. Indianapolis, IN: Hackett Publishing Co., 1980.

Butler, J. Donald. *Four Philosophies and Their Practice in Education and Religion*. 3d ed. New York: Harper & Row, 1968.

_____. *Idealism in Education*. New York: Harper & Row, 1966.

Calvin, John. *Institutes of the Christian Religion*, 2 vols. Translated by Ford Lewis Battles. Edited by John T. McNeill. Philadelphia: Westminster Press, 1960.

Camus, Albert. *The Myth of Sisyphus and Other Essays*. Translated by Justin O'Brien. New York: Vintage Books, 1955.

Carper, James C., and Hunt, Thomas C., eds. *Religious Schooling in America*. Birmingham, AL: Religious Education Press, 1984.

Chambliss, J. J., ed. *Philosophy of Education: An Encyclopedia*. New York: Garland Publishers, 1996.

Chapman, J. Crosby, and Counts, George S. *Principles of Education*. Boston: Houghton Mifflin Co., 1924.

Clark, Gordon H. *A Christian Philosophy of Education*. Grand Rapids, MI: Wm. B. Eerdmans Publishing Co., 1946.

Clouser, Roy A. *The Myth of Religious Neutrality: An Essay on the Hidden Role of Religious Belief in Theories*. Notre Dame, IN: University of Notre Dame Press, 1991.

Coleman, James S. et al. *Equality of Educational Opportunity*. Washington, DC: U.S. Department of Health, Education, and Welfare, 1966.

College Board. *Academic Preparation for College*. New York: The College Board, 1983.

Conant, James B. *The American High School Today*. New York: McGraw-Hill Book Co., 1959.

Cone, James H. *A Black Theology of Liberation*, 2d ed. Maryknoll, NY: Orbis Books, 1986.

Copleston, Frederick. *Contemporary Philosophy: Studies of Logical Positivism and Existentialism.* Rev. ed. London: Search Press, 1972.

Counts, George S. *Dare the School Build a New Social Order?* New York: John Day Co., 1932.

_____. *Education and American Civilization.* New York: Teachers College, Columbia University, Bureau of Publications, 1952.

_____. *Education and the Foundations of Human Freedom.* Pittsburgh: University of Pittsburgh Press, 1962.

_____. *The Soviet Challenge to America.* New York: John Day Co., 1931.

Cremin, Lawrence A. *The Genius of American Education.* New York: Vintage Books, 1965.

_____. *Public Education.* New York: Basic Books, 1976.

_____. *The Transformation of the School: Progressivism In American Education, 1876-1957.* New York: Vintage Books, 1964.

Dennison, George. *The Lives of Children.* New York: Random House, 1969.

Derrida, Jacques. *On Grammatology.* Baltimore: The Johns Hopkins University Press, 1976.

Dewey, John. *Art as Experience.* New York: Minton, Balch & Co., 1934.

_____. *Democracy and Education.* New York: The Macmillan Company, 1916.

_____. *Experience and Education.* New York: The Macmillan Company, 1938.

_____. *How We Think: A Restatement of the Relation of Reflective Thinking to the Educative Process.* New ed. New York: D. C. Heath and Co., 1933.

_____. *The School and Society.* Rev. ed. Chicago: University of Chicago Press, 1915.

Diggins, John Patrick. *The Promise of Pragmatism: Modernism and the Crisis of Knowledge and Authority.* Chicago: University of Chicago Press, 1994.

Ditmanson, Harold H.; Hong, Howard V.; and Quanbeck, Warren A., eds. *Christian Faith and the Liberal Arts.* Minneapolis: Augsburg Publishing House, 1960.

Doll, William E., Jr. *A Post-modern Perspective on Curriculum.* New York: Teachers College Press, Columbia University, 1993.

Eavey, C. B. "Aims and Objectives of Christian Education." In *An Introduction to Evangelical Christian Education.* Edited by J. Edward Hakes. Chicago: Moody Press, 1964.

Edlin, Richard J. *The Cause of Christian Education.* 2d ed. Northport, AL: Vision Press, 1998.

Eliot, T. S. "Religion and Literature." In *The Christian Imagination: Essays in Literature and the Arts.* Edited by Leland Ryken. Grand Rapids, MI: Baker Book House, 1981.

Falwell, Jerry. *Listen, America!* Garden City, NY: Doubleday & Co., 1980.

Feinberg, John S. *The Many Faces of Evil: Theological Systems and the Problem of Evil.* Grand Rapids, MI: Zondervan Publishing House, 1994.

Fletcher, Joseph. *Situation Ethics: The New Morality.* Philadelphia: The Westminster Press, 1966.

Foucault, Michel. *The Archeology of Knowledge and the Discourse on Language.* New York: Pantheon Books, 1972.

Frankl, Viktor E. *Man's Search for Meaning: An Introduction to Logotherapy.* New York: Washington Square Press, 1963.

Freire, Paulo. *Pedagogy of the Oppressed.* Translated by Myra Bergman Ramos. New York: Seabury Press, 1968.

Gaarder, Jostein. *Sophie's World: A Novel About the History of Philosophy.* [London]: Phoenix House, 1995.

Gaebelein, Frank E. *The Christian, The Arts, and Truth: Regaining the Vision of Greatness.* Portland, OR: Multnomoah Press, 1985.

_____. "The Greatest Educational Force." *Christianity Today* 8 (August 28, 1964): 28-29.

_____. *The Pattern of God's Truth: Problems of Integration in Christian Education.* Chicago: Moody Press, 1968.

_____. "Toward a Philosophy of Christian Education." In *An Introduction to Evangelical Christian Education.* Edited by J. Edward Hakes. Chicago: Moody Press, 1964.

Gardner, John W. *Self-Renewal: The Individual in the Innovative Society.* New York: Harper & Row, 1964.

Garrick, Gene. "Developing Educational Objectives for the Christian School." In *The Philosophy of Christian School Education,* 2d ed. Edited by Paul A. Kienel. Whittier, CA: Association of Christian Schools International, 1978.

Geisler, Norman L. *The Roots of Evil.* Grand Rapids, MI: Zondervan Publishing House, 1978.

Geisler, Norman L., and Watkins, William D. *Worlds Apart: A Handbook of World Views.* 2d ed. Grand Rapids, MI: Baker Book House, 1989.

Giroux, Henry A. *Pedagogy and the Politics of Hope: Theory, Culture, and Schooling.* Boulder, CO: Westview Press, 1997.

Glasser, William. *Schools Without Failure.* New York: Harper & Row, Perennial Library, 1975.

Graybill, Virginia Lowell. "English Literature." In *Christ and the Modern Mind.* Edited by Robert W. Smith. Downers Grove, IL: InterVarsity Press, 1972.

Greene, Maxine. *Teacher as Stranger: Educational Philosophy for the Modern Age.* Belmont, CA: Wadsworth Publishing Co., 1973.

Grenz, Stanley J. *A Primer on Postmodernism.* Grand Rapids, MI: Wm. B. Eerdmans Pub. Co., 1996.

Gross, Beatrice, and Gross, Ronald, eds. *The Great School Debate: Which Way for American Education?* New York: Simon & Shuster, 1985.

Gutek, Gerald L. *Philosophical and Ideological Perspectives in Education.* Englewood Cliffs, NJ: Prentice Hall, 1988.

Gutiérrez, Gustavo. *A Theology of Liberation: History, Politics, and Salvation,* rev. ed. Maryknoll, NY: Orbis Books, 1988.

Habermas, Ronald, and Issler, Klaus. *Teaching for Reconciliation: Foundations and Practice of Christian Educational Ministry.* Grand Rapids, MI: Baker Book House, 1992.

Heie, Harold, and Wolfe, David L., eds. *The Reality of Christian Learning: Strategies for Faith-Discipline Integration.* Grand Rapids, MI: Wm. B. Eerdmans Publishing Co., 1987.

Henry, Carl F. H. *Christian Personal Ethics.* Grand Rapids, MI: Wm. B. Eerdmans Publishing Co., 1957.

Heslop, Robert D. "Analytic Philosophy," in *Philosophy of Education: An Encyclo-*

pedia, ed. J. J. Chambliss. New York: Garland Publishing, 1996.

Hick, John. *Evil and the God of Love.* Rev. ed. New York: Harper & Row, 1978.

Hilgard, Ernest R., and Bower, Gordon H. *Theories of Learning.* 3d ed. New York: Appleton-Century-Crofts, 1966.

Hill, Brian V. *Faith at the Blackboard: Issues Facing the Christian Teacher.* Grand Rapids, MI: Wm. B. Eerdmans Publishing Co., 1982.

Hirsch, E. D., Jr. *Cultural Literacy: What Every American Needs to Know,* updated and expanded ed. New York: Vintage Books, 1988.

_____. *The Schools We Need and Why We Don't Have Them.* New York: Doubleday, 1996.

Hocking, William Ernest. *Types of Philosophy.* 3d ed. New York: Charles Scribner's Sons, 1959.

Holmes, Arthur F. *All Truth Is God's Truth.* Grand Rapids, MI: Wm. B. Eerdmans Publishing Co., 1977.

_____. *Contours of a World View.* Grand Rapids, MI: Wm. B. Eerdmans Publishing Co., 1983.

_____. *Faith Seeks Understanding: A Christian Approach to Knowledge.* Grand Rapids, MI: Wm. B. Eerdmans Publishing Co., 1971.

_____. *The Idea of a Christian College.* Grand Rapids, MI: Wm. B. Eerdmans Publishing Co., 1975.

_____. *Shaping Character: Moral Education in the Christian College.* Grand Rapids, MI: Wm. B. Eerdmans Publishing Co., 1991.

Holt, John. *Freedom and Beyond.* New York: Dell Publishing Co., Laurel Edition, 1972.

_____. *How Children Fail.* New York: Pitman Publishing Corp., 1964.

Horne, Herman Harrell. *The Democratic Philosophy of Education.* New York: The Macmillan Co., 1932.

_____. "An Idealistic Philosophy of Education." In *Philosophies of Education.* National Society for the Study of Education, Forty-first Yearbook, Part I. Chicago: University of Chicago Press, 1942.

_____. *The Philosophy of Christian Education.* New York: Fleming H. Revell Co., 1937.

Hummel, Charles E. *The Galileo Connection: Resolving Conflicts between Science & the Bible.* Downers Grove, IL: InterVarsity Press, 1986.

Hutchins, Robert M. *The Conflict in Education.* New York: Harper & Brothers, 1953.

_____. *The Higher Learning in America.* New Haven, CT: Yale University Press, 1936.

_____. *The Learning Society.* New York: New American Library, 1968.

Illich, Ivan. *Deschooling Society.* New York: Harper & Row, 1970.

_____ et al. *After Deschooling, What?* New York: Harper & Row, Perennial Library, 1973.

James, William. *Essays In Pragmatism.* Edited by Alburey Castell. New York: Hafner Publishing Co., 1948.

_____. *Pragmatism.* New York: Longmans, Green, and Co., 1907.

Jencks, Christopher et al. *Inequality: A Reassessment of the Effect of Family and Schooling in America.* New York: Harper & Row, 1972.

Jervis, Kathe, and Montag, Carol, eds. *Progressive Education for the 1990s: Trans-*

forming Practice. New York: Teachers College Press, Columbia University, 1991.

Kaplan, Abraham. *The New World of Philosophy.* New York: Random House, 1961.

Kaufmann, Walter. *Existentialism from Dostoevsky to Sartre.* Rev. ed. New York: New American Library, 1975.

Keniston, Kenneth et al. *All Our Children: The American Family under Pressure.* New York: Harcourt Brace Jovanovich, 1977.

Kincheloe, Joe L. *Toward a Critical Politics of Teacher Thinking: Mapping the Postmodern.* Westport, CT: Bergin and Garvey, 1993.

Kneller, George. *Existentialism and Education.* New York: John Wiley & Sons, 1958.

_____. *Introduction to the Philosophy of Education.* 2d ed. New York: John Wiley & Sons, 1971.

Knight, George R. "How Did the Galaxies Come into Existence?" *These Times,* September 1, 1978, pp. 8-12.

_____. "Reschooling Society: A New Road to Utopia." *Phi Delta Kappan* 60 (December 1978): 289-91.

_____. "The Transformation of Change and the Future Role of Education." *Philosophic Research and Analysis* 8 (Early Spring 1980): 10-11.

Kohl, Herbert R. *The Open Classroom: A Practical Guide to a New Way of Teaching.* New York: New York Review, 1969.

_____. *36 Children.* New York: New American Library, 1967.

Kozol, Jonathan. *Death at an Early Age.* Boston: Houghton Mifflin Co., 1967.

_____. *Free Schools.* Boston: Houghton Mifflin Co., 1972.

Kraemer, Hendrik. *Why Christianity of All Religions?* Translated by Hubert Hoskins. Philadelphia: The Westminster Press, 1962.

LaHaye, Tim. *The Battle for the Mind.* Old Tappan, NJ: Fleming H. Revell, 1980.

Lambert, Ian, and Mitchell, Suzanne, eds. *The Crumbling Walls of Certainty: Towards a Christian Critique of Postmodernity and Education.* Sydney: Centre for the Study of Australian Christianity, 1997.

Land, Gary. "The Challenge of Postmodernism." *Dialogue* 8:1:5-8.

Laska, John A. *Schooling and Education: Basic Concepts and Problems.* New York: D. Van Nostrand Company, 1976.

Lewis, C. S. *Mere Christianity.* New York: The Macmillan Company, 1960.

Lucas, Christopher J., ed. *Challenge and Choice in Contemporary Education: Six Major Ideological Perspectives.* New York: Macmillan Publishing Co., 1976.

Luther, Martin. "Sermon on the Duty of Sending Children to School." In *Luther on Education,* by F. V. N. Painter. Philadelphia: Lutheran Publication Society, 1889.

Lyotard, Jean-François. *The Postmodern Condition: A Report on Knowledge.* Minneapolis: University of Minnesota Press, 1984.

Maritain, Jacques. *Education at the Crossroads.* New Haven, CT: Yale University Press, 1943.

Marler, Charles D. *Philosophy and Schooling.* Boston: Allyn and Bacon, 1975.

Marquis, John A. *Learning to Teach from the Master Teacher.* Philadelphia: The Westminster Press, 1925.

Martin, Wm. Oliver. *Realism in Education.* New York: Harper & Row, 1969.

McLaren, Peter. *Life in Schools: An Introduction to Critical Pedagogy in the Foundations of Education,* 3d ed. New York: Longman, 1998.

Morris, Charles. *Varieties of Human Value.* Chicago: The University of Chicago Press, 1956.

Morris, Leon. *I Believe in Revelation.* Grand Rapids, MI: Wm. B. Eerdmans Publishing Co., 1976.

Morris, Van Cleve. *Existentialism in Education: What it Means.* New York: Harper & Row, 1966.

_____. *Philosophy and the American School.* Boston: Houghton Mifflin Company, 1961.

Nash, Paul. *Models of Man: Explorations in the Western Educational Tradition.* New York: John Wiley & Sons, 1968.

Nash, Paul; Kazamias, Andreas M.; and Perkinson, Henry J. *The Educated Man: Studies in the History of Educational Thought.* New York: John Wiley & Sons, 1966.

Nash, Ronald H. *The Closing of the American Heart: What's Really Wrong with America's Schools.* [Dallas]: Probe Books, 1990.

National Commission on Excellence in Education. *A Nation at Risk: The Imperative for Educational Reform.* Washington, DC: U.S. Government Printing Office, 1983.

Neff, Frederick C. *Philosophy and American Education.* New York: The Center for Applied Research in Education, 1966.

Neill, A. S. *Summerhill: A Radical Approach to Child Rearing.* New York: Hart Publishing Co., 1960.

Newman, John Henry. *The Idea of a University.* Notre Dame, IN: University of Notre Dame Press, 1982.

Niebuhr, H. Richard. *Christ and Culture.* New York: Harper & Brothers, Torchbook ed., 1956.

Niebuhr, Reinhold. *The Nature and Destiny of Man: A Christian Interpretation.* 2 vols. New York: Charles Scribner's Sons, 1964.

Noddings, Nel. *The Challenge to Care in Schools: An Alternative Approach to Education.* New York: Teachers College Press, Columbia University, 1992.

Nygren, Anders. *Agape and Eros.* Translated by Philip S. Watson. Philadelphia: Westminster Press, 1953.

O'Neill, William F. *Educational Ideologies: Contemporary Expressions of Educational Philosophy.* Santa Monica, CA: Goodyear Publishing Co., 1981.

Oppewal, Donald. *Biblical Knowing and Teaching.* Calvin College Monograph Series. Grand Rapids, MI: Calvin College, 1985.

Ornstein, Allan C. *An Introduction to the Foundations of Education.* Chicago: Rand McNally College Publishing Co., 1977.

Ozmon, Howard, and Craver, Sam. *Philosophical Foundations of Education.* Columbus, OH: Charles E. Merrill Publishing Co., 1976.

Painter, F. V. N. *Luther on Education.* Philadelphia: Lutheran Publication Society, 1889.

Pazmiño, Robert W. *By What Authority Do We Teach? Sources for Empowering Christian Educators.* Grand Rapids, MI: Baker Books, 1994.

_____. *Foundational Issues in Christian Education: An Introduction in Evangelical Perspective,* 2d ed. Grand Rapids, MI: Baker Books, 1997.

_____. *Principles and Practices of Christian Education: An Evangelical Per-*

spective. Grand Rapids, MI: Baker Book House, 1992.

Perkinson, Henry J. *The Imperfect Panacea: American Faith in Education, 1865-1976.* 2d ed. New York: Random House, 1977.

Peter, J. Laurence, and Hull, Raymond. *The Peter Principle.* New York: William Morrow and Co., 1969.

Peters, R. S. *Ethics and Education.* London: George Allen & Unwin, 1966.

Plato. *The Dialogues.* 4 vols. Translated by B. Jowett. New York: Charles Scribner's Sons, 1872.

Postman, Neil, and Weingartner, Charles. *The School Book: For People Who Want to Know What All the Hollering Is About.* New York: Dell Publishing Co., 1973.

Powell, John. *The Secret of Staying in Love.* Niles, IL: Argus Communications, 1974.

Pratte, Richard. *Philosophy of Education: Two Traditions.* Springfield, IL: Charles C. Thomas, Publisher, 1992.

Price, J. M. *Jesus the Teacher.* Nashville: The Sunday School Board of the Southern Baptist Convention, 1946.

Ramm, Bernard. *Offense to Reason: A Theology of Sin.* San Francisco: Harper & Row, 1985.

_____. *The Pattern of Religious Authority.* Grand Rapids, MI: Wm. B. Eerdmans Co., 1959.

Rian, Edwin H. "The Need: A World View." In *Toward a Christian Philosophy of Higher Education.* Edited by John Paul von Grueningen. Philadelphia: Westminster Press, 1957.

Rich, John Martin. *Education and Human Values.* Reading, MA: Addison-Wesley Publishing Co., 1968.

Rickover, H. G. *American Education—A National Failure: The Problem of Our Schools and What We Can Learn from England.* New York: E. P. Dutton & Co., 1963.

_____. *Education and Freedom.* New York: E. P. Dutton & Co., 1960.

Rogers, Carl R. *Freedom to Learn.* Columbus, OH: Charles E. Merrill Publishing Co., 1969.

_____. *On Becoming a Person: A Therapist's View of Psychotherapy.* Boston: Houghton Mifflin Co., 1961.

Romanowski, William D. *Pop Culture Wars: Religion and the Role of Entertainment in American Life.* Downers Grove, IL: InterVarsity Press, 1996.

Rookmaaker, H. R. *Art Needs No Justification.* Downers Grove, IL: InterVarsity Press, 1978.

_____. *Modern Art and the Death of a Culture.* Downers Grove, IL: InterVarsity Press, 1971.

Rorty, Richard. *Philosophy and the Mirror of Nature.* Princeton, NJ: Princeton University Press, 1979.

Rousseau, Jean-Jacques. *Emile, or On Education.* Translated by Allen Bloom. New York: Basic Books, 1979.

Ryken, Leland. *Culture in Christian Perspective: A Door to Understanding & Enjoying the Arts.* Portland, OR: Multnomah Press, 1986.

_____, ed. *The Christian Imagination: Essays on Literature and the Arts.* Grand Rapids, MI: Baker Book House, 1981.

Sartre, Jean-Paul. *Existentialism and Human Emotions*. New York: Philosophical Library, 1957.

Schaeffer, Francis A. *Art and the Bible: Two Essays*. Downers Grove, IL: Inter-Varsity Press, 1973.

————. *Escape from Reason*. Downers Grove, IL: InterVarsity Press, 1968.

————. *He Is There and He Is Not Silent*. Wheaton, IL: Tyndale House, 1972.

————. *True Spirituality*. Wheaton, IL: Tyndale House, 1971.

Schofield, Harry. *The Philosophy of Education: An Introduction*. London: George Allen & Unwin, 1972.

Schumacher, E. F. *A Guide for the Perplexed*. New York: Harper & Row, 1977.

————. *Small is Beautiful: Economics as if People Mattered*. New York: Harper & Row, 1973.

Searle, John R. *The Construction of Social Reality*. New York: The Free Press, 1995.

Seeveld, Calvin. "Christian Art." In *The Christian Imagination: Essays on Literature and the Arts*. Edited by Leland Ryken. Grand Rapids, MI: Baker Book House, 1981.

Shane, Harold G. *The Educational Significance of the Future*. Bloomington, IN: Phi Delta Kappa, 1973.

Shermis, S. Samuel. *Philosophic Foundations of Education*. New York: D. Van Nostrand Company, 1967.

Shor, Ira. *Empowering Education: Critical Teaching for Social Change*. Chicago: University of Chicago Press, 1992.

Silberman, Charles E. *Crisis in the Classroom: The Remaking of American Education*. New York: Vintage Books, 1970.

Sire, James W. *Discipleship of the Mind: Learning to Love God in the Ways We Think*. Downers Grove, IL: InterVarsity Press, 1990.

————. *How to Read Slowly: A Christian Guide to Reading With the Mind*. Downers Grove, IL: InterVarsity Press, 1978.

————. *The Universe Next Door: A Basic Worldview Catalog*, 3d ed. Downers Grove, IL: InterVarsity Press, 1997.

Skinner, B. F. *About Behaviorism*. New York: Vintage Books, 1976.

————. *Beyond Freedom and Dignity*. New York: Alfred A. Knopf, 1971.

————. *Science and Human Behavior*. New York: The Macmillan Co., 1953.

————. *Walden Two*. New York: The Macmillan Co., 1948.

Slattery, Patrick. *Curriculum Development in the Postmodern Era*. New York: Garland Publishing, 1995.

Sleeter, Christine E. *Multicultural Education as Social Activism*. Albany, NY: State University of New York Press, 1996.

Smith, Philip G. *Philosophy of Education: Introductory Studies*. New York: Harper & Row, 1965.

Snow, C. P. *The Two Cultures and the Scientific Revolution*. New York: Cambridge University Press, 1959.

Soltis, Jonas F. *An Introduction to the Analysis of Educational Concepts*. 2d ed. Reading, MA: Addison-Wesley Publishing Co., 1978.

Spencer, Herbert. *Education: Intellectual, Moral, and Physical*. New York: D. Appleton and Company, 1909.

Stronks, Gloria Goris, and Blomberg, Doug, eds. *A Vision With a Task: Christian*

Schooling for Responsive Discipleship. Grand Rapids, MI: Baker Books, 1993.

Stretch, Bonnie Barrett. "The Rise of the 'Free School.'" In *Curriculum: Quest for Relevance.* 2d ed. Edited by William Van Til. Boston: Houghton Mifflin Co., 1974.

Sutherland, E. A. *Studies in Christian Education.* Leominster, MA: The Eusey Press, 1952.

Task Force on Education for Economic Growth. *Action for Excellence.* Denver: Education Commission of the States, 1983.

Thorndike, Edward L. "The Nature, Purposes, and General Methods of Measurement of Educational Products." In *The Measurement of Educational Products.* National Society for the Study of Education, Seventeenth Yearbook, Part II. Bloomington, IL: Public School Publishing Co., 1918.

Tillich, Paul. "Existentialist Aspects of Modern Art." In *Christianity and the Existentialists.* Edited by Carl Michalson. New York: Charles Scribner's Sons, 1956.

Titus, Harold, and Smith, Marilyn S. *Living Issues in Philosophy.* 6th ed. New York: D. Van Nostrand Co., 1974.

Toffler, Alvin. *Future Shock.* New York: Random House, 1970.

_____. *Power Shift: Knowledge, Wealth, and Violence at the Edge of the 21st Century.* New York: Bantam Books, 1990.

_____. *The Third Wave.* New York: Bantam Books, 1980.

_____, ed. *Learning for Tomorrow: The Role of the Future in Education.* New York: Vintage Books, 1974.

Trueblood, David Elton. *General Philosophy.* New York: Harper & Row, 1963.

_____. *Philosophy of Religion.* New York: Harper & Row, 1957.

_____. *A Place to Stand.* New York: Harper & Row, 1969.

Unamuno, Miguel de. *Tragic Sense of Life.* Translated by J. E. C. Flitch. New York: Dover Publications, 1954.

Van Brummelen, Harro. *Walking With God in the Classroom.* Burlington, Ontario: Welch Publishing, 1988.

Van Doren, Mark. *Liberal Education.* Boston: Beacon Press, 1959.

Walsh, Brian J. "Education in Precarious Times: Postmodernity and a Christian World View," in Ian Lambert and Suzanne Mitchell, eds. *The Crumbling Walls of Certainty: Towards a Christian Critique of Postmodernity and Education.* Sydney: Centre for the Study of Australian Christianity, 1997.

Walsh, Brian J., and Middleton, J. Richard. *The Transforming Vision: Shaping a Christian World View.* Downers Grove, IL: InterVarsity Press, 1984.

Warnock, Mary. *Ethics Since 1900.* 3d ed. New York: Oxford University Press, 1978.

Wayson, William W. et al. *Up From Excellence: The Impact of the Excellence Movement on Schools.* Bloomington, IN: Phi Delta Kappa Educational Foundation, 1988.

Welch, Herbert. "The Ideals and Aims of the Christian College." In *The Christian College.* New York: Methodist Book Concern, 1916.

Wenham, John W. *The Enigma of Evil: Can We Believe in the Goodness of God?* Grand Rapids, MI: Zondervan Publishing House, 1985.

White, Ellen G. *Education.* Mountain View, CA: Pacific Press Publishing Association, 1903.

Whitehead, Alfred North. *The Aims of Education and Other Essays.* New York: The Free Press, 1967.

Wild, John. *The Challenge of Existentialism.* Bloomington, IN: University Press, 1955.

Wilhoit, Jim. *Christian Education and the Search for Meaning,* 2d ed. Grand Rapids, MI: Baker Book House, 1991.

Wittgenstein, Ludwig. *Tractatus Logico-Philosophicus.* Translated by D. F. Pears and B. F. McGuinness. London: Routledge and Kegan Paul, 1961.

Wolterstorff, Nicholas. *Art In Action: Toward a Christian Aesthetic.* Grand Rapids, MI: Wm. B. Eerdmans Publishing Co., 1980.

_____. *Educating for Responsible Action.* Grand Rapids, MI: Wm. B. Eerdmans Publishing Co., 1980.

Zahorik, John A. *Constructivist Teaching.* Bloomington, IN: Phi Delta Kappa Educational Foundation, 1995.

Zuck, Roy B. *Teaching as Jesus Taught.* Grand Rapids, MI: Baker Books, 1995.

_____. *Teaching as Paul Taught.* Grand Rapids, MI: Baker Books, 1998.

Index